Family Farming
in Europe and America

Rural Studies Series

Rural Public Services: International Comparisons, edited by Richard E. Lonsdale and György Enyedi

The Social Consequences and Challenges of New Agricultural Technologies, edited by Gigi M. Berardi and Charles C. Geisler

†*Rural Society in the U.S.: Issues for the 1980s*, edited by Don A. Dillman and Daryl J. Hobbs

Technology and Social Change in Rural Areas: A Festschrift for Eugene A. Wilkening, edited by Gene F. Summers

†*Science, Agriculture, and the Politics of Research*, Lawrence Busch and William B. Lacy

†*The Cooperative Extension Service: A National Assessment*, Paul D. Warner and James A. Christenson

The Organization of Work in Rural and Urban Labor Markets, Patrick M. Horan and Charles M. Tolbert II

The Impact of Population Change on Business Activity in Rural America, Kenneth M. Johnson

Small Farms: Persistence with Legitimation, Alessandro Bonanno

Studies in the Transformation of U.S. Agriculture, edited by Eugene Havens with Gregory Hooks, Patrick H. Mooney, and Max J. Pfeffer

Family Farming in Europe and America, edited by Boguslaw Galeski and Eugene Wilkening

†Available in hardcover and paperback.

About the Book and Editors

Much has happened since agricultural economists and rural sociologists met at the University of Chicago in 1946 to discuss family farming. The problems and issues related to the structure of agriculture have been intensified by current economic considerations, which promote the growth of larger-scale commercial farming operations and edge out many smaller farms owned, operated, and worked by families.

In this book, contributors from eleven nations in Europe and North America provide a comparison of farm structure under different economic and political systems, including Poland as an example of a non-market economy. In addition to providing information on how local, state, and international policies have affected the agricultural enterprise, they look at the role of farmers' organizations in policy formulation and take note of changes in farm patterns and policies that have had an impact on farm production, off-farm work, and the welfare of farm families and rural communities.

Boguslaw Galeski is visiting professor in the Department of Sociology and Anthropology at the University of Wisconsin-Stevens Point. He has served as the head of the Department of Rural Sociology, Institute of Philosophy and Sociology, Polish Academy of Sciences at Warsaw, and has taught in Britain, Italy, and New Zealand as well.

Eugene Wilkening is professor in the Department of Rural Sociology at the University of Wisconsin-Madison. He has served as president of the Rural Sociological Society and was honored as Distinguished Rural Sociologist by that society in 1981.

Family Farming
in Europe and America

edited by Boguslaw Galeski
and Eugene Wilkening

Westview Press / **Boulder and London**

Rural Studies Series, Sponsored by the Rural Sociological Society

This Westview softcover edition is printed on acid-free paper and bound in softcovers that carry the highest rating of the National Association of State Textbook Administrators, in consultation with the Association of American Publishers and the Book Manufacturers' Institute.

Published in 1987 in the United States of America by Westview Press, Inc.; Frederick A. Praeger, Publisher; 5500 Central Avenue, Boulder, Colorado 80301

Library of Congress Cataloging-in-Publication Data
Family Farming in Europe and America.
    (Rural studies series)
    1. Family farms--Europe--Case studies. 2. Family
farms--United States--Case studies. 3. Family farms--
Canada--Case studies. I. Galeski, Boguslaw.
II. Wilkening, Eugene A. III. Series: Rural studies
series of the Rural Sociological Society.
HD1476.E85F35 1987   338.1'6   87-2041
ISBN 0-8133-7340-9

Composition for this book was provided by the editors.
This book was produced without formal editing by the publisher.

Printed and bound in the United States of America

The paper used in this publication meets the requirements of the American National Standard for Permanence of Paper for Printed Library Materials Z39.48-1984.

6   5   4   3   2   1

Contents

1 INTRODUCTION 1

2 FAMILY FARMING IN BRITAIN, Ruth Gasson 5

3 FAMILY FARMING IN IRELAND, D.F. Hannan
   and R. Breen 39

4 FAMILY FARMING IN NORWAY, Reidar Almas 71

5 A PERSISTENT CULTURE: SOME REFLECTIONS ON
   SWEDISH FAMILY FARMING, Ulrich Nitsch 95

6 POSTWAR TECHNOLOGICAL AND SOCIAL DEVELOPMENT
   ON FAMILY FARMS: THE CASE OF FINLAND,
   Nils Westermarck 117

7 FAMILY FARMING AND THE AGRICULTURAL CRISIS
   IN DENMARK, Torben Bager 137

8 THE FAMILY FARM IN THE FEDERAL REPUBLIC
   OF GERMANY, Ulrich Planck (translated by
   Max J. Pfeffer) 155

9 FAMILY FARMING IN FRANCE: CRISIS AND
   REVIVAL, Hugues Lamarche (translated by
   Jacques Marre and Keith M. Moore) 193

10 FAMILY FARMING IN POLAND, Boguslaw Galeski 217

11 THE SOCIAL ECONOMY OF CANADIAN AGRICULTURE:
   FAMILY FARMING AND ALTERNATIVE FUTURES,
   Michael E. Gertler and Thomas Murphy 239

12 FAMILY FARMING IN THE UNITED STATES,
    Eugene Wilkening and Jess Gilbert 271

13 CONCLUSIONS 303

ABOUT THE CONTRIBUTORS 311

1
Introduction

Food production has continued to be a family enterprise in most countries of the world, even with increased industrialization and urbanization. The family owned and operated enterprise has provided the incentives and the commitment of people to produce for their own needs and for others under a wide range of natural, economic, and political conditions. The family farm also provides the basis for self-sustaining family and community life, as well as a way of producing for the market. But farming is increasingly influenced by the market for its products and by the investments in land and other resources by nonfamily interests. So family farms must respond to changing technology and market forces if they are to provide the income and opportunities comparable to nonfarm enterprises. As these forces change, it becomes more difficult for the famliy farmers to survive without local and national policies to support them.

Values other than economic must be considered as they relate to structure of agriculture. These include the maintenance of stable communities and rural population throughout the country. Families who live on the land require adequate social as well as economic opportunities to maintain a good quality of life for the family as well as for the nation. There must also be concern for the maintenance of the natural resources upon which the farm is based. As the family farm appears to be in crisis in the industrialized nations, it is an appropriate time to examine the family farm as it relates to these considerations.

While definitions of the family farm vary among the countries, it is generally regarded as a farm which is owned and operated by a family which may include one or

1

more generations. Most of the land and capital is provided by the family, although additional land may be rented for expansion of the operation and capital may be borrowed for supplies, machinery, and improvements. Most of the labor is provided by members of the family living on the farm, but additional labor may be hired, most often on a seasonal basis. This indicates that the concept of the "family farm" is an "ideal type" in which the farm is owned and operated by a family. This conception varies among countries and is undergoing change as larger operations with improved technology are needed to utilize family resources and to provide an adequate income. Thus, the concept of family farming must be used with flexibility to refer to the extent to which the social as well as economic goals and values of the family are considered in the decisions and policies related to the farm. For example, the average family farm in North America is larger, more specialized, and commercialized than those in Europe, but the family is the risk taking manager and provides most of the labor.

In Europe the family farm has grown out of a range of conditions. In some countries the abolishment of serfdom provided land to peasant families and economic independence in relationship to markets. In some countries the farms were not isolated family units but part of a village and pastureland, with residential areas and services being shared within the community. In North America, farming families were generally free from feudal bonds, tending to live on their land in isolated settlements which provided more flexibility in size and services and more opportunity for expansion. In this sense the family farm in America may be regarded as the fulfillment of dreams of European peasantry in its striving for land and individual freedom. Most European settlers have brought with them and maintained certain traditional patterns of farming, but from the beginning these patterns have been influenced by the nature of land disposition in the region, market forces, and various public policies affecting access to land, water resources, and public services.

Overproduction and low prices have presented a problem in the market economies, while Poland and other non-market economies of Eastern Europe are suffering from a shortage of food products. How is the increasing concentration and global competition of the food industry related to the structure of agricultural production? What policies are needed in response to the present

crisis for the long-term sustainability of food production without severe economic, social, and environmental costs? In general, there has been little
opportunity to go beyond the current issues of market
price and production to see how the people and producers
of the rural areas are affected. The chapters which
follow should assist those who want to preserve the
family farm for social and ecological as well as economic
reasons. They should also be useful for developing
countries in considering the alternative paths of development to avoid the undesirable consequences of large-
scale, nonfamily farming.

In order to understand what is happening to the
structure of agriculture and its consequences authors
from nine European and two North American countries have
responded to the following issues related to the family
farm:

1. As a general basis for a comparative perspective
on the family farm, what historical forces have produced
the current patterns of farming?

2. What is happening to the structure of agriculture
with respect to size, labor, and management and why?
What are the consequences of these structures for the
income, market, and maintenance of rural life and the
natural resources of these countries?

3. How have government policies affected the family
farm in nonmarket as well as market economies? How do
such policies affect the maintenance of the land and
water resources as well as the welfare of the people
operating the land as compared to nonfarm families?

4. What are the prospects for the family farm in the
future and how are these prospects likely to be affected
by local, state, and international policy regarding agriculture and the food industry?

5. What are the alternatives to the family farm and
the consequences of those in different countries and cultures?

The countries providing contributions to this book
from Europe and North America have certain historical
similarities. This is important for a comparative study
of the issues. Although Poland is from the Eastern block
of nonmarket economies, it has maintained its family farm
rather than shift a major part of its food production to
State and collective farms as in other East European
countries. While only France provides a contribution
from Southern Europe, other chapters in this volume

should have significance for that part of Europe, as well as other industrial nations around the world.

The contributors to the volume have reaffirmed a concern for the structure of agriculture and the well-being of those associated with it in the industrialized nations. They indicate that while the farm population has declined, it still represents an important element in the economy and rural life that is of national concern. The nature of this concern and the policies following from it is a major justification for this volume. The effect on farm organizations, political parties, local groups, and cultural patterns are revealed. While there are some common concerns among the various countries, each country has dealt with the problem of the family farm and the crisis affecting it in a different manner. This underscores agriculture's dependence upon national and international conditions and policies.

2
Family Farming in Britain

Ruth Gasson

Although "the family farm" is highly regarded in Britain, there seems to be no general agreement on what is meant by family farming. The term implies a close association between the farm and the family running it, with business control, capital supply, and investment patterns determined largely by such factors as the farmer's age, size of family, and interpersonal relationships. A measure of business continuity could be expected from one generation to the next, as well as a close correspondence between phases of the business cycle and phases of the family cycle.

Virtually all farms in the United Kingdom could be described as family farms in the sense that they are run by and on behalf of families. Even some of the largest enterprises, which are operated along strictly commercial lines and are highly capitalized and heavily dependent upon hired labor, are nevertheless strongly identified with families. According to one authority, 94% of agricultural holdings are run by individual proprietors, partnerships, or private (usually family) companies (Commission, 1981). Another authority has suggested that no less than 97.5% of all English farms are genuinely family businesses in that all the business principals, if more than one, are closely related by blood or marriage (Harrison, 1975).

The much publicized purchase of farms by financial institutions during the 1970s raised fears about the survival of the family farm. A Government Committee of Inquiry, the Northfield Committee set up to investigate trends in agricultural land acquisition and ownership, established that institutions owned only 1.2% of the agricultural land in Great Britain and they were directly involved in farming only a fraction of that figure (North-field, 1979). By 1982 the proportion had only risen to 2% (Burrell, Hill and Medland, 1984).

The family farm is perhaps best understood as an ideal type which can be contrasted with another ideal type, the large-scale capitalist farm. Family farming implies that the family which owns and controls the farm business also provides the capital, management, and some, if not all, of the labor. It need not own the land, for in Great Britain, where roughly two-thirds of farmland is owner occupied, no distinction seems to be made between family farming on rented and owned land. Under the capitalist system, land, labor, capital, management, and business control could all be supplied from different sources.

In everyday use, "family farming" has come to mean farming on a small scale, and it will be used in that sense here. The term may also have gathered connotations, justified or otherwise, of traditionalism, inefficiency, and a disregard for economic rationality. Newby (1979), for instance, characterizes the family farmer as one who spends most of his time working on the land, is low in market orientation, whose behavior is "molded not so much by economic incentives as by family, social, and even religious values."

Accepting that the small size of the business, rather than identification with a family, has become the distinguishing feature of family farming in Britain, the question is where the boundaries should be drawn. As there are no policies directed toward family farming as such, there is no official definition, leaving the way open for a variety of approaches to suit different needs.

DEFINING THE "FAMILY FARM"

The Smallfarmers' Association, a pressure group set up to promote the family farm, has not been able to agree on a precise definition of family farming. The organization wants farms to be of a size which can be worked by "an efficient average sized family." The family-worked farm has been depicted as "a unit large enough to support two members of a family or one member of a family and one employee, possibly part time, with a standard of living fully comparable to urban occupations but probably with a higher quality of life" (Buccleuch, 1981) Another definition describes the family farm as one that would enable "an efficient family unit, plus some outside labor, to make a reasonable living using accepted modern techniques for the production of wholesome food or other products on a sustainable basis" (Hunter-Smith, 1982).

On this basis, the family farm would be a two- to four-man unit, but other definitions would include the one-man unit as well. Most family farms would, therefore, be in the range of 250 to 1,000 standard man days (smds) where 250 smds represents one man year of work. The smd factors, which are periodically revised to reflect improvements in work rates, have now been superceded by European Size Units (ESUs), one ESU being 1,000 European Units of Account of Gross Margin. Farms between 4 and 24 ESUs are described as "small and family-sized farms" (Furness, 1983). The family farm can also be defined in terms of labor use, the ceiling being where hired workers make up half of the labor force. Britton and Hill (1975), using data for 1970 and 1971, identified a threshold at 800 to 850 smds, this being where hired labor made up half of the total labor bill.

In Britain, then, the boundary between the family farm and the large-scale capitalist farm is ill-defined but conventionally located in the region of the three- to four-man unit, between 750 and 1,000 smds or 16 to 24 ESUs. For present purposes, all farms below this threshold will be described as "family farms." Those which in theory provide insufficient employment for two persons, that is, below 500 smds (previously 600 smds) are referred to as "smaller family farms." The term "larger-than-family farm" will be used to denote all types of "large-scale capitalist business," "industrial-type enterprise," and "megafarm" above the threshold.

IMPORTANCE OF FAMILY FARMING IN BRITAIN

Farms in the United Kingdom are large by West European standards. In 1982, half of the 242,300 agricultural census holdings were capable of providing full-time work for at least one person, and they averaged almost 300 acres. Half of the total cultivated acreage was on holdings of 250 acres and above. Individual enterprises are also large, with the average cereal acreage on cereal growing farms being 100 acres, and average size dairy herd 55 cows.

Larger-than-family farms dominate in terms of production. Table 2.1, relating to England and Wales, indicates that farms above 1,000 smds, although representing less than 12% of all holdings, occupied 40% of the farmland and accounted for 52% of the total smds, which is a rough guide to their importance for production.

Table 2.1. Distribution of agricultural census holdings, crops & grass acreage and total standard man days by size of farm business, England and Wales, 1977

Size of farm business (smds)	Percent of holdings	Percent of crops & grass	Percent of total smds
Under 250	48.6	15.1	8.1
250 - 499	21.0	17.8	14.7
500 - 999	18.5	26.6	25.0
1000 - 1999	8.2	21.3	21.8
2000 and over	3.7	19.2	30.4
All holdings	100.0	100.0	100.0

Source: Ministry of Agriculture, Fisheries and Food, 1979.

The top 4% of farms contributed more than 30% of the output of British agriculture. Although family farms of less than 1,000 smds are numerically the most important, accounting for almost 90% of holdings, they contributed less than half of the output. Taking ESUs as the yardstick, family farms accounted for 88% of all UK holdings in 1982, occupied 42% of the total cultivated area, and contributed 30% of total business activity, measured by aggregate Standard Gross Margin (Furness, 1983).

Although output is skewed towards larger-than-family farms, Britton and Hill have demonstrated that there is more agricultural activity taking place on two-man holdings than on any other size interval of equal range. When they plotted the number of holdings within each 50 smd interval against the total number of smds those successive batches of holdings contained, the curve peaked at about 550 smds and fell off quite steeply thereafter. This gave substance to the image of British agriculture as an industry still dominated by family sized businesses, both in numbers and in productive activity.

The nature of the labor force further underlines the importance of family farming. Of the 702,000 persons working on UK farms at the 1983 agricultural census, 421,000, or 60% were farmers, partners or directors, spouses of farmers, or other family workers. More than three-quarters of British farms employ no workers apart from members of the family on a full-time basis, and a further 10% employ only one. Larger-than-family farms employing more than one man full time account for only 12% of the holdings in England and Wales, although they employ 85% of the nonfamily labor.

Using any definition, then, family farms dominate UK agriculture in terms of numbers. They are especially important in Wales and Northern Ireland, where about nine farms out of ten are family farms, accounting for more than half of the total farm business activity. Family farms contribute between a quarter and a third of total farm business activity in the north and west of England and in Scotland but only about 15% in eastern England. This is consistent with their emphasis on livestock production. Family farms produce over half of the nation's output of cattle and sheep, much of this coming from Scotland, Wales and the west of England. They are responsible for 40% of dairy production, with the west and north of England, Wales, and Northern Ireland contributing most. Although many family farms specialize in pigs, poultry, and horticultural crops, larger-than-family farms now dominate these lines of production, as they do in cropping, which is especially significant in the southeastern half of England (Furness, 1983).

BASIC TYPES OF FAMILY FARMS

A distinction has been made between family farms and large-scale capitalist farms. Family farms can be subdivided according to the family's involvement in other work and their dependence on nonfarm sources of income. Part-time farming is not confined to small- or family-sized farms, but the great majority of British farmers or farm families with other gainful activities (at least 90%) operate in the family farm size range.

In 1983, 25% of UK farm occupiers had other gainful

activities, and the proportion is rising. For a majority
of farmers who are dual job holders, the other job is the
main activity. Many are proprietors of second businesses,
which may be enterprises on the farm, such as a caravan
site or farm shop; or businesses which take them to other
farms, like agricultural contracting, or off-farm
businesses quite unrelated to agriculture. The larger the
farm, the more likely it is that if the farmer has a
second job, he runs another business. Manual work comes
next as a second activity for farmers, while if wives have
off-farm employment, they are most likely to be engaged in
professions or other white collar jobs. The other
activity may well provide most of the income. In a
national survey, nearly two-thirds of farmers or farming
couples with second jobs declared that they were earning
more from other sources than from the farm; only about
one farmer in three was making more from the farm (Gasson,
1986).

A number of countries divide part-time farms into
two classes--Class I, where the farm family depends mainly
on farming for its earned income but also has other work;
and Class II, where the farm household spends the greater
part of its working time in nonfarm activities and derives
the greater part of its income from those activities.
Class II part-time farms are more numerous and are
becoming increasingly important in many of the world's
industrialized countries, while Class I farms are on the
decline. In the British survey there were two Class II
farms to each one in Class I.

There is a measure of correspondence between the
part-time farm classification and farm size, although size
is by no means the only determining factor. In the
British study, the dividing line appeared to be somewhere
in the region of 250 smds. Below this threshold, a
majority of part-time farms were mainly dependent upon
other income sources, above it mainly dependent on farming.

Four basic types have now been defined.
Larger-than-family farms are those variously measured as
above 24 ESUs or 1,000 smds, employing more than one
full-time, nonfamily worker, or where more than half the
labor is hired. Although they account for only about 12%
of all holdings, they occupy relatively more of the land,
employ four-fifths of the hired workers and account for a
disproportionate share of output.

Family farms are now divided into full-time, Class
I and Class II part-time farms. Class II farms are
generally the smallest, usually below 500 smds and often

below 250 smds or 4 ESUs, and they contribute a negligible amount to the nation's farm output. Most of the available family labor is employed off the farm and most, if not all of the current income is from other sources.

Class I part-time farms, where farming is the main but not the only source of family employment and earnings, are in many ways intermediate between Class II part-time and full-time family farms. For some purposes they can be grouped with the latter as "main living farms." It is these main living farms which have been disappearing most rapidly in the post-war period.

TRENDS IN NUMBERS

Agricultural statistics indicate that since the Second World War, agricultural holdings below 300 acres have been disappearing and numbers of agricultural holdings above that size rising. While the total number of holdings in England and Wales declined by 43% between 1945 and 1975, the number above 300 acres actually increased by 43%.

Although this suggests the disappearance of many small family farms, other influences have been at work, too. Some small holdings are not independent units but parts of larger farms. Attempts have been made to encourage farmers to complete a single census return for all the land they farm. Some 10,000 holdings disappeared from the census in England and Wales between 1969 and 1970 as a result of "statistical amalgamation." In addition to this, successive statistical revisions have purged many of the smallest units which could not by any stretch of the imagination be regarded as "farms." In 1973, for instance, the threshold for inclusion in the census was raised from 26 to 40 smds, which had the effect of removing some 14,000 holdings from the UK total.

In view of the changing statistical base, a better indicator is the proportion of land farmed in small and large units. Between 1965 and 1975, the share of land in holdings below 300 acres in Great Britain declined from 67% to 57% (Commission, 1981).

Furness (1983) has interpolated changes in the size structure of farm businesses over the period 1970 to 1979, making allowance for changes in smd factors. Decline was occurring across the whole of the family farm size range, with heaviest losses among smaller family farms of 250 to 500 smds. Very small units below 250 smds and larger family farms of 500 to 1,000 smds declined by a smaller amount, while larger-than-family farms increased. The last column in Table 2.2 brings the analysis almost up to date. Since 1977, the 250-500 smd group has shrunk most rapidly, with negligible changes among other family farm categories. Larger-than-family farms have continued to grow. Analysis based on ESUs, though only extending back to 1980, shows the same pattern.

Although all the measures based on farm size show a consistent decline in family farming, this decline being greatest among one- to two-man farms, measures based on the labor force tell a different story. The number of farms and farmers has been dropping since the Second

Table 2.2. Changes in farm business structure in the United Kingdom, 1970 to 1982

Size of farm business (in 1976 smds or equivalent)	Percent change in numbers of holdings	
	1980-1979	1977-1982
Under 250	− 17	+ 1
250 − 499	− 27	− 14
500 − 999	− 8	− 1
1,000 and over	+ 18	+ 7
All holdings	− 14	+ 2

Sources: Furness, 1983; Annual Review of Agriculture 1983, HMSO.

World War, but the decline among hired workers has been steeper still. In 1960 the ratio of workers to farmers was about two to one; today this ratio is nearly one to one. On this basis, family farming is on the increase, while the larger-than-family farms employing more than one worker have shrunk from 21% to 12% of all farms. Taking these trends into consideration together, the total number of family farms is being eroded, but the threshold between family worked farms and larger-than-family farms is creeping upwards.

SOME CHARACTERISTICS COMPARED

In many respects the "typical" farming family in
Britain today is indistinguishable from any other family.
The small nuclear group is the norm, three generation
households being quite uncommon. Younger farm families,
in particular, share many of the goals and aspirations,
consumption patterns, and leisure pursuits of urban
families or, more likely still, of their urban employed
but rural dwelling neighbors. This is especially true of
Class II part-time farming families who, although they
live on farms, may identify with the lifestyle appropriate
to the main occupation. In other respects, farming
families are quite distinct, as the following pages show.

Age of Farmers

Farmers are, on average, older than hired farm workers
or the working population at large. In the 1971
Population Census, 20% of farmers but only 10% of all
British working people were aged 60 and over. This is
hardly surprising in an occupation dominated by small
family businesses; the age distribution of farmers is, in
fact, very close to that for all employers and
self-employed persons. Somewhat more surprising is the
contention that English farmers today are, on average,
younger and beginning their careers earlier than their
counterparts of 50 years ago (Harrison, 1975).
In general, the smaller the farm, the older the
farmer; but this statement needs to be qualified in one
respect. The census category of "farmers, partners, and
directors" includes farmers' sons who are junior partners,
and these are more often found on large farms. The
association of elderly farmers with small holdings is,
however, more than a statistical artifact. From the 1975
EC Farm Structure Survey comes evidence that farmers 65
and over have smaller than average farms and are less
intensive users of land and labor, as indicated by lower
stocking rates and fewer acres per person. Farmers in the
35 to 45 age group have the largest farms, carry the most
livestock and operate with the highest ratios of land to
labor (Commission, 1981).
Three factors help to account for the association
between older farmers and small farms. One is the
preference for full-time farmers to move to smaller
holdings on retirement. Second, the ranks of Class II

part timers are swollen by the influx of newcomers, often
wealthy, who purchase small farms when they retire from
other occupations. Third, for reasons which will be
discussed later, operators of smaller holdings are less
likely than those on larger farms to have successors and
so are under less pressure to retire in favor of the
younger generation.

Education, Qualifications and Training

Size of farm and the farmer's age both have a bearing
on his formal education and qualifications. Broadly
speaking, the larger the farm and the younger the farmer,
the higher the levels of both general and agricultural
education attained. Families on larger farms are likely
to have greater resources, enabling children to stay on at
school and to attend agricultural college. Added to this,
farmers with larger businesses are, on average, younger,
and younger farmers are better qualified.

In England and Wales the typical family farmer,
employing not more than one worker, left school before he
was 15 with only a one in six chance of obtaining a school
leaving certificate and a one in thirteen chance of an
agricultural college education. By contrast, those
larger-than-family farmers, with five or more workers,
left school at an average age of 16 years, nearly half
with some form of school leaving certificate and more than
a quarter going on to obtain an agricultural qualification
(Agriculture EDC, 1972). The pattern continues, with
operators of very large farms showing the same
tendencies. Among a sample of East Anglian farmers with
1,000 acres or more, the average school leaving age was 17
years, half the farmers hold an agricultural
qualification, and 59% having had some type of further
education (Newby, et al., 1978).

Although occupiers on the very smallest holdings are
the least likely to have been trained in agricultural
subjects, they may be qualified in other spheres. A
majority of Class II part-time farmers on holdings of less
than 100 smds came into farming from some other career.
Some are qualified members of professions (doctors,
lawyers, teachers), and some of the businessmen are also
qualified, for instance as engineers or accountants. This
suggests a U-shaped distribution of higher education among
farmers, with larger- than-family farmers the most likely
to hold qualifications in agricultural subjects and Class

II part-time farmers, at the other end of the spectrum, the most likely to be qualified in other fields. Most disadvantaged in terms of formal qualifications are those on small family farms including Class I part-timers.

Background and Entry Into Farming

Most farmers in Britain today are sons of farmers, grew up on the land, and, more often than not, inherited the family business. In the past such a high degree of immobility might have been attributed to lack of alternatives, but nowadays the reasons are largely financial. The increasing size of unit necessary to make a living in farming, soaring land prices, and growing requirements for working capital are making it harder for all but the very wealthy to enter agriculture by purchasing a farm. At the same time, a shrinking tenanted sector has effectively cut off the supply of new farms to rent. Also, the disappearance of small holdings in the one- to two-man range is making it harder for those on the bottom rungs of the farming ladder to climb. Consequently, entry into farming is becoming restricted to members of farming families who inherit and those with substantial capital behind them.

The larger the farm, the higher the costs of entry. It is, therefore, among the largest farms that inheritance plays the most important part. "Overall mobility rates in farming are low precisely because entry into farming at the top level is so highly circumscribed" (Newby, et al., 1978). The backgrounds of three groups of farmers in eastern England illustrate the point. Newby and colleagues compared a sample of East Anglian farmers with 1,000 acres and over (the large farm sample) with a control group of Suffolk farmers drawn from all size groups (the Suffolk sample). Gasson (1969) had previously interviewed a sample of farmers in the eastern counties with holdings of between 275 and 600 smds (the small farm sample).

Table 2.3 shows that more farmers in the large farm sample than the Suffolk sample had inherited their farms, more were sons of farmers, and more were born and brought up on their present farms. "Stability rather than mobility is the most obvious facet of the lives of the larger farmers," (Newby, et al., 1978). Small family farmers were lowest on all counts. On the other hand, among those who had not inherited, most small farmers were

born and brought up in the same locality, whereas those
with large farms were the most likely to have moved into
the area from elsewhere.

Among part-time farming families, the inheritance rate
is lower still. Only a quarter of part-time farmers in
England and Wales inherited their farms (Gasson, 1986).
The small size of most part-time farms is one reason.
Besides this, many part-time farmers run other businesses
which generally yield more income than the farm. Children
may take over these enterprises rather than the farm.
Where the family is new to agriculture, too, as is the
case with many part-time farming families, sons are less
likely to follow on than where the farming tradition has
continued over several generations.

Table 2.3. Backgrounds of farmers in three samples in
eastern England

	Small farm sample	Suffolk sample	Large farm sample
	percent of farmers		
Son of a farmer	65	72	80
Inherited farm	50	56	70
Grew up on present farm	26.5	33.3	47.5
in same parish	24.5	10.5	1.0
in next parish	20.6	7.0	3.0
elsewhere	28.4	49.2	48.5
Number in sample	102	57	101

Sources: Gasson, 1969; Newby, et al., 1978.

Succession

Looking to the future, the tendency for farms to be
handed down within families is likely to persist and may
even be intensified. Nearly two-thirds of all English
farmers are thought to have successors, very rarely from

outside the immediate family, willing and able to take over from them (Harrison, 1975). The link between size of farm and probability of succession is again evident, with small and part-time farmers less likely to be planning on succession. In a recent survey of farmers' retirement plans, for instance, three out of four farmers with 250 acres or more expected to hand the property on to a successor, compared to less than half on farms of less than 100 acres (Farmers Weekly, 1984). In Scotland, too, three-quarters of larger-than-family farms, compared to only about half of all smaller family farms, have potential successors (Rettie, 1975). Only 40% of part timers have successors for the farm.

With farms becoming larger and fewer, successors are increasingly likely to remain at home rather than begin farming on small holdings of their own. Transfer of business control from father to son should ideally be a gradual process, allowing both successor and retiring farmer enough time to adjust to their new roles. Timing can be crucial for the survival of the business. If succession occurs too early, the son may not be familiar with all aspects of the business; but if it is too late, the successor's motivation, confidence, and competence to take decisions may be undermined (Hastings, 1984).

Family farms often create problems for succession. Father and son do not have sufficient space to get away from one another, the scope for management decision making is limited, and it is difficult to delegate part of the responsibility to the successor. It may prove impossible for father and son to work together, and the son may have to leave and find other employment, at least temporarily. On larger-than-family farms with a hired labor force and several enterprises, there are more opportunities to involve sons in management, and fathers can allocate specific areas of decision making without feeling they have lost control of the business (Hastings, 1984). In Scotland, a strong link between the size of the farm business and the successor's already being on the holding confirms this tendency (Rettie, 1975). In the East Anglian study, too, only 6.3% of sons in the large farm sample were not involved in running the farm in some capacity. In the Suffolk sample, the proportion of sons not involved was 62.5% (Newby, et. al, 1978).

Housing is another factor which may militate against succession on the smaller farm. In Britain today it is normal for young couples to start their married life in their own home rather than share the parents' house.

Smaller farms are less likely to have spare dwellings or the means to build another house, so the successor and his family may be forced to live elsewhere until the parents retire and move off the farm. Any separation of the potential successor from the family farm, in employment or housing, will lessen the chances of his taking over the farm eventually.

Roles of Farmers' Wives

Most British farmers are male and most are married. The larger the farm, the more likely the farmer is to have a wife. One study shows the proportion of farmers who are married rising from under 77% on farms employing no workers to 89% on farms with five or more employees (Agriculture EDC, 1972). Paradoxically, it is the smaller so-called family farms which are the most likely not to be run by families.

Table 2.4. Wives' involvement in farm tasks on small and large farms

Percent of wives who regularly	Small family farms	Larger-than-family farms
Rear calves or lambs	58	32
Feed hens, collect eggs	44	29
Round up straying animals	33	24
Milk cows	27	3
Drive a tractor	19	4

Source: Farmers Weekly, 1980.

Only a minority of British farmers' wives are not involved in running the farm in some capacity. On family farms, and especially those without regular workers, more wives are involved and they work for longer hours than on larger-than-family farms. Table 2.4 compares the contribution of wives on small family farms of 50 to 100 acres with that on larger-than-family farms of 500 acres and above. Wives on family farms are more likely to be involved in every kind of task, the differences being especially marked in respect to predominantly "male" tasks like milking and tractor driving.

Regular involvement in manual work is one of the few activities of farmers' wives which varies significantly by farm size (Errington, 1983). Two ideal role types, "working farmwife" and "farm housewife" encapsulate many of the differences in woman's work between family farms and larger-than-family businesses (Gasson, 1980). On smaller family farms where no other labor is employed, the wife may be called upon to help her husband in any task requiring more than one pair of hands. Typically she does not take sole responsibility for any of the farm activities but plays the role of assistant. Final responsibility for day-to-day decisions will probably rest with the husband. The wife's role in decision making tends to be supportive rather than equal. The working farmwife, involved with the daily running of the farm, may however be consulted to a greater extent than the wife on a larger farm.

The farm housewife on a larger, labor employing farm, is not expected to help regularly on the farm, although she is liable to be called upon at busy times and in emergencies. Being somewhat remote from daily events on the farm, she is not likely to be consulted on management questions, although her knowledge of the financial state of the business, if she does the farm accounts, will make her a valuable and informed adviser. Symes and Marsden (1983) have drawn attention to the increasingly asymmetrical roles of husbands and wives on large, arable farms. Some farm housewives are home centered and place a high value on children's development and domestic skills. Others channel their surplus energy into voluntary work or careers off the farm.

Errington (1983) has predicted that British agriculture will become increasingly polarized between smaller family farms and larger-than-family farms and that wives will correspondingly become more clearly identified with the roles of either working farmwife or farm housewife. The former are likely to become still more involved in the manual work on the farm, while the latter become still more marginal to the day-to-day running of the business and may take up employment off the farm.

Value Systems

The farm-centered background, upbringing and socialization of the majority of farmers is reflected in a distinctive set of values. British farmers as a whole bring a predominantly "intrinsic" approach to their work as compared to the instrumental, bureaucratic, or solidarity orientations attributed to other occupations. Typically they emphasize the satisfactions derived from the work itself, such as working outdoors, performing varied and enjoyable tasks, seeing things grow, and being in control of the whole process from sowing to harvest. Independence, meeting a challenge, and the risk and gamble involved in farming are also valued highly, while purely instrumental goals tend to be given low priority.

Research in East Anglia (Gasson, 1974; Newby, et al., 1978) has revealed some differences in value systems between family farmers and those operating on a larger scale. While intrinsic aspects of the farming occupation are valued highly throughout the size range, it is family farmers who give them the most weight. Newby and colleagues noticed that "husbandry" was rated higher by the Suffolk sample, which included family farmers, than by the large farm sample. When Gasson asked them how they defined "a good farmer," larger-than-family farmers gave more assent to "one who is up-to-date, progressive, and willing to experiment." More conservative values embodied in statements like "one who preserves the beauty of the countryside" or "one who leaves the land better than he found it" were more highly regarded by family farmers.

The most striking difference was the high value attached to "independence" by smaller family farmers. In one comparison, twice as many family farmers as larger-than- family farmers believed independence was the greatest attraction of their job. This might be a reflection of the alternatives facing each group. Farmers with larger businesses might see the alternative as managing a different business, where they would still enjoy a degree of autonomy. For family farmers, the alternative could be a manual or routine nonmanual job, where their freedom would be severely curtailed.

While no group of farmers is likely to give blatantly instrumental replies to value laden questions, Gasson found larger-than-family farmers were twice as likely as those on smaller farms to mention economic benefits of being a farmer. The importance attached to economic goals in the business increased regularly with farm size. While

attributes concerned with growth -- "expanding the
business" and "making as high an income as possible" --
were preferred by larger-than-family farmers, statements
implying stability, such as "making a reasonable living"
and "job security," appealed more to family farmers.
Small family farmers as a group valued stability above
growth, while the preference for growth over stability
rose progressively with the size of the farm.

The approach of part-time farmers is different again.
As farming is not the only source of income and frequently
makes a very minor contribution to the household budget,
instrumental values in farming tend to be played down.
Few of them would agree that "making a living out of
farming" is the most important reason for living on a
farm. Many have chosen to live on farms to improve their
quality of life.

Among the sample of part-time farmers (Gasson, 1986),
the two most important attributes of their situation were
"living in the country" and "doing the kind of work you
enjoy." Class II subjects were more strongly oriented to
the farming lifestyle, while Class I approached it more as
an occupation.

Nowhere can these differences in emphasis be better
seen than in regard to farmers' attitudes towards the
natural environment. At the present time British farmers
are very sensitive to charges of causing environmental
damage. Among the part-time farming families interviewed,
three out of four expressed themselves "strongly in favor"
or "somewhat in favor" of conserving the natural
environment on their farms, with only a minority neutral
or opposed. The proportion strongly in favor ranged from
26% in Class I to 42% among Class II part-time farmers
with no income from farming. Newby and colleagues also
found significant differences in attitudes towards
conservation. In general the large-scale farmers were
more hostile; for example, they were more than twice as
likely as farmers in the Suffolk sample to regard concern
for the environment as "a problem manufactured by
environmentalists."

To summarize, farmers running larger-than-family
businesses appear more immobile and inward looking than
family farmers only in the sense that the farm is more
likely to remain with the family for several generations.
In most other respects, those running larger farms appear
more outward looking than family farmers, being on average
younger, better educated, more likely to have had a formal
training in agriculture, and married to women who may

pursue off-farm careers of their own. These characteristics are reflected in and reinforced by differences in their approach to the farm business. Family farmers place a high value on maintaining their independence and tend to be conservative and cautious, valuing security and stability in the farm business where operators of larger-than-family farms are more likely to pursue expansionist policies. These characteristics help to shape the farmer's response to the changing economic environment in which he has to work.

AGRICULTURAL POLICY

As a small, densely populated island, Britain has historically been one of the world's largest markets for food. Until the Second World War the cheap food policy pursued by successive governments depended heavily on imports, much to the detriment of home agriculture. The war brought about a fundamental revision of policy, prominence being given to the goals of food security and stability as well as to low prices. Since that time, much greater and more consistent support has been given to domestic producers. The framework for Britain's post-war agricultural policy was laid down in the 1947 Agriculture Act which aimed:

...promote a stable and efficient industry capable of producing such part of the nation's food as in the national interest it is desirable to produce in the United Kingdom and to produce it at minimum prices consistent with proper remuneration and living conditions for farmers and workers in agriculture and with an adequate return on capital invested.
(Agriculture Act 1947)

The instruments used to achieve a stable and prosperous agriculture have varied over the post-war period, but the mainstay has always been price support. A system of fixed prices at the end of the war was replaced by one of minimum guaranteed prices. The level at which prices were set, together with grants and subsidies on the cost of some inputs, enabled farmers to expand production and plan ahead with confidence while virtually free entry to food supplies from abroad gave consumers the benefit of low prices. Since Britain's entry into the EEC, prices have been underpinned by direct intervention in the market. This has meant that consumers have no longer been able to benefit from cheap food in the shops, while prices to British farmers have mostly been above those prevailing under the earlier system.

Any support system based on product prices must favor larger farmers who not only produce more but can be expected to achieve lower costs due to economies of size. As shown earlier, the 12% of larger-than-family farmers now account for over half of the total output of British agriculture. Because expansion is mainly financed by retained profits, the smaller farmer is less well placed than the larger operator to increase production. A growing emphasis on improving productivity also puts the smaller farmer at a disadvantage. The cost structure of agriculture makes it easier to raise productivity by increasing output than by cutting costs. The small farm in particular has a large element of fixed costs. Together these trends result in a polarization between expansionist, larger-than-family farmers, and the great majority of family farmers whose share of the market is falling and whose future prospects in the industry appear increasingly questionable.

Support for Family Farming?

These trends point to the inherent contradiction in British agricultural policy. Promoting a stable and efficient industry capable of producing cheap food implies larger farms and fewer farmers, whereas maintaining proper remuneration and living conditions for farmers means keeping the smaller producer in business. If prices are set at a level sufficient to provide an adequate livelihood for the marginal producer, the lion's share will go to larger producers who are least in need of income support, as well as stimulating an unwanted increase in output. The alternative of channeling money directly to farmers most in need would be costly and open to attack on the grounds of promoting inefficiency (Crow, 1984).

The crucial question seems to be how much the nation is prepared to pay to help the smaller farmer continue in business. Although the notion of family farming is warmly embraced by British politicians and farming leaders alike, it is difficult to point to any specific measures which have been taken to promote family farming at the expense of the larger farm.

One way of encouraging family farming might be to
arrest the trend towards larger units, through capital
taxation or legislation, and to redistribute the land in
smaller holdings. The Northfield Committee rejected the
idea of setting limits on the amount of land that one
occupier might farm as inappropriate, impracticable, and
unnecessary in the circumstances of British agriculture.
One objection was that if the ceiling were too high,
redistributing land would have a negligible effect on the
total number of farms while if it were low, an intolerable
amount of upheaval would be caused throughout the farming
industry. Perhaps more significant was the argument that
losses in efficiency by imposing a farm size limit would
be too high a price for the social benefits of creating
smaller farms (Munton, 1982). The Northfield Committee
appeared to have been swayed by the argument that:

The country has a limited number of really able
farmers. They are to be found running enterprises of
every type and size, ranging from the smallest to the
very largest. It is, therefore, desirable to create
conditions in which it is less difficult for farm
enterprises to grow bigger in order that the ability
of such men can be fully extended
(Northfield Report, 1979).

The possibility of making direct payments to smaller
farmers has often been mooted but rarely pursued. Various
schemes to help farmers in upland areas might be classed
as social payments. Earlier it was shown that smaller
farmers are disproportionately represented in the upland
areas of Wales, Scotland, northern England, and Northern
Ireland, where they tend to concentrate on cattle and
sheep production. Headage payments and preferential terms
of grants for farmers in Less Favored Areas could be said
to channel funds directly to smaller farmers. Even so,
those with the largest flocks and herds still obtain the
greatest amount of support.
The one government scheme aimed specifically at
encouraging the survival of the family farm, the 1959
Small Farmer Scheme, was short lived. Within a few years
it was superceded by schemes to hasten farm structural
change. This new approach was outlined by the Government
in 1965:

The Government believes that one of the more important
problems facing agriculture is that of the small

farmer trying to win a livelihood from insufficient land. As time passes, his difficulties will increase. He will find it harder to keep pace with technical advance. He will find it more and more difficult to maintain a standard of living in keeping with modern times

(The Development of Agriculture, 1965).

Attention was focused on those full-time farmers "who, however hard they work and however well they manage their businesses, just cannot hope to get a decent living from their farms at prices which the taxpayer and consumer could afford." The problem was to be tackled from three angles -- encouraging these farmers to enlarge their farms where possible, to resettle or retire from farming where they wanted "to give up an unrewarding struggle," and to cooperate with others to gain some of the benefits of farming or marketing on a bigger scale.

One scheme offered assistance with the costs of farm amalgamation and boundary adjustment. Under a second, farmers who gave up "uncommercial units" of between 100 and 600 smds for approved amalgamations and whose main income was derived from farming, were eligible for annuities or lump sum payments. Response to these two schemes for structural change was small. In the first few years the Payments to Outgoers Scheme attracted about 400 successful applicants a year, although small farms were disappearing at about ten times that rate. Among the objections to the scheme were the low level of incentives, administrative difficulties, and the loss of independence and other intrinsic satisfactions of farming. Whatever the arguments in favor of the schemes, their economic impact on the industry was quite small (Hine and Houston, 1973).

Cooperation was seen as a third possibility for the smaller farmer. Despite considerable inducements offered by the Government to encourage farmers to cooperate, formal cooperation still seems to have a limited appeal for British farmers. For a combination of historical and economic reasons, most produce is marketed through other channels. While the great majority of cooperative measures use their organization for the purchase of requisites, many are wary of sharing machines for fear that they will not be able to use them at the critical time. Moreover, while cooperation has made some progress in recent years among the larger farmers, there has been much less interest among smaller farmers who, it might appear, have more to gain. The proportion of farmers in England and Wales belonging to cooperatives in 1975 was 29% on holdings of 275 smds and over, 11% on smaller holdings. Corresponding proportions of members who used their cooperative for marketing produce were 31% and 19% (Ministry of Agriculture, Fisheries and Food, 1976). Perhaps it is the high value placed on independence which discourages the smaller farmer from committing himself wholeheartedly to the cooperative movement. Family farmers may prefer to cooperate on an informal basis, exchanging labor and sharing machines with relatives or neighbors.

Government policy towards part-time farmers is overtly neutral. In the 1965 policy statement, for instance, it was argued:

> There is nothing to prevent these part-time farmers from continuing in agriculture if that is what they wish. If they do, however, they cannot expect farming to give them their main livelihood.

In practice, part-time farmers operating on a small scale stand to gain much less than larger farmers from high farm prices and other state aids to the industry. Under the Agricultural and Horticultural Development and Grant Schemes, for example, full-time farmers were able to receive grants of up to 50,000 British pounds per farm to invest in approved projects. These substantial aids (which have since been reduced) were not available to farmers with units below 275 smds or to those who received less than half their income from farming. This had the effect of widening the gap between very small and larger farms.

Finally, there is no political movement of any consequence which represents the interests of small and family farmers as opposed to larger farmers. Movements like the Farmers' Union of Wales and the Smallfarmers' Association focus on the needs of family farms, but their efforts are dwarfed in comparison with the National Farmers' Union. With a membership thought to embrace 75% of all farmers (Newby, 1979), the NFU can justly claim to speak for all farmers. Its strength lies in being able to hold together its membership despite the conflicting interests between, for example, owner occupiers and tenants, arable and livestock producers, small- and large-scale farmers. In its latest policy statement, the

NFU affirms that, "For social, economic, and environmental reasons the family farm should remain the basic unit of the industry," (NFU, 1984). Yet it must simultaneously promote the cause of its larger-than-family farmer members. In short, while "survival of the family farm" continues to be a popular slogan, winning approval from most parts of the political spectrum, few positive steps have been taken to make it a reality. In a competitive free market economy, all the advantages in the form of price support, access to investment funds, tax benefits, and opportunities for growth appear to lie with the larger-than-family farm. The Government's "laissez faire" approach to the family farm may be criticized, but if it is true, as Bowler (1979) maintains, that, "No government has as yet found the means of helping small farms without helping large farms more," the alternatives could be worse. At least the present situation avoids the danger of unforeseen side effects which so often defeat the purpose of state intervention in the farming sector.

PERFORMANCE OF THE FAMILY FARM

Intensity of Land Use

It is a widely held opinion that the family farm uses its land more intensively than the larger farm, and this is often used as an argument for retaining the smaller unit. Much of the evidence in Britain suggests, however, that larger businesses use land more intensively than smaller ones. Furness (1983) has produced detailed figures to show that intensity, measured in terms of Gross Margin per hectare, increases steadily with size of farm business. This relationship holds true for dairy, livestock, and cropping farms separately and is consistent throughout the size range. Intensity of land use on the very smallest holdings may be only half that of larger-than-family farms. Other measures, like stocking density and output per cow, also tend to improve with size of farm or herd.

Total Factor Productivity

Investigating economies of size in farming, Britton and Hill (1975) detected a kind of threshold somewhere about 800 to 850 smds, between the two- and three-man farm and slightly below the ceiling for family farms. If the threshold is not reached, it is likely that resources in the farm business are not being used effectively. On the other hand, there does not appear to be any great advantage in expanding the business above that size, for little evidence could be found for greater economies on very large farms.

On the whole, Britton and Hill considered that "marketing economies" in the form of reduced input costs were of modest proportions in Britain. Larger UK producers did not appear to benefit to any great extent by obtaining higher prices for the larger quantities they marketed. The major source of economies of size is the spreading of costs of production over a larger volume of output. Smaller farms tend to suffer from the relative underemployment of family labor, including that of the farmer and wife. The problem is most acute on family farms where the lack of alternative employment and obstacles to structural change prevent the family from reorganizing its resources in order to utilize the available labor more fully (Agriculture EDC, 1973). In part-time farming families, where a second occupation helps to absorb the labor surplus, efficiency of labor use is likely to be much improved (Cavazzani and Fuller, 1982).

The conclusion on efficiency of resource use seems to be that smaller family farms are at a disadvantage compared to those at the top of the family farming range. While there are few benefits in economic efficiency which cannot be enjoyed by the large family farm, the well run two- to four-man unit, there are other reasons why farmers in this category should want their businesses to grow.

Farm Incomes and Profitability

While it is in the national interest to achieve the most efficient use of resources, the individual farmer has to consider his total profit and income. Whereas maximum efficiency may be achieved on quite small farms, maximum profits accrue to much larger businesses. In 1981-1982, for instance, two-thirds of the small family farms in the UK received net incomes of less than 6,000 British pounds, which was the average income of the nonfarming population at the time. Three-quarters of the larger-than-family farmers with farms of 40 ESUs and more were estimated to be earning over 10,000 British pounds in the same year

(Furness, 1983). There is, consequently a strong incentive for the operator of an efficient family farm to expand and push his business into the larger-than-family league.

Size related differences in income within types of farming can be very great indeed. In Wales in 1981-1982, for instance, larger-than-family dairy farms had average net incomes ten times greater than those of specialized dairy farms between 4 and 8 ESUs. Differences between types of farming compound the disadvantage of the family farm. Since the early 1970s, incomes on cropping farms have been rising much faster than on livestock and dairy farms, where most of the family farmers operate (Furness, 1983).

Many family farmers in Britain, therefore, have reason to feel dissatisfied if they compare the returns for their labor with wages and salaries in other occupations. When interest charges are deducted, the residual sum for family living expenses appears still less adequate. Yet without higher incomes these farmers find it difficult to expand their businesses and, as will be shown, expansion has been the key to economic survival.

Investment and Growth

The cost-price squeeze forces farmers to improve productivity if they are to remain competitive. The two ways of achieving this are to reduce costs or to increase output. As already pointed out, the cost structure of agriculture offers little scope for cost cutting, especially on smaller units where the farmer's and wife's own labor looms large among total costs. Most farmers, therefore, need to find ways of increasing output if they are to survive and enjoy an acceptable level of living. Yet this option, too, seems to be receding. Since April, 1984, the imposition of milk quotas has effectively prevented expansion in the dairy sector and at the present time, cereal growers are wondering whether they will have to face quotas or lower prices.

Increasing output by more intensive farming methods is a possibility but one that brings its own problems. It demands better management, for instance, to prevent the build up of disease in animals or crops, and this may be a limiting factor. Their higher average age, lack of agricultural training, and preference for security may discourage the smaller family farmer from experimenting with new technologies to improve output on a limited acreage.

Increasing output by buying or renting more land is often a preferred option, but here again the smaller farmer is at a disadvantage. Farm development is largely financed out of retained profits; on average between 80 and 90% of new investment on British farms comes from personal sources, the rest being made up of government grants and borrowing. The lower profitability of smaller farms, therefore, fuels a vicious circle. Without higher incomes or access to other sources of capital, they are not able to buy more land or finance farm improvements in order to expand their businesses. But without growth they cannot realize higher profits. Table 2.5 clearly illustrates the dilemma of the smaller farmer. Net investment from income retained on farms of 4 to 16 ESUs in 1981-1982 was less than a tenth of that on larger-than-family farms in the owner-occupied sector. Among tenanted farms, retained incomes in the 4 to 16 ESU size band were actually negative (Furness, 1983).

For other reasons, too, larger farms may be able to support investment and growth more easily than small farms. The biggest lenders to British agriculture are the commmercial banks, who assess any request for funds on its merits and on an equal footing with requests from nonfarming clients. Return on capital, a good indicator of profitability, is likely to be low on smaller farms, making them less attractive as potential borrowers. Government grants are the next most important source of outside funds. As already pointed out, many small units may not be eligible because their businesses are too small or because too large a share of the income is derived from nonfarm sources. Third, while agricultural land prices have been rising in real terms, farmers paying high marginal rates of income tax have had a strong incentive to plow surplus profits back into buying more land. Interest on money borrowed for land purchase can be deducted from income before tax, so the greater the income, the greater the benefit to the farmer buying more land. Small farms with poorer performance and those handicapped by poor soils, difficult terrain, or unfavorable climatic conditions have little opportunity to develop. The gap between dynamic, larger-than-family farms and smaller family farms is thus likely to widen.

Part-time farming families are not locked into their situation to the same extent. In Britain, a majority of them rely mainly on other income sources, which relieves

Table 2.5.   Net investment from retained income by size of
            business, England 1981-1982

Size of business in ESU	Net investment from retained income British pounds per farm
Owner occupied farms	
4 - 15.9	835
16 - 39.9	5,305
40 and over	9,040
Tenanted farms	
4 - 15.9	- 361
16 - 39.9	1,730
40 and over	5,578
Mixed tenure farms	
4 - 15.9	1,764
16 - 39.9	3,355
40 and over	13,514

Source: Furness, 1983.

them both of the need to wrest a living from the farm and
from having to expand in order to stay in the same
relative income position. Many seem content for their
farm businesses to remain static, but if expansion is the
goal, it may be possible to finance it from other income
sources. If the family is able to subsist on the nonfarm
earnings, farm profits can be retained in the business to
hasten growth.

EVALUATION

The family farm can be evaluated as a form of business
organization which has certain strengths and weaknesses as
compared with other forms. The family provides most of
the resources of land, labor, capital, and management.
Once these factors of production have been acquired, they
do not have to show market rates of return. The family

farm does not depend on hired labor to any extent and so
is not vulnerable to demands for better wages or improved
working conditions which could threaten the larger farm
business. The family farmer can weather bad times, for a
while at least, by tightening his belt.

On the debit side, difficulties can arise on family
farms if the labor demands of the farm cannot be varied
responding to stages in the family cycle. Many small
farms also suffer chronic underemployment of family labor,
especially that of the farmer and wife, which lowers their
productivity. Incomes which are, on average, lower than
those in other occupations represents a threat to the
future of the smaller farm. Children may not choose to
follow in their fathers' footsteps. Difficulties of
phasing in a successor on a farm which is too small to
support two families further reduce the chances of the
farm remaining in the family. Shortage of capital,
coupled with generally lower levels of formal training in
agriculture, tends to make smaller farmers less receptive
to technological change. Technical advice is less likely
to be offered and less often sought by the smaller farmer
than by larger operators. Low income farms have fewer
opportunities for growth, since growth is largely financed
out of current profits. These influences are likely to
reinforce one another and widen the gap between large,
progressive, dynamic, growing farm businesses and smaller,
static or declining ones. Some of the larger family farms
will be in the first category, but inevitably many smaller
family farms will be in the second.

It is the smaller family farms, those requiring less
than two man-years, and certainly the less-than-one-man
farms, which are at an increasing disadvantage in the
competitive climate of British agriculture today. Small
farmers may be locked into their situation with few
opportunities to expand their farms, seeing no future in
farming for themselves or their children but unable to
break away through a combination of age and lack of
alternative skills or opportunities. On the other hand,
the smaller farmer may be reconciled to his position.
The farming occupation itself, independence, and country
living may be enough to compensate for low financial
rewards. Some small farmers may consciously prefer
satisfactory incomes to higher incomes with more risk
attached, valuing continuity more highly than change. For
others, part-time farming may be the solution. Having a
second and often larger source of income allows a large
number of families to live on small farms in Britain,

enjoying the lifestyle and participating in farming activities without having to accept a declining standard of living.

Family farming can also be evaluated from the point of view of the wider community, considering how it contributes to the well being and quality of life of the whole nation. What is a strength for the individual farm business may be seen as a weakness in the eyes of the wider community and vice versa.

While growing food surpluses and the mounting cost of agricultural support have been leading up to a crisis in the Common Agricultural Policy, the farmer's standing in the eyes of the British public has suffered a severe blow. No longer regarded as the savior of the nation, the farmer has been caricatured in some quarters as one who has grown rich at the taxpayer's expense, wasting resources to produce food which has to be stockpiled while millions starve. Politicians like Body (1982, 1984) have attacked the whole system of agricultural support. Economists like Bowers and Cheshire (1983) have based their critique of agricultural policy not just on costs of support generally but on misuse of the countryside. They are supported by naturalists like Shoard (1980), who has made a powerful attack on the environmental effects of modern farming in her book The Theft of the Countryside.

The family farmer probably emerges from this chorus of accusation rather better than the large capitalist farmer. Owning fewer acres, he has not become so blatantly wealthy (on paper at least) as the larger farmer due to the land price boom. Producing less, he has not profited as much from the artificially high level of prices under the Community regime. Producing beef, sheep, or milk rather than cereals, his income has not risen as rapidly as on the larger cropping farms. Obliged to finance farm improvements from his own more limited resources and not enjoying easy access to borrowed funds or grants, the smaller farmer has not been able to change the physical appearance of his farm as rapidly or as systematically as his larger neighbor. In Potter's terms, he is more likely to be a constrained than an enabled subject (Potter, 1985). Removing trees and hedgerows in order to enlarge fields to accommodate bigger machines, draining wetlands, heavy use of agricultural chemicals, and so on are associated in the public mind with large arable farms rather than with the "typical" family farm. Hence the smaller farmer who, whether he likes it or not, tends to farm on more conservative and traditional lines is less likely to antagonize the increasingly vocal conservation lobby.

Family farms may help to keep an agricultural population in employment, with all that this implies for maintaining services and holding together the fabric of rural society. Perhaps the real strength of family farming lies not so much in reversing current trends towards farm modernization, concentration of enterprises, and farm enlargement, which must necessarily follow from technological change, but in slowing down the pace of change to a more acceptable level. The family farm, then, may have a significant role to play in conserving the natural and man-made environment in a recognizable and valued form. In the long run, this quality may be judged more important than its contribution to agricultural production and prosperity.

35

REFERENCES

Agriculture Act 1947. HMSO.
Agriculture EDC. 1972. Agricultural Manpower in England
  and Wales. London: HMSO.
Agriculture EDC. 1973. Farm Productivity: A Report on
  Factors affecting Productivity at the Farm Level.
  London: HMSO.
Annual Review of Agriculture. 1983. Cmd. 8804. London:
  HMSO.
Body, Richard. 1982. Agriculture: The Triumph and the
  Shame. London: Temple Smith.
Body, Richard. 1984. Farming in the Clouds. London:
  Temple Smith.
Bowers, J. K. and Paul Chesire. 1983. Agriculture, the
  Countryside and Land Use. London: Meuthen.
Bowler, Ian. 1979. Government and Agriculture: A Spatial
  Perspective. Harlow: Longman.
Britton, D. K. and Berkeley Hill. 1975. Size and
  Efficiency in Farming. Farnborough: Saxon House.
Buccleuch and Queensberry, Duke of. 1981. Smallfarming: A
  Landowner's View. pp. 21-26 in R. B. Tranter (ed.)
  Smallfarming and the Nation. Centre for Agricultural
  Strategy, University of Reading. CAS Paper 9.
Burrell, Alison, Berkeley Hill and John Medland. 1984.
  Statistical Handbook of UK Agriculture. London:
  Macmillan.
Cavazzani, Ada and Anthony M. Fuller. 1982. "Inter-
  national perspectives on part-time farming: a review"
  GeoJournal 6(4): 383-389.
Commission of the European Communities. 1981. Factors
  Influencing Ownership, Tenancy, Mobility and Use of
  Farmland in the United Kingdom. Brussels/Luxembourg.
  Information on Agriculture No. 74.
Crow, Graham. 1984. The Impact of the Common Agricultural
  Policy on Family Farming. Unpublished paper presented
  to the British Association for the Advancement of
  Science, Norwich.
The Development of Agriculture. 1965. Cmnd. 2738. London:
  HMSO.
Errington, A. J. 1983. The farmer's wife: her role in the
  farm business. Pp. 223-228 in R. B. Tranter (ed.)
  Strategies for Family-Worked Farms in the UK. Centre
  for Agricultural Strategy, University of Reading. CAS
  Paper 15.

36

Farmers Weekly. 1980. Women on the Farm Survey Report.
September 26 and October 3.
Farmers Weekly. 1984. Retirement: A Special Survey and
Guide. October 19.
Furness, G. W. 1983. The Importance, Distribution and Net
Incomes of Small Farm Businesses in the UK. pp. 12-41
in R. B. Tranter (ed.) Strategies for Family-Worked
Farms in the UK. Centre for Agricultural Strategy,
University of Reading. CAS Paper 15.
Gasson, Ruth. 1969. Occupational Immobility of Small
Farmers. Farm Economics Branch, Cambridge University.
Occasional Paper No. 13.
Gasson, Ruth. 1974. "Socioeconomic status and orientation
to work: the case of farmers" Sociologia Ruralis XIV
(3): 127-141.
Gasson, Ruth. 1980. "Roles of farm women in England"
Sociologia Ruralis XX (3): 165-180.
Gasson, Ruth. 1986. Farm Families with Other Gainful
Activities. Dept. of Agricultural Economics, Economics;
Wye College.
Harrison, Alan. 1975. Farmers and Farm Businesses in
England. Department of Agricultural Economics and
Management, University of Reading. Miscellaneous Study
No. 62.
Hastings, M. R. 1984. "Succession on farms."
Agricultural Manpower. 8:4-8.
Hine, R. C. and A. M. Houston. 1973. Government and
Structural Change in Agriculture. Universities of
Nottingham and Exeter.
Hunter-Smith, J. D. 1982. Opening Address. pp. 9-11 in B.
J. Marshall and R. B. Tranter (eds.) Smallfarming and
the Rural Community. Centre for Agricultural
Strategy, University of Reading. CAS Paper 11.
Ministry of Agriculture, Fisheries and Food. 1976. EEC
Survey on the Structure of Agricultural Holdings,
1975: England and Wales. Press release, Guildford.
Ministry of Agriculture, Fisheries and Food. 1976.
Unpublished results of June Census.
Munton, R. J. C., 1982. The Northfield Committee Report on
Small Farms. pp. 18-27 in B. J. Marshall and R. B.
Tranter (eds.) Smallfarming and the Rural Community.
Centre for Agricultural Strategy, University of
Reading. CAS Paper 11.
National Farmers' Union. 1984. The Way Forward: New
Directions for Agricultural Policy. London: NFU.

Newby, Howard, Colin Bell, David Rose and Peter Saunders.
1978. Property, Paternalism and Power: Class and
Control in Rural England London: Hutchinson.
Newby, Howard. 1979. Green and Pleasant Land? Social
Change in Rural England. London: Hutchinson.
Northfield, Lord. 1979. Report of the Committee of
Inquiry into the Acquisition and Occupancy of
Agricultural Land. Cmnd. 7599. London: HMSO.
Potter, Clive. 1985. The Farmer as an Enabled and
Constrained Subject. Unpublished paper presented to
the Rural Economy and Society Study Group conference,
Oxford.
Rettie, W. J. 1975. "Scotland's farm occupiers,"
Scottish Agricultural Economics XXV:387-393.
Shoard, Marion. 1980. The Theft of the Countryside.
London: Temple Smith.
Symes, David G. and Terry K. Marsden. 1983. "Complementary
roles and asymmetrical lives: farmers' wives in a
large farm environment" Sociologia Ruralis XXIII
(3/4): 229-241.

3
Family Farming in Ireland

D.F. Hannan and R. Breen

INTRODUCTION: FAMILY FARMING IN IRELAND*

In Ireland, the term "family farm" is synonymous with the term "farm" itself, since the degree of penetration of agriculture by commercial interests or "agribusiness" remains relatively small. The virtual absence of tenant farmers, a tiny employee farm labor force, and a minute proportion of very large farms means that almost all Irish farms are family owned and, for the most part, family run. Thus, the notion of the "family farm" is not a particularly useful one in the Irish context. Instead it serves to obscure the large differences that exist among family farms in their economic interests and in their social characteristics. In particular, it masks the extent to which these differential interests are influenced by historical forces and state policies, which in general have had quite different consequences for large and small farmers.

Broadly speaking, there are three overlapping dimensions along which important distinctions between family farms occur in Ireland. These are (1) farm size, (2) the regional location of the farm, and (3) the type of farming carried out. The recent trend in these areas are declining numbers of smaller farms along with their marginalization and relative impoverishment, unless farming is combined with off-farm employment. Since small-scale farming is most characteristic of the western half of the country where less off-farm employment is

---

* In this paper the word "Ireland" will be used only to refer to the Republic of Ireland.

available, the situation of the smaller producers there has declined into almost complete marginality. So the viable and even vibrant pattern of economic and social life described by Arensberg and Kimball (1940) as characteristic of these small farm communities in the late 1920s and early 1930s, has almost completely vanished. Either these farms are now operated by generally very poor and rather old bachelors, heirless married farmers, or, where contiguous to expanding industrializing towns, by part-time farmers (Rottman, Hannan, et al., 1982; Kelleher and O'Mahony, 1984).

Output and income arising in agriculture have been growing rapidly over the past 20 years but have been increasingly concentrated in the large, more specialized and more capital intensive dairying, tillage, or, less frequently, beef enterprises in the east and south. Economic inequalities have widened dramatically, so that the farming sector now comprises some of the poorest but also a small minority of some of the richest families in Ireland (Rottman, et al., 1979).

In this paper we begin with a broad review of historical changes in the pattern of Irish family farming. We examine the role of government and EEC policy in bringing about these changes. We examine some of the effects of these changes on the economic and social structure and environment of rural Ireland. Lastly, we shall discuss the prospects for the different kinds of family farm in Ireland today. As a preliminary, however, we need to place Irish farming within the context of its regional and wider European perspective.

REGIONAL AND FARM SIZE DIFFERENCES

By British and North American standards Irish farms are very small. The median size of holding is 16 hectares—half that of Britain—and we have almost none of the very large commercial farms one finds in England. However, compared with the EEC as a whole, the Irish farm size is somewhat over the average (Harrison, 1982). However, given the extremely wide differences in land quality and in the level of commercialization—in which Ireland stands at one extreme—this completely overstates the relative economic position of Irish farmers.

Unlike most other West European countries, the process of land consolidation in Ireland has shown a decline in the number of very large farms, due primarily to the action of a land reform program beginning in the late 1870s which initially transferred ownership of holdings from landlords to tenants. Subsequently, the authorities appropriated and redistributed even farmer-owned larger holdings to create a number of more viable small farms. The very large farms--over 500 acres--have, therefore, generally declined in number over the 20th century. But there also has been a decline in the number of very small farms (under 15 acres). Increases have occurred in farms of the middle sized category (50-150 acres).

Within Ireland a generally accepted figure of 20 hectares (about 50 acres) is considered the minimum necessary for a viable farm unit. Only 42% of Irish farms are over that figure. When farms were categorized by their commercial or development potential using the most comprehensive data available and using more liberal Irish rather than EEC standards, 45% were considered viable (Commins, 1983). Using these standards, 15% of Irish farms were found to reach commercial standards--with a clear commercial market orientation and incomes roughly equivalent to the nonfarm sector in the local region. Another 30% were categorized as "development"--capable of becoming commercially viable given adequate farm development aid. A majority of Irish farms are, therefore, regarded as "marginal"--not capable of becoming commercially viable. Under the somewhat different criteria employed by the EEC's "Farm Modernization Scheme," only 33% of all Irish farms were categorized as commercial or development status in 1982, (Commins, 1983; Kelleher and O'Mahony, 1984). This highly marginal status of the majority of Irish farms, even under the most liberal criteria, has emerged only over the past 40 years, with the pace of marginalization accelerating from the mid 1960s onwards.

Since almost all Irish farmland is owner-occupied (97%), compared to an EEC average of 65%, we face much greater rigidities in structural reform than almost all other EEC countries. While peasant proprietorship was a highly sought after political goal, its achievement has had certain serious costs in much lower land mobility rates. Over a third of our agricultural land is now in the hands of older farmers whose farm output and incomes are very low and who depend to a large extent on maintenance payments from the state. At the same time, a large proportion of younger and potentially viable farmers cannot get their hands on the necessary land to bring their holdings up to a potentially commercial size.

42

Within Ireland, however, there are pronounced regional differences in all of these respects. In the western and northwestern regions, the province of Connaught and the three counties of Ulster which lie within the Republic, less than 25% of farms exceed 20 hectares, compared to over 50% in the more commercialized East and South. Even these size differences understate regional inequalities, since land quality in the western counties, in terms of yielding ability, is about half that of the east and south. Over two-thirds of the land in these western counties was in fact categorized as "marginal" for most commercial agricultural purposes in 1980, compared to around a quarter of the land in the more commercialized counties (The National Soil Survey of Ireland, 1980). It is not surprising, therefore, that family farm incomes in the western counties are less than half that in the eastern and southern counties.

It is in this western region, therefore, that the most serious farm structural problem arises. In the early part of this century, however, it was in this very region that the most viable, in terms of any measure of social reproduction, family farming system existed; a system whose structure and dynamics were made widely known by Arensberg and Kimball's (1940) classic study.

THE HISTORICAL BACKGROUND

The majority of family farmers in Ireland today, therefore, hold a rather marginal position within the economy, being extremely unlikely to reproduce themselves. To understand their position we need to know the base from which the problem has developed and the process by which it occurred. This crisis in small-scale farming is, in fact, a relatively recent phenomenon. At the time that Arensberg (1937) and Arensberg and Kimball (1940) painted such an Arcadian image of these western small farm communities in the early 1930s, the independent demographic and economic evidence shows that despite being located in the poorest and least market favored region, these small farm communities possessed a highly self-sustaining subsistence economy and had the highest marriage and reproduction rates of all farming regions in Ireland. In terms of any index of social reproduction, this small farm region was the most viable of all farming regions in Ireland (Hannan, 1979, pp. 27-68). But its

origins were much more recent and its structure much less
stable than Arensberg and Kimball indicated.
    In the 19th century the pattern of Irish agriculture
and Irish society as a whole underwent a series of almost
cataclysmic changes. There was a very rapid growth in
population until the Famine in the mid 1840s. The
increasing subdivision of holdings and establishment of
new households was encouraged by the landlords,
particularly during the period of high prices for tillage
crops on the English market, which held until the end of
the Napoleonic wars. It was also facilitated by the rapid
spread of potato culture (O'Tuathaigh, 1972; Crotty,
1966). Although there is clear evidence of a slowdown in
population growth before the Famine, as a reaction to
changing economic and land tenure conditions, this early
expansionary phase was brought to a dramatic end by the
million deaths during the Great Famine of 1846-1847 and by
the contemporary massive emigration which continued well
into the late 19th century, (Lee, 1973; Kennedy, 1973).
This hiatus, however, was highly class selective. Both
famine and emigration were disproportionately selective of
the class of propertyless farm laborers, cottiers, and
very small tenant farmers. As Lee (1973, p.3) puts it:
"Between 1845 and 1851 the number of laborers and cottiers
fell by 40%, the number of farmers by 20%. During the
following 60 years the number of laborers and cottiers
again fell by 40%, the number of farmers by 5%. Within
the rural community the class balance swung sharply in
favor of farmers. Within the farm community it swung even
more sharply in favor of bigger farmers as against small
farmers."
    This newly emerging class of smallholders and
middle-sized farmers became increasingly secure in their
tenancies as the 19th century drew to a close. But faced
with the long-lasting agricultural depression starting in
the 1870s, this group fought the successful "Land War"
against their exploitative landlords. By the beginning of
the 20th century the population of most rural communities
had been reduced and transformed from a teeming mass of
impoverished laborers, small cottiers, and very small
tenant farmers, into a stable, conservative, land owning
peasantry. Famine, emigration, a longlasting agricultural
recession, increasing opposition to subdivision, and a
steep decline in local and migrant agricultural laboring
opportunities combined in a very severe process of
marginalization of the poorest and weakest section of the
agricultural population. This first eliminated the class

of landless laborers and small cottiers which had so
dominated the farm population before the Famine. But from
the late 1870s onwards, the noninheriting sons of even
larger farmers found themselves equally disadvantaged
(Lee, 1973; Crotty, 1966; Hannan and Hardiman, 1978).

So by the time Arensberg and Kimball came to the small
farm communities of County Clare in the early 1930s, they
were dealing with a particular local economy and a
particular social structure which had only recently
established its apparently very solid foundations,
foundations which in cultural and social structural terms
appeared to them to be almost as timeless as the history
of the Irish people themselves (Arensberg, 1937:16-34).
The society they studied and its "customs" were viewed
primarily as "an unbroken ancient tradition that goes
back, perhaps long into pre-Christian times" (pp. 16-17).
The "ancient and unbroken tradition" (p. 18) in terms of
its economic and social structure and in many aspects of
its culture, had a very recent history indeed. One
particular irony of Arensberg and Kimball's study is that
even as they described it, this rural social structure was
nourishing the seeds of its own destruction (Hannan,
1979:51-65).

Arensberg and Kimball's ethnographically based model
of the social and economic structure of these small farm
communities in the west of Ireland in the early 1930s is
accepted here as a generally reliable and valid one,
however. As an economic system, almost all production
took place within small family farms with very little
employed labor. It was dominantly a subsistence
production system. The evidence available for the 1930s
shows that around one-third of total agricultural
production in Ireland was consumed on farms, without
process of sale (Agricultural Statistics, 1934-1956).
Estimates for the western region of small farms would put
that figure close to 60% for that time. Even in 1956,
between 30 and 40% of total agricultural output on the
smaller western farms (under 30 acres) was estimated as
being consumed within the farm gate (National Farm Survey
1955-58). In comparison, the more commercialized eastern
and southern farming regions, with average farm sizes
almost double that of the west, had family farm
subsistence rates almost half that of the west, even at
the same farm size levels (Hannan, 1979:32-33). In the
western region in the 1920s and 1930s, we had a relatively
stable small farm subsistence economy, with use values
rather than exchange values being dominant. In the

eastern and southern regions this was clearly not the case.

By this time, impartible inheritance had become the norm, and familial arrangements followed the so-called "stem family" pattern. Thus, only one son inherited the undivided patrimony, the rest had to find employment elsewhere, although they may have had temporary aid from "the stem" in early adulthood before migrating or later if in distress. Occasionally, noninheriting sons might be settled on neighboring farms acquired through purchase or inheritance from other relatives.

Just as one son inherited, generally, one daughter received a dowry. As Arensberg puts it: "Usually only the heir and one daughter are married and dowered, the one with the farm, the other with the fortune. All the rest, in the words of the Luogh residents, 'must travel'." (Arensberg 1937:79). The system, in other words, guaranteed generational replacement of the father by his chosen heir; the result was a high marriage rate for heirs, high levels of emigration amongst the noninheriting siblings, or prolonged dependency with attendant nonmarriage for those who chose to stay "surplus" at home. A continuous process of emigration and population decline coexisted with the persistence of strong local familial and communal systems.

Table 3.1 summarizes some basic indices of social reproduction for the two most contrasting regions within the country in 1926--where these regional differences are most marked. Father-son replacements were substantially greater on western farms of all sizes in 1926, but particularly so on the smaller farms. Of course, there were very few off-farm opportunities in the Western region at that time, but what is striking about the figures is that despite this oversupply of potential heirs, the actual selected heir was far more likely to marry, and especially so on the smaller farms. In the Western regions as a whole, only between 8 and 15% of older male farmers (over 45) remained unmarried in 1926 compared to over 30% in most Eastern and Southern commercial farming counties.

What is equally surprising is the extraordinary effectiveness of these smaller Western farmers in dispersing the noninheriting sons. Although substantially more sons initially entered the farm occupation, almost four times the proportion subsequently left farming than in the more commercialized eastern province--mostly to emigrate.

Table 3.1. Some indices of social reproduction for the Western subsistence and Eastern commercial farm regions in Ireland in 1926.

Two most extreme regions	No. of farmers' sons working on farms per 1000 male farmers		Percentage of male farmers, 35-44 who are married i.e. by 1946		Percentage of male farm entrants at ages 15-24 in 1926 who are estimated to have remained of left home 20 years later,		
	Farms less than 30 acres	Farms 50-100 acres	Farms 15-30 acres	Farms 50-100 acres	% as family dependent	% as farmers (inheritors)	% who had left home
Connaught (West)	750	820	73	69	27	36	37
Leinster (East)	542	714	59	65	39	51	10

Source: Hannan, 1979, pp. 40-50.

It appears that the process of demographic replacement—of sons replacing fathers on farms and of this new family reproducing itself—was far more effective in the west than in the more commercialized farming regions, and this pattern held until the late 1940s. This poorer region also was more efficient in its process of dispersal of noninheritors, leaving relatively fewer sons in prolonged dependency on their fathers or on inheriting brothers. The viability of the stem-family system, as described by Arensberg (1937) and Arensberg and Kimball (1940), is strongly supported by these independent indices of reproduction and dispersal. The "archaic pattern" of high marriage rates that had been so characteristic of most of peasant farming regions of Ireland in the mid 19th century and was assumed by most demographers to have ended by the beginning of the 20th century (Cousens, 1964, 1968; Kennedy, 1973; Walsh, 1970), was still clearly characteristic of small farmers in the western region even in 1926 and 1936.

As to the characteristic structure of family relationships within these farm communities at that time, particularly the position of women, all of the independent evidence available suggests that Arensberg and Kimball's ethnographic model is a reliable, valid one. With the growing dominance of peasant proprietorship and of female impartible inheritance after the 1870s, patriarchy increased in significance. Increasing incorporation into a market economy, declining local nonfarm opportunities, and increasing impartibility of inheritance all combined to restrict the local economic and marriage opportunities of women to almost one adult role—that of farm wife and mother. Women's economic position, therefore, became increasingly dependent on paternal endowment on marriage and subsequently on husband owned resources. As a result, the classic description of the Irish small-scale farm family by Arensberg and Kimball (1940) appears to be generally a valid and reliable one. This description includes a rigid division of labor between the sexes in farm, household, and childrearing tasks, with strong patriarchical authority patterns, considerable role autonomy for wives within their restricted task role specialties, and a maternally dominant social emotional structure (Hannan and Katsiaouni, 1977). Both the stability and the longevity of these farm and family patterns were much less sturdy, however, than Arensberg and Kimball's work had indicated.

THE CHANGING STRUCTURE OF FAMILY FARMING IN THE
POST-WAR PERIOD

The Dissolution of the Smallholding System

The unique pattern of farm economy, family living,
inheritance arrangements, family cycle patterns, and
kinship and communal arrangements which was so graphically
described by Arensberg and Kimball (1940) for the 1920s
and 1930s, gave way to increasing class and regional
differentiation in the post-war period. The pace of
dissolution of the smallholding system gathered speed as
time passed. By the 1980s we are left with a large number
of Western smallholders whose economic position is among
the worst of any social group in the community (Rottman,
et al., 1979), but who hold on tenaciously to their farms,
allowing little land mobility. The result is a
marginalized class of small farmers who are untouched by
agricultural and land policy and who increasingly rely on
direct social welfare payments from the State for their
support (Commins, et al., 1978; Hannan, 1979; Kelleher and
O'Mahony, 1984).

Hannan (1979), examining a number of indices of social
reproduction, shows clearly that the regional differences
in farming and family system isolated for the 1920s and
1930s remained relatively stable until 1946 or so (Hannan,
1979:51-59). But after 1946 there was a growing decline
in father-son replacements and in the marriage rate of
successors, as well as increasing farm size differentials
in social reproduction. Table 3.2 summarizes these
changes for the two main contrasting regions.

Two trends are evident. In the earlier period, farm
size differences were clearly reflected in marriage
chances in the commercialized eastern region, but not in
the western small farming region. Marriage rates, in
fact, do not change very much in commercial farming
regions over the whole period from 1926 to 1971--except
that the chances of the large commercial farmers have
progressively improved, particularly in recent decades, as
market conditions improved. On the other hand, the poor
economic and social situation of very small farmers in
commercial regions had already become quite obvious by
1926. But in the western region, while the position of
the small farming sector has markedly worsened, the
relative advantage of the larger farmer has significantly
improved. As we shall see later, income inequalities grew

rapidly in the post-war period and, as a result, farm size differences and related life chances widened considerably. By 1961 regional differences in the farm-size/marriage-rate relationship had almost disappeared. However, these figures understate the inequalities that have developed in the Western region particularly. Here the extent of marginalization of the small farming group had proceeded much further than elsewhere. One study (Scully, 1971) showed that 51% of all farmers over 55 in Connaught in the mid 1960s were either single or had no direct heir willing to take over the farm. Among farmers with less than 30 acres, the percentage was considerably higher.

Table 3.2. Percentage of male farmers, aged 35-44 who were single in 1926, 1946, 1961, and 1971, in 2 farm regions and farm sizes.

Region	Farm Size	1926	1946	1961	1971
Connaught	Less than 15 acres	28	38	43	49
(west)	15-30 acres	27	38	43	49
	Over 100 acres	36	38	29	30
Leinster	Less than 15 acres	45	38	43	49
(east)	15-30 acres	41	39	46	47
	Over 100 acres	34	32	27	23

One of the main underlying reasons for the declining reproduction of the smallholding system was the increasing reluctance of young women to confine themselves to the opportunities it allowed. The daughters of farmers, particularly small farmers, started to desert these confining opportunities at a much earlier stage than their brothers. The trend toward rapidly increasing outmigration rates for young farm women turns sharply upward after 1936, whereas for men such trends only occur after 1946 (Hannan, 1979:52-55). Although there is nothing but anecdotal evidence for the period, it appears that the main reason for this trend is that women developed highly negative attitudes toward their much more constrained and dependent opportunities. The image of the farm woman with "the dirty apron and the wellington boots"

was one that had high saliency at that time. As a result
of these trends, by the mid 1960s almost half of all
farmers on smaller acreages were not able to marry unless
they combined farming with off-farm employment. By this
stage, in fact, prescriptive farm inheritance arrangements
had become onerous family obligations for which sons had
to pay a heavy price both economically and socially.

Increasing Farm Size Inequalities

The recent processes of change in Irish agriculture
have led to a greater and increasing differentiation of
life chances. Income from agriculture has become heavily
concentrated in fewer and increasingly prosperous hands.
The process of change toward a class differentiated system
of farming is neatly illustrated by the finding that up
until the mid 1950s net output per acre and per man
declined with increasing farm size. But from that time
onward, and at an increasing pace, the position reversed;
and now productivity and farm size are highly positively
correlated (Johnson and Conway, 1976).

Aggregate output growth on Irish farms has been
slightly greater than the EEC average since 1974 (Eurostat
National Accounts, 1985). This rapid growth of output is
mostly attributable to the more commercialized and
development status farmers. On the other side of the
coin, output has been declining on the smaller, more
marginalized farms as the older, and generally heirless,
farm population retire from active farming.

The effect of EEC policies, since entry in 1973, has
been to accelerate this process of marginalization.
Direct State policies have also strongly shifted their
emphasis from small farm development in the 1960s toward
larger farm commercialization, and the development of
off-farm employment and direct income support measures for
smaller farms (Commins, et al., 1978). Inequalities in
output and incomes arising in agriculture have grown
rapidly in recent times, to a point where variances in
market incomes are now greater than in the nonfarm sector
(Cox, et al., 1982; Kelleher and O'Mahony, 1984). While
one of the goals of price support policies is to help
equalize farm and nonfarm incomes, a very high proportion
of these transfers goes to the larger farmers whose
incomes were initially greater than the national average.
It is estimated, for instance, that the top 11% of farmers
having over 100 acres captured roughly 40% of price
support expenditure. At the same time, the bottom

third of farm incomes are roughly equivalent to those in the households of unskilled manual workers, where the level of unemployment is very high (Rottman, et al., 1982). These farmers receive almost none of the price support expenditure (Matthews, 1982).

About 25% of farmers are part-timers, who have quite good incomes. Their presence in the small farm communities of the west depends mainly on distance from developing industrial locations. Where these industrial centers have developed--and national policy since the mid 1960s has emphasized the dispersion of new industry--such outlets have had remarkably positive effects on local rural communities. Between 1961 and 1966, for instance, 78% of mainly open country rural districts declined in population. This had fallen to 57% for the period 1966-71. But between 1971 and 1981, only 18% of such districts declined in population. The dispersed nature of industrialization that occurred in the 1970s appears responsible for the slow down, rather than any growth in farm prosperity. Only those places remote from towns and developing industrial centers declined in population in the 1970s.

This emergent duality of Irish agriculture, a highly commercialized large farming sector coexisting with a highly marginalized small farm sector, has a pronounced regional distribution. It is in the western and northwestern small farm region, where once the most viable "peasant" farming system had existed, that now has the least commercially viable farms. Over 90% of farms in this region are now categorized as "marginal"--effectively not capable of becoming commercially viable under the EEC Farm Modernization Scheme. In the eastern and southern regions, over half of the farms were defined as viable or potentially viable in this sense. Such State defined categories clearly indicate the preferences and role of the State in the farm development process, as we shall see in the following section.

This relative economic viability of farms is now highly predictive of the position and role of women in farming. Only a minute proportion of farms are inherited directly by women, and usually only when there is no son. So marriage to farmers, now no longer mediated by "match-making" or dowries, is still the main avenue to farming for women. Now, however, a significant proportion of younger marriages are by women with continuing off-farm employment, usually with jobs in nursing, teaching or related semi-professional or clerical employment. On

average, wives also receive a much better education than
their husbands, a relative advantage which becomes
apparent in their higher participation in household and
farm account keeping and management decisionmaking (Hannan
and Katsiaouni, 1977).

Within farm families the position of women and the
structure of family relationships varies widely. Only
around a quarter of farm families now approximate to the
"traditional" structure - one with rigid segregation of
task roles in household and farm, a high degree of
patriarchical dominance, and clear maternal specialization
in social-emotional functions. And where these classic
patterns are most evident, they constitute the least
satisfactory of all family arrangements. In other words,
the most "traditional" is now the least legitimized
pattern.

At the other extreme are around one-fourth of farm
families which approximate to what was the most "modern"
urban, middle class model of the 1960s--low sex role
segregation in household and childrearing roles, joint
farm and family decisionmaking, and a mutually supportive
spousal and parental social-emotional structure. Most
families, therefore, fall between these two extremes--with
interaction patterns varying widely across the three
dimensions of task role specialization, decisionmaking,
and social-emotional patterns. Normative, situational,
and social-emotional factors interact in various ways to
explain differences in these family interaction outcomes.
But two clear conclusions are obvious: (1) the
"traditional" patterning of husband-wife and parental-
child relationships is the least institutionalized of all
patterns, and (2) the outcome that appears the most
desirable is that which approximates the typical middle
class urban pattern of the 1960s--with women generally not
participating in farm task roles but with shared spousal
and parental roles as well as shared decisionmaking and
social-emotional functions (Hannan and Katsiaouni, 1977).
Up to the present time there is little evidence of a trend
toward more egalitarian ownership or task role patterns
within farm families.

STATE POLICY AND POLARIZATION

The growing polarization within agriculture--between
small and large farms, and between farms of the west and
the east--has been the result of the particular processes

of agricultural development that have taken place in Ireland. Of course, it is possible that within the agricultural sector modernization per se need not have led to increasing inequalities. However, many features characteristic of this process will tend towards this result unless government policy dictates otherwise. So, for example, technological developments in farming have tended to reduce the marginal costs of production and to increase the scale of operations. Large farms have benefited most from this process because they can more easily adjust their scale of output to an optimal level and also because the fixed costs of new techniques are often too high to make it worthwhile for smaller producers to adopt them. Even if technological innovation occurs in small farm products, the emergence of associated economies of scale will lead to the development of much larger and more efficient production units which, in turn, will drive these products off of small farms. In Ireland, such has been the case with pigs and poultry, both of which were small farm products within mixed farming until the late 1950s and early 1960s, but are now produced in large specialized units (Matthews, 1981:121).

A similar situation holds with respect to the availability and use of credit and, more generally, of resources for investment in agriculture. If, for example, banks and the lending agencies allocate their funds to farmers on the basis of the assets already held by farmers, then clearly this will lead to divergent farm growth. We shall see that, to some extent, such a situation has persisted to the present day. Perhaps of equal, if not greater, importance in the Irish context is the attitude of farmers towards credit. Hannan (1972) has argued that, within the context of agriculture in the poorer western half of the country, there were social conventions which placed obstacles in the path of any individual who sought to increase his output beyond the level of his neighbors. Farmers in these areas had traditionally adopted a pattern of mixed farming with limited marketing of produce, which was a strategy that appears to have insulated them, as far as possible, from market fluctuations. These farmers depended heavily on neighbors and local kin for their labor requirements, since hired labor was rare and family labor insufficient at times of peak demand, such as harvest. As Hannan (1972:171) notes, however: "One will not for long be given communal help to augment one's own status which only creates a greater social distance between one's self and

54

one's helpers." In this context, farmers had to withdraw, to some degree, from traditional local social relationships in order to develop. Hannan argues that to do so the farmer required the support of both kin and the local agricultural advisor. Additionally, however, the individual also had to reject many of those beliefs that underpinned such social relationships—the preference for mixed farming, limited marketing of produce, and the traditional aversion to borrowing.

Thus, the majority of these western farmers proved to be markedly risk averse, not using credit and not innovating technically as both processes rapidly expanded from the mid 1950s onwards. Both their small size and historically conditioned culture and social structure militated against their adaptation to modern commercial farming. The use of credit and technical innovation expanded rapidly, however, in the more commercialized eastern and southern farm regions, as well as among the large farmers in the west (Matthews, 1981:123).

Relative price changes for products accompanying modernization tend to change the distribution of income arising in agriculture if the "income multiplier" (i.e., the ratio of gross revenue to farm income) differs between farms of different sizes. These relative price changes also depend on the actual pattern of price changes across the various products of large and small farms. In addition to the immediate effects arising on farm incomes, price shifts may also cause changes in the income distribution if farms of different sizes show different abilities to adjust to new sets of prices.

As Matthews (1981:125) has pointed out, "income multipliers" have varied greatly according to farm size, as Table 3.3 shows. Here we see that, over the 1955-1978 period, the ratio of multipliers for the different farm size categories has been relatively stable, increasing with increasing farm size, implying that unit price increases for products will benefit the largest farmers to a somewhat greater extent (1.7 times greater in the case of the smallest farmers) than the smaller. Conversely, Table 3.3 shows that a fall in prices will tend to hurt the large farmer more than the smaller. However, the post-war period has been one of generally rising prices for Irish agricultural products (in part due to government price support policy) as the graph (Figure 3.1) of average milk prices over roughly the same period as that covered by Table 3.3 shows.

Agricultural production takes place within a structure

of State and later EEC price subsidies and guarantees, protective tariffs, and, in some cases, direct cash payments. The range of instruments used by the Irish State and the EEC in pursuance of their agricultural policies has been wide: production grants and subsidies, direct aid, taxation incentives, price support, and land policy.

Table 3.3. Income Multipliers by Size of Farm – All Farms (Gross Output/Family Farm Income).

| Year | \multicolumn{6}{c}{Size Class – Acres} |
	5-15	15-30	30-50	50-100	100-200	200+
1955-58	1.53	1.54	1.68	1.87	2.17	2.52
1966-69	1.67	1.73	1.69	1.77	2.00	2.24
1972-74	1.71	1.66	1.88	1.86	2.01	2.39
1976-78	1.51	1.62	1.70	1.97	2.16	2.82

Source: Mathews, 1981:125.

Irish farm policy has done little to ameliorate the growing inequalities in farm incomes; and, indeed, since the 1970s, the introduction of EEC schemes has accelerated the process of differentiation. As Table 3.4 shows, the rate of income growth has been positively associated with farm size since the mid 1950s. But the rate of differentiation in the post-1966 decade is a multiple of the rate in the previous decade. Up until the late 1960s a number of policies were deliberately designed to help the smaller "traditional" farmer modernize—the Small Farm (Incentive Bonus) Scheme, Pilot Areas Scheme, as well as some price support schemes which graded subsidies according to the size of enterprise. (see Scully, 1971; Commins, et al., 1978; Kelleher and O'Mahony, 1984). Since the publication of the Third Economic Development Plan in 1969, where off-farm employment rather than specific small farm development schemes were seen as the main instrument for small farm and rural area development, policy objectives have changed to focus on the larger

Figure 3.1. Price of milk, 1956–1976.

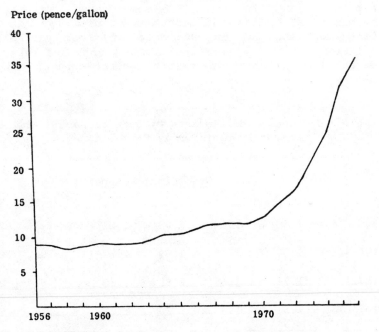

Price (pence/gallon)

Source: Breen, 1981, p. 127

commercial or commercially viable farm sector (Commins, et al., 1978; Commins, 1982; Kelleher and O'Mahony, 1984).

Over the post-war period a major aspect of Irish agricultural policy has been price support. Figures presented by Matthews (1982:257) show that in 1980, State plus EEC expenditure on farm price support accounted for almost 60% of income arising in Irish agriculture. Such supports were first introduced to an appreciable extent in the 1930s and were later taken over by the EEC. Since, as we have noted earlier, price increases favor the larger producer (all other things being equal), it follows that a government policy of price support will lead to the same result unless the commodities which receive such support are those of the smaller rather than the larger farms. In Ireland, cereals and older store cattle have been typical of the larger farms. Sheep and younger store cattle together with, until recently, poultry and pigs, have been typical of the smaller farms. Dairying was traditionally found on farms of all sizes, though recently there has

Table 3.4. Index Changes in Family Farm Incomes per Farm,
1955-1978

		Size Class	- Acres			
Year	5-15	15-30	30-50	50-100	100-200	200+
1955-58	100	100	100	100	100	100
1966-69	86	77	104	121	123	116
1972-74	137	164	227	263	323	323
1976-78	326	403	550	624	684	690

Source: Matthews, 1981:115.

been a very marked trend towards larger production units which can take advantage of technological developments in dairying (Tovey, 1982).

Those farm commodities which have benefited most from government and later EEC price supports are dairy products and cereals. Poultry, sheep, and cattle have been less favorably treated. Hence, in general, the allocation of price supports across products has been biased toward those products requiring large acreages and/or capital intensive operations. The effect of this generally, has been to increase inequality in the farm income distribution.

Of course, price supports have not been the only instruments of farm policy. Direct investment grants to farmers have also been an important tool that governments have used to encourage increased output. In Ireland the major schemes of this type before EEC entry were the Land Project and Farm Buildings Scheme, with the Small Farm (Incentive Bonus) Scheme operating in the West. After entry into EEC, these were replaced by the Farm Modernization Scheme. This latter scheme provides the most generous grants to those farmers in the "development" category. It has been argued that this scheme is less favorable to small farmers, particularly those in the West, than was the pre-existing set of schemes. In discussing this, Matthews (1981:129) concludes that, in fact, the recent trend does clearly show a concentration of investment in the better-off counties. Though no data are available to show how this aid is distributed across farm sizes, all indirect indicators suggest that the distribution of such grants and subsidies is highly regressive.

Matthews (1981:133) also argues that government interest subsidies or loans to farmers are regressive for the simple reason that the utilization of farm credit is very uneven across farm sizes. By the mid 1970s, 90% of farm credit went to that upper third of farms of 50 acres and over, and over 60% of farm credit went to the 13% of farms greater than 100 acres. Virtually no credit went to the bottom 42% of farms under 30 acres (Matthews, 1981:133).

There are, however, two types of agricultural policy which clearly favor the smaller farmers and may be expected to improve the distribution of agricultural incomes. These are subsidy payments not related to sales and the Small Holders Assistance (SHA) Scheme. Since entry to the EEC, subsidies have been paid chiefly in the form of cattle and sheep headage payments to "disadvantaged areas." Payments to any one farmer under these schemes is limited. Although these subsidies only amounted to 2.6% of family farm income in 1977 (Matthews, 1981:131), they are targeted toward farms in the poorest agricultural areas of the country, with over half of these payments accruing to farms in the poorest counties.

The SHA scheme was introduced in 1966, but has undergone major reviews since. Under the scheme farmers whose acreage valuation was of a particularly low level--generally under 30 acres in the west of Ireland--received a weekly social welfare payment somewhat lower than that received by the long-term unemployed. Since 1983 the amount payable depends on a means test but has the same equivalent maximum amount. Despite some anomalies, this scheme is of great benefit to the smaller, poorer farmers. For 1973 it was estimated that 26% of the gross income on farms of under 30 acres came from this and other sources of direct state transfers (such as pensions), and that 50% of households in that category had more than 30% of gross income from such state transfer sources (Rottman, Hannan, et al., 1979:82,84). Small farm families are more dependent on state subsidies than households from unskilled manual backgrounds. In other words, their poverty levels are greater than lower working class households.

In the area of land policy little progress has been made. A major land problem exists in Ireland, with a great deal of agricultural land in holdings too small to be viable or owned by those who have no incentive to work it, chiefly the old and the heirless. Paradoxically, despite the growing marginalization of the small farm sector, there has been no significant land consolidation. Rather, most smallholders, despite being poor and often lacking any direct heir, have held on tenaciously to their land. If they have no off-farm employment, they have come increasingly to depend on direct cash (social welfare) payments either in the form of old age pensions or Small Holders Assistance (Commins, et al., 1978; Kelleher and O'Mahony, 1984). And in an extraordinary but not yet fully understood process, the properties of these older and generally heirless farm owners do not enter the land market. Instead, their properties pass to more distantly related and often quite elderly heirs who appear to claim their limited farm inheritance as soon as the old people have passed away. A very high proportion of farm holdings in Ireland are in this type of "refuge" agriculture, providing very poor current economic returns, but obviously providing substantial capital and psychological security for an impoverished sector of the farm community (Commins, et al., 1978; Kelleher and O'Mahony, 1984).

For the most part, Irish land policy has concentrated on creating a number of relatively small holdings through the subdivision of large estates, rather than the amalgamation of nonviable farms. Over the post-war period in the open market, land has tended to accrue to large farmers, while the Land Commission's activities in allocating land to farmers of 50 acres or less acted as a counterbalance. The net result has been a striking lack of change in the size of distribution of farms in recent years, as, for example, Embleton (1978) has shown. Despite a number of official discussion papers and pressure from almost all quarters of the farming community (Commins, 1982), State intervention in the land market has been very limited over the past 10 years. Also there have not been any attempts to tackle such pressing issues as the lack of availability of land on long-term leases. The result is a great deal of immobility in the land market, with 80% of all transfers occurring through inheritance.

The recent history of State policies for agriculture in Ireland is, at its simplest, one of growing polarization between, on the one hand, measures that seek to stimulate and/or reward commercial agricultural production and, on the other hand, those measures that simply attempt to maintain the income of poorer farmers at or around the poverty level. These two sorts of policies are, of course, related. Those State policies aimed at

60

encouraging greater output have had differential impacts, by and large favoring the larger farmer over the smaller and the farms of Leinster and East Munster over those of the poorer western and northwestern counties. As the smaller farmer on poorer land has become increasingly marginalized, so has his need grown for direct income support from the State.

Finally, the efforts of the agricultural advisory (extension) service have become increasingly concentrated on the larger commercial or development status farmer. Even by the mid 1960s a number of studies had clearly shown that the agricultural advisory service had become concentrated on the larger, more commercially oriented farmers (Spain, 1968). But this had been largely an unplanned consequence of both the low density of farm advisors and the spontaneously occurring selective nature of contact and interaction between advisory officers. The advisors are highly educated and generally of high social status, while their potential clientele's education and social and cultural characteristics are highly correlated with the size of their enterprise. But in 1983 the newly reorganized advisory service came to an explicit policy decision, primarily stimulated by certain cutbacks in expenditure, to concentrate almost all their efforts on the larger, commercially oriented farmers and to ignore, unless explicitly requested otherwise, the smaller and numerically more important marginal sector of farmers (Downey, 1983; Kelleher and O'Mahony, 1984).

To conclude, then, state policy in the 1960s seriously and imaginatively tried to address the peculiar structural and development problems of Irish agriculture. However, native state structural policy making seems to have virtually ceased since EEC entry, being concerned mainly with maximizing the total transfers from Brussels irrespective of their often quite perverse effects. The main "successful" policies, from the point of view of the majority of farmers who are small-scale, have been those implemented by other government departments: mainly rural industrialization, and social welfare policies.

ENVIRONMENTAL CONSEQUENCES OF INTENSIVE AGRICULTURE

In recent years concern has grown in Ireland over the environmental consequences of the growing intensity of agricultural production, particularly arising from the increased use of fertilizers and other agri-chemicals and

from the greater stocking density of farm livestock.
Pollution of lakes and rivers is of particular concern.
The best documented case is that of Lough Sheelin in
County Cavan (Dodd and Champ, 1983). In this area pig
production expanded rapidly in the 1970s, and the bulk of
the slurry was disposed of by spreading it on the owners'
land. This resulted in the pollution of the lake, which
threatened the continued existence of trout fishing
there. The government responded by introducing a scheme
to transport slurry out of the area and dispose of it
elsewhere. This essentially stopgap measure illustrates
the general ad hoc nature of policy response to the
broader problem of water pollution from farming.

Overall, however, the most serious agricultural
pollutant is silage effluent. There have been innumerable
cases of farmers contaminating rivers and their own water
supply as a result (Fitzmaurice, 1983:151). On the other
hand, in a review of the effects of intensive fertilizer
use, Morgan (1983:145) concludes that even large increases
in nitrogen, potassium, and phosphorus use could, "be
absorbed by the Irish environment without appreciable
risk." Our much lower density of population and lower
levels of agricultural commercialization, combined with
substantially higher rainfall, make Ireland significantly
less susceptible to serious environmental damage. State
and local government policy has had very little to do with
our good fortune in this respect.

Problems of pollution and environmental deterioration
exist at a local or regional level, rather than
nationally. For example, the Index of Structural
Agricultural Pollution (ISAP) measures a country's ability
to cope with animal manure by expressing the minimum area
of cropland required for the dispersal of manures as a
proportion of the total agricultural area. In Ireland
this measure scores 0.4, indicating that "there is ample
cropland to sustain our present animal manure load" (Dodd
and Champ, 1983:115). This contrasts with countries such
as Belgium, The Netherlands, and Denmark where the ISAP
figure exceeds 1.0.

Pollution and environmental damage in Ireland arising
out of agricultural intensification occurs, in part,
because of inadequate enforcement of existing legislation
(see Fitzmaurice, 1983 and Scannell, 1983). For example,
it is often impossible to prove the source of groundwater
contamination and thus take action against the offenders.
Related to inadequate enforcement is the existence of
inadequate legal controls. Laws are often not enforced in

this area, one suspects because of difficulties with the relevant legislation. For example, a farmer requires a license to discharge effluent from a point source, under the Local Government (Water Pollution) Act, 1977. However, much pollution from farms is from nonpoint sources (particularly run-off of slurry and other effluents) and thus is not subject to license (Scannell, 1983:106-7). Finally, there are problems associated with the absence of relevant legislation and the exemptions from legal provisions granted to farmers. For example, under the Local Government (Planning and Development) Regulations, 1977, farm buildings of up to 400 square meters used to house animals do not require planning permission, nor do subsequent additions to these buildings. Thus, the planning laws fix no limit on animal density, nor do they provide any environmental safeguards or safeguards against nuisance to other local residents. Reforms in both legislation and its enforcement are clearly required if localized environmental damage is not to escalate into a more widespread pattern.

PROSPECTS FOR THE FAMILY FARM

Irish agriculture enjoyed an unprecedented boom during the mid 1970s in the period of adjustment to EEC membership. Real prices rose 43% from 1970 to 1979 in anticipation of EEC entry. This was accompanied by a growth in output of just under 4% per annum (O'Connor, et al., 1983:43). In the 1960s, the ratio of per capita income in farming to average industrial earnings had fallen by over 7% (Sheehy, 1980:297). By the 1970s, this ratio increased rapidly and in some years came to exceed unity. The improved prices for agricultural products were due to EEC alignment during the transitional period as well as common price increases and monetary adjustments. However, once the transitional period ended, Irish farmers received only the common price increases agreed for the EEC as a whole (plus some special measures). Since the Irish inflation rate was higher than in most other EEC countries, this led to a sharp reversal of the pre-existing trend: after 1978, Irish farmers experienced a net fall in incomes. To some degree this was also due to difficult weather and other conditions in 1979 and 1980, but in each year of the period from 1979 to 1983, Irish farmers experienced a fall in real prices for their products. In 1984, however, there was a substantial recovery. But 1985 and 1986 saw substantial income declines.

The future prospects for farming in Ireland are now intimately linked to the fate of the Common Agricultural Policy. At present the EEC is facing difficulties in funding a farm policy based primarily on price supports. In many respects, these parallel the problems encountered by the Irish government in the pre-EEC period when it had to meet the cost of farm price support policies (Matthews, 1982). The Irish government adopted various coresponsibility measures to attempt to resolve these difficulties, though these were, naturally, unpopular among farmers. The future of Irish agriculture appears to be very sensitive to the particular measures that the EEC chooses to adopt to curb farm spending, as well as the likelihood of negotiating exemptions from such measures (e.g., the recent partial exemption from the so-called milk "super-levy"). EEC policy on dairying is particularly vital to Ireland, given that this has been the most dynamic agricultural sector in recent times (O'Connor, et al., 1983:138). Sheehy (1982/83) has examined some of the implications of different sorts of EEC dairy policies for Irish dairying. Although Ireland would fare better under some of these (e.g., quota limitations on farm production) than others (e.g., price reductions), there is no doubt that the heady days of agricultural development such as we saw in the 1970s are unlikely to return in the short to medium term.

A slower or zero rate of growth in agricultural production will have several important consequences for the Irish economy as a whole since agriculture, fishing, and forestry account for around 30% of the total value of exports. However, we shall concentrate on those consequences that relate to issues discussed earlier. First, a slower rate of agricultural growth should slow down the growth in the environmental threat from intensive farming. Boyle and Kearney (1983:96) point out that economic factors have proved to be the dominant force shaping the pace and pattern of intensification in Irish agriculture. Therefore, given only a very limited increase in the price/cost ratio, the pace of future intensification will most probably be less than in the 1970s. However, there is little room for complacency in this respect. In the area of commercial agriculture, even a lower rate of growth in intensification seems likely to lead to increased localized environmental problems, particularly given the weakness of regulatory bodies and a widespread belief among the farming community that pollution is not a serious problem. In the poorer farming regions of the west and northwest, increasing marginalization suggests that the environmental threat stems from farmers' reduced concern for the physical environment.

What are the implications of this changed scenario for the distribution of incomes within farming? Just as large farmers with greater income multipliers benefit most from increasing prices, so they suffer most from a relative price fall, all other things being equal. Thus, a slower rate of increase in farm product prices should, at the very least, lead to a less rapid increase in income inequality than we witnessed over the post war period to 1978. And, indeed, there is evidence that post 1978 the marked trend of polarization within the agricultural sector was not sustained, at least over the years 1979 and 1980 (Matthews, 1981). However, the overall effects of price changes will depend upon differential price changes among commodities. More generally, the results of policies to curb production will depend upon which commodities are most severly curbed and how these policies are put into effect. For example, although a milk quota system may be the least damaging option of those considered by Sheehy (1982/83), from the point of view of the Irish economy as a whole, it is clear that it will hit farmers who are still seeking to expand their production more than those who have already reached their full potential (O'Connor, et al., 1983:136). This implies that the medium-sized, developing farmer, rather than the very large or very small farmer, is the most likely to suffer under such a regime. Such farmers are likely to experience particular difficulty if they borrowed heavily to finance expansion in the mid 1970s.

Given the highly vulnerable position of these middle-sized farmers (50 to 100 acres) and the fact that the threshold of viability has been moving up rapidly since the 1950s, unless there is a clear switch toward a more successful structural policy--particularly in land acquisition and allocation--it cannot be very long before their position is not very different from their smaller neighbors.

As for the smaller marginal farmers, EEC policy has had very little positive effect on their welfare, and it has been the State--through industrialization and social welfare policy--that has picked up the tab for the effects of a poorly distributed farm policy. Yet these State

65

policies have had some clearly undesirable
effects—particularly in rewarding "land hoarding"
behavior among a smallholding class which attaches
enormous value to land both as a symbol and for security.
A serious attempt to integrate social welfare, rural
industrial, land transfer, and small farm development
policy is urgently needed (see Commins, et al., 1978).
Yet in recent times, government policy has been moving in
the opposite direction—toward means testing on small
farms where previously Small Holders Assistance was given
irrespective of output and toward dismantling the
structure, power, and resources of the Land Commission.
These arrangements had previously been uniquely effective
in European land distribution policy.

To conclude, unless there are substantial changes in
the Common Agricultural Policy which would increasingly
channel resources toward structural reform and promote
effective planning and administrative action in this area,
the immediate future appears to be one of little change.
The future points to continued concentration of production
and incomes at the top. At the same time a process of
withdrawal from production, dependence on off-farm
employment, or direct income maintenance payments will
continue for almost half the farm population (those with
the smallest farms and the lowest incomes). At a time
when the pace of industrialization has almost stopped,
such a policy stance appears absurd. Yet there is no
evidence of any change in this respect. We hesitate to
end on the same pessimistic note as a recent report on the
marginalized farm sector by Kelleher and O'Mahony (1984),
but it appears highly appropriate: "State intervention
functions in such a way as to reproduce the very
conditions which call for State support in the first
place. Current trends in agricultural development,
agricultural advisory work, and land policy do not suggest
that any amelioration of marginal farming and its
associated problems can be expected in the immediate
future" (p. 113).

66

REFERENCES

Agricultural Statistics 1934-1956. Central Statistics
    Office, Dublin. 1960.
Arensberg, C. 1937. The Irish Countryman. New York:
    Macmillan.
Arensberg, C. and S. Kimball. 1940. Family and Community
    in Ireland. Cambridge, Mass: Harvard University
    Press. (Reissued in 1968)
Boyle, G.E. and B. Kearney. 1983. "Intensification in
    Agriculture--Trends and Prospects" in J. Blackwell and
    F.J. Convey, (eds.). Promise and Performance: Irish
    Environmental Policies Analyzed. Dublin: REPC, pp.
    77-102.
Breen, R. 1981. Change and Development in an Irish Rural
    Community, 1936-1978. Unpublished Ph.D. thesis,
    University of Cambridge, England.
Commins, P. 1982. "Land Policies and Agricultural
    Development" in P.J. Drudy (ed.). Ireland: Land,
    Politics, and People. Cambridge: Cambridge
    University Press, pp. 217-240.
Commins, P. 1983. The Land Question: Is Leasing the
    Answer? In Adjustment and Structural Problems in the
    Agricultural Sector. Papers of the Agricultural
    Institute, Economic and Rural Welfare Annual
    Conference, 1983, Dublin.
Commins, P., P. Cox, and J. Curry. 1978. Rural Areas:
    Change and Development. National Economic and Social
    Council. Paper No. 41. Dublin.
Cousens, S.H. 1964. Regional Variation in Population
    Change in Ireland, 1861-1881." Economic History
    Review, 17, 301-332.
Cousens, S.H. 1968. "Population Trends in Ireland at the
    Beginning of the 20th Century." Irish Geography, 5,
    387-401.
Cox. P. 1982. "The West of Ireland: Problems and
    Policies." Paper presented to the European
    Association of Agricultural Economists. Belgrade.
Cox, P., J. Higgins, and B. Kearney. 1982. Farm Incomes:
    Analysis and Policy, National Economic and Social
    Council, Report No. 65, Dublin.
Crotty, R. 1966. Irish Agricultural Production. Cork:
    Cork University Press.
Dodd, V.A. and W.S.T. Champ. 1983. "Environmental
    Problems. Associated with Intensive Animal Production
    Units, with Reference to the Catchment Area of Lough

67

Sheelin" in J. Blackwell and F.J. Convery (eds).
Promise and Performance: Irish Environmental Policies
Analyzed. REPC, pp. 111-130.
Downey, L. 1983. "Role of ACOT (the agricultural advisory
service) in Rural Development". Paper read at
Agricultural Science Assoc. Conference, Kilkenny,
Ireland, 1983.
Embleton, F.A. 1978. "Developments of Structure of Irish
Farming, 1960-1975, with Special Reference to the
Situation in 1975." Journal of Statistical and Social
Inquiry Society of Ireland, 1977-1978. 23, 5, pp.
29-74.
Eurostat National Accounts (ESA) Detailed Tables by Sector,
1970-1982. Office of Official Publications, European
Community; Luxembourg, 1985.
Fitzmaurice, P. 1983. "Farming and the Enforcement of
Water Pollution Control" in J. Blackwell and F.J.
Convery (eds.). Promise and Performance: Irish
Environmental Policies Analyzed. REPC, pp. 147-154.
Hannan, D.F. 1972. "Kinship, Neighborhood and Social
Change in Irish Rural Communities." The Economic and
Social Review, 3, 2, pp. 163-188.
Hannan, D.F. 1979. Displacement and Development: Class,
Kinship and Social Change in Rural Communities.
Economic and Social Research Institute. Paper No. 96.
Hannan, D.F. and N. Hardiman. 1978. "Peasant
Proprietorship and Changes in the Irish Marriage Rate
in the Late Nineteenth Century." Economic and Social
Research Institute. Seminar Paper Series.
Hannan, D.F. and L. Katsiaouni. 1977. Traditional
Families: From Culturally Prescribed to Negotiated
Roles in Farm Families. ESRI Paper No. 87. Dublin.
Harrison. 1982. Factors Influencing Ownership, Tenancy,
Mobility and Use of Farmland in the Member States of
the European Community, Commission of the European
Communities, Info. on Agric. No. 86, Luxembourg.
Johnson, R. and A.G. Conway. 1976. "Factors Associated
with Growth in Farm Output." Paper to the
Agricultural Economics Society of Ireland, Dublin.
Kelleher, C. and A. O'Mahoney. 1984. Marginalization in
Irish Agriculture. Economic and Rural Welfare
Research Centre of the Agricultural Institute,
Socio-Economic Research Series, Paper No. 4. Dublin.
Kennedy, R. 1973. The Irish Emigration, Marriage and
Fertility. University of California Press.
Lee, J. 1973. The Modernization of Ireland. Dublin:
Gill and Macmillan.

68

Local Government (Water Pollution) Act, 1977. Stationery Office, Dublin. 1977.

Matthews, A. 1981. "The Changing Distribution of Income in Irish Agriculture." Proceedings of the Agricultural Economics Society of Ireland, 1981, pp. 114-142.

Matthews, A. 1982. "The State of Irish Agriculture, 1950-1980" in P.J. Drudy (ed.). Ireland: Land, Politics and People. Cambridge: Cambridge University Press.

Morgan, M.A. 1983. "Fertilizers and Environmental Quality" in J. Blackwell and F.J. Convery (eds). Promise and Performance: Irish Environmental Policies Analyzed. REPC, pp. 131-146.

National Farm Survey, 1955-58. Final Report. Central Statistics Office, Dublin, 1961.

O'Connor, R., C. Guiomard and J. Devereux. 1983. A Review of the Common Agricultural Policy and the Implications of Modified Systems for Ireland. Dublin: The Economic and Social Research Institute, Broadsheet No. 21.

O'Tuathaigh, G. 1972. Ireland Before the Famine. Gill and Macmillan, Dublin.

Rottman, D.B., D.F. Hannan, et al. 1982. The Distribution of Income in the Republic of Ireland: A Study in Social Class and Family Cycle Inequalities. The Economic and Social Research Institute, Paper No. 109. Dublin.

Scannell, Y. 1983. "Agriculture and Environmental Law" in Blackwell and F.J. Convery (eds). Promise and Performance: Irish Environmental Policies Analyzed. REPC, pp. 103-110.

Scully, J. 1971. Agriculture in the West of Ireland. Dublin: Department of Agriculture and Fisheries.

Sheehy, S.J. 1980. "The Impact of EEC Membership on Irish Agriculture," The Journal of Agricultural Economics, 31, 3, pp. 297-310.

Sheehy, S.J. 1982/83. "Co-responsibility and the Future of Irish Agriculture." Journal of Statistical and Social Inquiry Society of Ireland. Dublin.

Spain, H. 1968. "Agricultural Education and Extension" (in Ireland) Paper No. 10, Agricultural Adjustment Conference, Dublin.

Tovey, H. 1982. "Milking the Farmer? Modernization and Marginalization in Irish Dairy Farming" in M. Kelly, M. O'Dowd and J. Wickham (eds). Power, Conflict and Inequality. Dublin: Turoe Press, pp. 68-89.

Walsh, B. 1970. "Marriage Rates and Population Pressure, Ireland 1871-1911." Economic History Review, 23. 2.

4
Family Farming in Norway

Reidar Almas

A SHORT INTRODUCTION TO THE AGRARIAN HISTORY OF NORWAY

In some respects Norwegian agrarian history is very similar to European history. Most farms have been family farms for several generations. The first technological revolution took place in the late 19th century, with a new "great leap forward" after World War II. Cooperation is widespread in processing and marketing, but seldom to be found in primary production.

But the Norwegian case is also quite special in several respects. Peasant ownership of land survived the Middle Ages. No more than half the cultivated holdings were ever owned by the church or other feudal land owners. However, in the late 18th and early 19th centuries a new class of crofters was formed. These were landless farm workers who were allowed to cultivate a plot. This payment in kind secured a cheap labor force for the self-owners and provided a living for the growing rural population. Later, when crofting was abolished in the first part of this century, these people (who did not emigrate) formed the smallholder class. Combining agriculture with fishing, forestry, transport, and other rural industries, the smallholders constitute the bulk of the agrarian population throughout this century.

Compared to other advanced capitalist countries, the agrarian sector in Norway is quite large, employing 8% of

Extended version of a paper to the XII European Congress for Rural Sociology, Budapest, Hungary, July 24-29, 1983. I would like to thank the late Nigel McKenzie for his stimulating comments to this article.

71

the labor force. Most of the farms are small (below 10 hectares), and a substantial part of the income of many farm families comes from other sources. But many of these secondary occupations have disappeared. Technical innovations in food production, both on the farm and outside, have diminished the labor force. Partly because of this, there has been an exodus from the countryside. In the 1970s, however, there has been a turn-around trend in population movement. New industrial and service occupations are replacing the traditional rural ones. Commuting is extending the labor market for the rural population.

This opens a new challenge for the family farm. When all the new work and educational opportunities reach the rural areas, there are new possibilities for the farm family. The wife may wish to utilize her education, earn her own money, or simply be in touch with more people. The children may receive training for jobs outside their communities and come home just for holidays. Elderly farmers and farmers' wives look for something else to do when they retire. We have shown elsewhere how this leaves a single producer (plus machines) on the farm, a process described as "the masculinization of Norwegian agriculture" (Almas and Odegard, 1983).

This presents a new challenge in analyzing the "agricultural mode of production," which is still a simple commodity production. Many authors have shown the shortcomings of the traditional Marxian scheme of analysis when dealing with modern agriculture. One such author is Djurfeldt, who presents an adaptation of the "Marxian ground-rent theory" to the micro-economy of the family farm. He argues that, "Competition eliminated rent and landlordism and hampered the reproduction of capitalist farmers but permitted the middle farmers to reproduce themselves..." (Djurfeldt, 1981:187). While agreeing with Djurfeldt to a certain extent, he does forget some of the sociological consequences of the present development as discussed later in this article.

Another reason for reanalyzing the agrarian transition under modern capitalism is the development of the corporate state. This phenomenon, taken together with the internationalization of trade, demands micro-macro models of analysis that take into account market relations, state policy, and the strategies of the agricultural producers. Havens and Newby (1981) have put forward a tentative feedback model that makes it possible to use both micro and macro data in the same analysis. I will explore the

extent to which this model covers the Norwegian conditions
of a semi-closed market.[1]

THE MICRO-LOGIC OF THE FAMILY FARM

To evolve a micro-theory that makes the decisions of
the modern farmer without a hired labor force
understandable, I take Marx's ground-rent theory as a
starting point (Marx, 1983). However, along with
Djurfeldt, I consider the original theory to be
incongruent with the present state of affairs. I shall
not present the ground-rent theory in any detail, as it is
quite well known. The argument will also be understood
without detailed knowledge of Marxian theory.

In short, Djurfeldt argues that instead of the
capitalist categories--variable capital, constant capital,
profit and surplus profit (ground rent)--one should use
consumption funds, installment on loans, and interest on
loans categories. Figure 4.1 summarizes this argument.

Figure 4.1. A diagrammatic representation of the micro-
economy of a family farm in comparison with
family farming

Family farm categories (Djurfeldt)	Consumption funds (wage) of farmer's household	Installment on loans taken to purchase means of production & raw material	Interest on loans paid to bank capital	Installment & interest on loans taken to purchase land
Capitalist categories (Marx)	Variable capital	Constant capital	Profit	Surplus profit (ground rent)

I basically agree with Djurfeldt, but as he points out
himself, this illustrates the most unfavorable situation
when the farming family has no "capital" of its own. They
need to buy land and are not able to accumulate anything
on their own. This would be the situation for a family

74

establishing itself in agriculture with no family
background in the sector. Generally this is not the case
in Norway and probably not in any capitalist country.

Keeping the basic idea in the Djurfeldt scheme and
adjusting it to realistic circumstances, the gross farm
income can be divided in the following components:

1. Consumption fund, which could be supplemented by
   wage income. It could be much less than the
   household income, or even negative.
2. Reproduction of own "capital," which means
   maintaining animals, machines, buildings, and
   equipment to the same standard and supplying the
   production with raw material.
3. Enlarged reproduction of own "capital" to keep up
   with growing farm size and number of animals, new
   technologies, etc.
4. Installment on loans used to buy means of
   production and raw materials when components 2 and
   3 fail.
5. Interest on loans.

As the reader will see, the structure of this model is
the same as that of the Marxian scheme. Of these five
points the last three are crucial in understanding the
mechanisms for both the decline and survival of family
farms. Taking decline first, there are many farms that
cannot reproduce on an enlarged scale and keep up with the
development of modern agriculture. They drop further and
further behind and survive for only a short time by
accepting a small income, supplementing the household
income with income from wage labor or insurance, and/or
consuming their own "capital." Most often there is a
combination of these methods. Sooner or later the family
will leave the business or production will be reduced to
an insignificant level.

The survivors are able to reproduce their farms on an
enlarged scale. If they cannot manage it on their own,
they take loans from private or state banks. Then they
have to enlarge production to meet the new expenditures
(components 4 and 5). If they are lucky (good soil, large
farm, hard work), they can accumulate and enlarge their
own capital. But according to Norwegian farm accounts,
very few have been able to do that: only farmers with
more than than 30 hectares, or 7% of all farmers, have
been able to increase their capital regularly during the
last 20 years.

THE ROLE OF THE STATE IN ADVANCED CAPITALISM

Until now I have discussed the micro-economy of the family farm without giving much attention to the macro-level of the State. Combining these two levels of analysis enables us to develop a model that takes into consideration budget transfers, the negotiations between the State and the organizations, international market relations, and so on.
As a point of departure, I take a heuristic model developed by Havens and Newby (Figure 4.2).
In their explanation, the authors stress that it begins and ends with the transformation of the social structure of agriculture (Havens & Newby, 1981. p. 12). On the basis of this structure, the interests of the different groups are organized to put pressure upon the State and also to intervene in the market (for instance with the help of producer cooperatives). State policy is affected by the resource crisis and international relations, particularly with respect to trade. Out of this "cross-pressure," the State attempts to formulate a policy according to what it calls "public interests." Policy comes out of a process of negotiation with representatives of influence groups, the so called "policy influentials."
But this policy cannot support all interest groups, and sometimes it is contradictory because it tries to fulfill contradictory aims. The policy influences the survival strategies of the producers, together with the market structure. The relations of production in agriculture will then be changed because of all these factors, and the new structure establishes the base for the next "round." Or more correctly, as this is a dynamic process, the factors are changing simultaneously and there is no beginning or end.
This is a stimulating model, and, with a few exceptions, it is a valuable analytical tool. First of all, interest groups, while putting pressure upon the State from outside agriculture, are very important in understanding the outcome of the negotiation process and should be introduced into the model. For Norway, we also must remember that the connection between international relations and state/market structure might be incomplete. Even though many countries subsidize their agricultural production, Norway is one of the countries which has closed its food market most.

STRUCTURAL CHANGES

To get an impression of how this micro-logic of family farming has transformed the rural scene, I will give an introduction to the structural, technological, and demographical changes of Norwegian agriculture.[2]
I start my description with the year 1945. In that year a period of economic growth with social democratic governments (which lasted for 20 years) began in Norway. History handed an agriculture of small farmers over to the new rulers. In Europe we might compare Norwegian farming structure to the situation in the "smallholding belt" from France through southern Germany and Switzerland to Austria. But in contrast to these areas, there has been no feudal bondage in Norway, and throughout the Middle Ages, a substantial section of the Norwegian peasantry remained freeholders.
In the 18th and 19th centuries a new agricultural proletariat--the crofters--sprung up that generally outnumbered the freeholders. These crofters were not owners of small plots, but generally worked for the plot owner to pay ground rent.
In the late 19th and early 20th centuries this crofting institution was effectively abolished by the emigration to America and was later formally abolished by law. Crofters bought their plots, and their families were still there in 1945. In the crisis years of the 1930s and throughout the war, a "superfluous" labor force was stored on these and other farms, simply because they had no other place to go. This is some of the background for Table 4.1.
A superficial look might give the impression that the content of this table supports the Marxian theory of horizontal concentration. As we see, the smallest holdings have decreased both absolutely and relatively. There has been a limited increase in the number of holdings over 10 ha. But as I shall show below, there is no reason to believe that a farm gives its owner a better living, although the cultivated area might have doubled during the period. The increasing number of hectares simply reflects the rising demands of production in order to keep up with the internal and external competition.
Most of these farms, 60% in 1949 and 70% in 1979, do not provide the farm family with a living. Just after the war, the most usual types of work combined with farming were fishing, seasonal wage labor in agriculture and forestry, and other seasonal work (building work, road construction, etc.). Today, work in industry is more

77

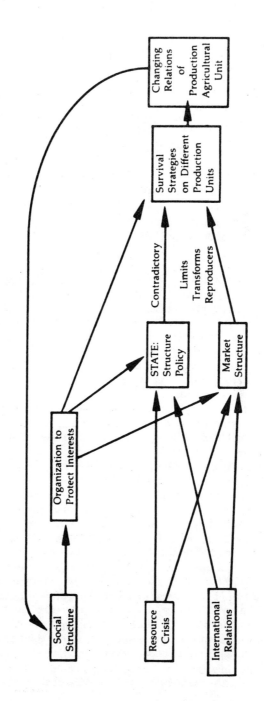

Figure 4.2. The role of the State in the changing structure of agriculture (Havens and Newby, 1981:13)

Table 4.1. Farms 1959-79 with own land in hectares, total and percent.

	1949		1959		1969		1979	
	Total	%	Total	%	Total	%	Total	%
0.5 - 4.9 ha	150,130	70	135,830	69	88.481	57	58.951	52
5.0 - 9.9 ha.	42,526	20	42,126	21	42.240	27	32.441	28
Above 10 ha.	20,785	10	20,359	10	24.256	16	23.217	20
Total	213,441	100	198,315	100	154.977	100	114.609	100

Source: Agricultural Census 1949, 1959, 1969 and 1979

common. Commuting is widespread, and even on relatively large farms, one or both of the family heads take wage labor outside the farm.

There are considerable differences between south and north and between lowland and highland, but we can indicate a "limit of livelihood" at 4-6 ha. in 1945 rising to 8-10 ha. today for dairy farming. That means that on farms below that size limit, the farming family has to supplement its farm income from other sources. In other types of production, the limit might be higher, for instance in grain cultivation where the "limit of livelihood" is three to four times that mentioned for dairy farming.

Most of the 100,000 farms that have disappeared in the period have been merged with neighboring farms. The farm house is often still in use by the family, either as a permanent or second home. In the northern part of the country and in peripheral parts of southern Norway, some of the land is not in use any more. Some of this land is also leased to neighboring farms, and land lease has been increasing, especially between 1969 and 1979, when it increased from 15% to 22% of the arable land. But less than 10% of the farms are wholly rented farms today.

Table 4.1 shows that the smallholders have been the most vulnerable social group. The process of proletarianization has speeded up, especially when there has been a generation shift at these farms. A rising level of living in society as a whole means that it is difficult to maintain the same standard of living, and young people have greater demands than the older generation. There are also different thresholds that are difficult to cross for small farmers. One such threshold is the purchase of a tractor, another is the purchase of a milking machine or milk tank.

But the proletarianization of the farming population has not increased the rural proletariat. On the contrary, this social class has declined very quickly from 94,000 in 1949 to 27,000 today. This means that the small farmers have gone to the secondary and tertiary sectors, and they have been followed by the bulk of the original proletariat. The remaining farm workers are also "modernized." New jobs in the farm relief service and other specialized professions have almost wiped out the unskilled proletariat. The remaining unskilled work has been taken over by machines, family labor, and school children.

To illustrate the point that more and more land is operated by fewer people, although they don't earn a greater income than the rest of the working population, we shall look at Table 4.2.

Table 4.2 shows a considerable rise in the standard of living, both in agriculture and industry. Even though the consumer price index rose to five times the level in 1949, the farm income rose seven times and the income in the manufacturing industries rose by 14 times the 1949 level. This shows that the farming population was better off during the period, but that the other sectors had a better relative position in the competition for labor and capital. Out of this situation of relative deprivation, three social consequences can be noted.

1. Much of the farming population left agriculture and took better paying jobs in other sectors.
2. Among the remaining farm population, there arose a growing discontent. (We shall discuss this in detail later.)
3. To keep up with the income level in the urban occupations, the farmers had to extend their arable land.

If we take a look at the last line of Table 4.2, we can see that the average amount of arable land per annual income in industry and mining doubled from from 1949 to 1969. From 1969 to 1979 there is a remarkable delay in the trend which we shall return to later (relating the new agricultural policy from 1975). The table shows that

80

Table 4.2. Annual farm income per hectare, arable land
per farm, average income per farm, annual
income in industry and mining, and arable land
which gives an industrial income, 1949-1972

	1949	1959	1969	1979
Annual farm income per ha.	930 N kr	1030 N kr	1870 N kr	6480 N kr
Average arable land per farm	3.8 ha.	4.2 ha.	6.4 ha.	7.8 ha.
Average income per farm	3500 N kr	4300 N kr	12000 N kr	50500 N kr
Annual income in industry and mining	5700 N kr	11600 N kr	23000 N kr	79700 N kr
Arable land per annual income in industry and mining	6.1 ha.	11.2 ha.	12.3 ha.	12.3 ha.

Source: Agriculture census 1949-79, Account results in
agriculture and forestry. Norges Landbruk-
sokonomiske Institutt.

though the average arable land per farm doubled during the
period, the "average farmer" still lags behind the
industrial worker. While the average farm had 3.8
hectares of arable land in 1949, a farm of 6.1 hectares
was needed to produce an income equivalent to that of an
industrial worker. In 1969, the same figures were 7.8
hectares and 12.3 hectares. Ten years later, a farmer
needs 60% more land than the average to reach an income
equivalent to the average income among industrial workers.

TECHNOLOGICAL CHANGES

The background of these structural changes is, of
course, not only the relative levels of income, but also

the technological innovations that are so well known in the industrialized world. We might call the period up to 1970 the "phase of tractorization." With this new energy source, there came an army of implements that were expensive but necessary.

For the largest farms, implements were not as expensive as hired labor, and the smaller farms could not get the necessary seasonal labor. So they had to follow the trend if they wanted to stay in the business. As Djurfeldt has mentioned, this meant the opening up of a broad road for bank capital to enter into agriculture (Djurfeldt, 1981).

Capital was also needed for buildings, various technical installations in these buildings, and new breeds of cattle. The main capital source for buildings was the state, via the state bank. Very few of the farmers were able to finance the capital equipment with their own money or private loans. A consequence of this was a firm State control over all farms that wanted to expand production, especially from the 1960s onward.

The technical standard of the farm varies, but almost all farms have one or two tractors. The most usual production, dairy farming, needs implements for soil dressing, sowing, weed killing, and harvesting as well as a tractor. For eight months the animals have to be kept inside. In the summer season the farmers are very busy producing fodder for the winter. Silos are the most usual storing method for grass. Very expensive installations are needed both to get it into and out of the silo. On the smallest farms much of this heavy work is done by hand. Milking machines are used by almost all dairy farmers now, but milk tanks are not so common on the smaller units.

Commerical fertilizing, liming, land leveling, and draining are also widespread on the small farms. Combined with the extensive use of concentrated feed, the rise in the use of commercial fertilizers has had a great impact on increased productivity in Norwegian agriculture. For instance, the production of milk per cow rose 2.5 times to 5600 kg. milk per cow form 1949 to 1979. And the wheat yield nearly doubled, up to 4000 kg. per hectare, in the same period. To a certain extent, animal husbandry has been released from some of the physical barriers that hampered it before. Concentrated fodder has been used to loosen the link between land and livestock production. But this also means that economies of scale are even more important than before.

The technological development has placed the agricultural producers in the middle of a chain from raw material to food consumption. This integration, not only of agriculture but also of the farmer in social production, tightens the grip of society's dominant mode of production on the family farm. An illustration of this is that the debt rose from 20% in 1945 to 40% in the late 1970s. Another aspect of the same process is the concentration of production on a few specialized units. In 1959, 150,000 or three-fourths of the farms produced milk, while 20 years later only 40,000 or one-fourth of the farms had milk cows.

It is difficult to say which is the most important factor in this conglomeration. But it seems that when the new technical equipment came in, capitalization and specialization followed partly because of the lack of labor and partly because of savings in expenditure on labor. Capitalization occurred because most of the farmers could not afford the investment needed; specialization occurred because the investment was less if the farmers concentrated on one production line. It is obvious that the smallholder had little to gain from this development, except from the partial separation of plant production and animal husbandry. For a few smallholders this meant that they could build up a modern, highly mechanized livestock production without much land. For many other farmers it meant that they were not able to compete.

THE EXODUS FROM FARMING AND DEMOGRAPHIC CHANGES

The first group to leave agriculture in the 1940s and 1950s was the hired labor force, mainly female labor. Later the family members also became superfluous. Before 1970 most of the family farms that were more than 5 hectares were left intact. In the 1970s, however, "the level of leaving" began to effect holdings of 6-7 hectares. The women left farming first and on a larger scale (Almas and Odegard, 1983).

Reliable total figures do not exist, but it seems that about 20% of full-time and 30% of part-time hired labor force in agriculture are women (Odegard, 1983). As a contrast, 40% of the farmers' wives take part in daily work on family farms (Odegard, 1983). In the early postwar years as many as 80% of the farmers' wives took part in the daily work on the farms. This reflects the decline in animal farming and the new role of the woman on the farm (Almas and Odegard, 1983)

Most of the farm workers of both sexes left farming and their farm houses in the period up to 1969. The current hired labor live in their own house away from the farm, and most of them work in forestry or in the farm relief service.

In 1949 every fourth Norwegian lived on a farm, while every seventh lived on a farm in 1969 and still does. During the same period, as the production of agricultural products was stable or rising, the labor force was more than halved. Although some of the superfluous smallholders remained on their holdings, the structural rationalizing led to a farm exodus. Up until the middle of the 1970s, urbanization continued at a pace similar to most industrialized countries. At the end of World War II, half of the population was living in sparsely populated areas. Today these areas still have about the same number of people, but the population in the densely settled areas has doubled.

This uneven development between town and country had the most dramatic consequences in the north, in the western coastal districts, and in the central highlands. Because these areas have offered few jobs outside agriculture, forestry and fishing, the decline in these sectors meant the end of a lot of small communities. When there were too few people to maintain the school, the shop, or the local organizations, the whole population moved away, often assisted by subsidies from the state. In the central areas there was still a lack of labor force, so the "immigrants" were welcomed by all authorities.

In the middle of the 1970s some of these well-known trends were no longer strong. First of all, the industrial crisis hit the big cities. The industrial growth period had ended in the late 1960s, and the decline started with the oil crisis in 1973. Companies looked for more favorable production costs. With the help of state and local subsidies in the marginal regions, it was more profitable to set up a business there. A reservoir of labor was already at hand, land transportation was not as expensive as it used to be because of state subsidies, and a better infrastructure existed.

Another factor concerning the turn-around trend was the blossoming public sector. In the 1950s and 1960s most of the growth in this sector occurred in densely populated areas. Most of the new jobs were created in education and public service. When the administrative system in the central areas was built up to the present level in the late 1960s, the small municipalities were still lacking both in administrative personnel and capacity to handle the new public tasks in education, health care, and social service, tasks that were required by law.

The rapid expansion of the public sector and the industrial growth in the rural areas lead to a consolidation of the settlement structure (Brox, 1980). The migration from north to south, from west to east, and from country to town slowed down, at least for a while. There was a local centralization around the district centers, but the long-distance migration was less favorable of the largest cities.

To what extent can we say that the development in agriculture and in the farm policy contributed to this turn-around trend? And how much of the structural and technological trends described above can be traced back to the political measures of the period? To find an answer to these questions, I move on to an analysis of post-war farm policy.

NORWEGIAN AGRICULTURAL POLICY 1945-1982

Rebuilding the Country, 1945-49

The political situation of 1945 must be seen against the background of the pre-war years. There was a Social Democratic minority government supported by the Farmer's Party and later the Liberals since 1935. This government had pursued a typical Keynesian line with public works, pensions for the elderley, and subsidies for agriculture to raise purchasing power. In spite of their strong anti-militarist inclinations and hesitant standpoint before and during the German attack in 1940, the Social Democrats came out of the war strengthened. Thanks to its strong anti-fascist attitude during the war and its willingness to use the State to promote economic development, the Social Democratic Party (DNA) got 41% of the votes and an absolute majority in the Parliament in 1945.

The Communists (NKP) were the other winners of the first post-war election. They had lost many of their legal leaders to German imprisonment, but their illegal political work and sabotage had secured them mass support. With 12% of the votes, NKP had to be taken into account by the DNA government.

Although agriculture needed new means of production, their claims were not heard. A considerable part of the population in the countryside looked forward to a life in the city or in the new industrial centers. The Farmer's Party was paralyzed by the "great industrial leap forward" launched by the Social Democrats. There were also some problems, as some of the Farmers' Party leaders had shown fascist inclinations before and during the war. The Norwegain Farmers Union showed some of these problems, as there was a close collaboration between these two organizations. The other general farm organization--the Norwegian Smallholders Union--was linked to the Social Democrats and promoted DNA farm policy.

Growth and Prosperity With Social Democratic Majority 1950-1961

The logic behind the DNA-approach was a transfer of the labor force and capital from agriculture, forestry, and fishing to manufacturing, industries, and mining. The public sector started to grow, through expansion and in public administration and education. The opposition was perplexed. After a political purge of "Titoists" and the Communist assumption of power in Czechoslovakia in 1948, NKP lost much of its mass support. On the right, there was no strong conservative party. They never gained more than 20% of the voters in this period and one of the reasons for this was their weak position in the rural areas. They had an urban-conservative profile and did not manage to utilize the protest against the rural decline. As an "economic growth" party, they could not support what they believed was a "reactionary" attitude to industrialization.

Concerning the world market for food, the DNA government gave some concessions to the farmers, which explains the lack of farmer unrest in the post-war period. The Norwegian market for important products such as milk, meat, and grain was protected from foreign competition. Milk and meat were protected by import prohibition, and the prices to producers were kept substantially above the world market prices by this "border defense." Grain prices were also kept higher than world market prices and imported grain (wheat for instance) was taxed to give correspondingly high prices.

To compensate for the higher price level, food prices were subsidized from the state budget. In that way, both workers and farmers were satisfied. In agriculture the DNA government had the stable support of most of the smallholders and the farm workers. These people were willing to "ally themselves with their own future" as wage laborers in the urban or urbanizing areas. As long as economic growth could provide safe jobs in other industries and these jobs were better paid, nobody complained.

The situation in the late 1950s was marked by internal migration and rising affluence. Income levels in rural areas and in agriculture were lower than in other sectors of society. Mechanization and expansion of production were the strategies used to increase the income level among farmers. State credit was available to make it easier to buy machines, especially tractors. "Viable farms" were given more land through amalgamation of farms and land lease. In that way, the Social Democrats won mass support for a policy that wiped out much of their own social base in the rural areas: the farm workers, the worker peasants, and the smallholders. Their policy helped to consolidate the classes that were politically alien to the labor movement: the middle-sized and big farmers. The social and political consequences of this policy are dealt with below.

Further Changes in the Farm Structure and the Social Democrats in Minority, 1961-75

From 1961 DNA governed with a Parliamentary minority, with support from the small and recently formed Socialist People's Party. This new left opposition was based on an anti-nuclear platform and dissatisfaction with the lack of radical measures from DNA. There was no opposition as yet to agricultural policy, which was still based on principles of increasing productivity through mechanization and enlarging production units.

In the mid 1960s, attention of State policy was directed to providing sufficient capital for the farmers who wanted to expand. The State Bank for Agriculture was given more financial support and became the principle source for investments. Loans were given by law and decree to those farms which were supposed to be "capable of providing a living." In this way, the State secured further control over the agriculture sector. Although

they won the election of 1965, the united center and right
parties (Conservatives, Liberals, Center Party (originally
the Farmers' Party) and Christian Democrats) did not
change agricultural policy in any significant way. The
new government--with a Center Party politician as prime
minister--continued along the same lines as the DNA.

The results were the same as in the 1950s: thousands
of people left the rural areas, with many people no longer
working their forefathers' holdings. Opposition sprung up
in the mid 1960s, first from Otter Brox and other
populists. Later the anti-centralization policy won
support in the left wing parties, in the Center Party, and
among the Liberals and Social Democrats. Much of this
criticism of urbanization and deruralization was based on
concern for rural communities which feared extinction.
After 1970, especially during the the campaign to take
Norway into the Common Market, the international situation
was also influential. The rural population feared even
greater discrimination from Brussels than Oslo.

The coalition government of 1965 was forced to resign
in 1971 on the Common Market issue. Politicians from the
political center could not come to terms with the
conservatives who advocated free trade and international
cooperation. Nevertheless, the farm policy survived
September 25, 1972, and the "no" vote to join the EEC.
Public opinion was, however, heartily shaken by these
events. The Social Democrats, together with the
Conservatives, were the losers in the Common Market
referendum and searched for a new rural policy to regain
their former rural strongholds.

In the international arena, a conference on food and
nutrition was held in Rome in 1973. The background was
the food crisis and the dramatic decline in the world's
food production in 1972. Out of this came a request to
all countries to increase their food production. The oil
boycott and the crisis in the manufacturing industries
also marked a shift in opinion in favor of the agrarian
sector.

Unrest in the Rural Areas and the New Agricultural Policy of 1975

A new agricultural policy, initiated by the Social
Democrats and supported by the Center Party, was
underway. The official committee working with the
question, proposed an increase in the level of

self-sufficiency in agricultural products from 40% to 50% by 1990. The proposal was approved by Parliament in 1975. But the rural population also wanted to have its voice heard. For the the first time in the post-war period a rural protest movement formed. It was a genuine grassroots movement, with no support from established political organizations. The connection with the "petty-revolution" was by nature a political event; the 1975 farmers strike was an economic and social protest.

This extra-parliamentary political action started among the smallholders of an island community in the middle of Norway and was thus named "the Hitra-action." Around 70 farmers voiced eight demands and refused to pay their taxes before the demands were met by the government (a Social Democratic minority government with support from the left socialists). Among these demands were higher prices for milk and meat, social security, more leisure time, and equal taxation with other groups (for a further documentation, see Almas, 1978).

I have dealt elsewhere with the different phases of the strike (Almas, 1978). It received immediate attention in the media and a wave of support spread over the country. Two groups were especially active in the support movement. In addition to other smallholders and their organizations, they received support from "the children of anti-EEC campaign." These were young and politically active people, mostly radicals, with anti-establishment attitudes on a number of questions. Some had a rural background, but others were city dwellers with "green" sympathies. They were organized into different parties and organizations, such as the Maoists, the left socialists, the agrarian intellectuals, and the populists. As professional activists, they provided the strike with the kind of expertise the smallholders did not have themselves.

The other significant support came from the influential middle farmers in the central and agriculturally rich areas of eastern Norway. Hitra—a marginal region in agrarian Norway—was seen by this group as an avant garde community for farmers' interests. The middle farmers ran big businesses but did not necessarily have big incomes with extended production. They belonged to the group of farms promoted by the State, with farms capable of providing a living. Now they joined a protest movement led by smallholders and supported by radicals.

To explain these events, we have to go back to some earlier theoretical propositions. It is very easy to

understand why the unrest originated among the
smallholders. What is more difficult to understand is why
it came so late, at a time when the government itself was
searching for a new policy. The politicalization of 1972
brought into the foreground some very important questions
of regional policy and relations between center and
periphery. An even more important factor to explain the
upsurge was the changing world situation (a crisis of
overproduction, oil boycott, food crisis). This
frightened the smallholders who feared for their future,
giving the radicals ammunition for their pamphlets.

Concerning the middle farmers, we must look at their
opportunities for extending the reproduction (Djurfeldt,
1981). From the late 1960s, the farmers of this group
were not able to extend their reproduction in line with
the rising level at which farms were capable of providing
a living. They had to choose between greater debt and
interest on the one hand and a more activist political
activity than the Farmer's Union had promoted on the other.

The established parties and the farmers' union faced
difficult political problems as a result of the strike,
which lasted from July to October, 1975. Members and
voters were protesting, but the protest could not be
supported because government and union were both partly
responsible for the situation which led to the strike.

From this social and economic unrest and fluid
political situation came the Norwegian Parliament's
unanimous decision of December 1, 1975, to implement
equality of income between farmers and workers within six
years. That was the most important result of the strike
and the following political campaign. That decision was
the end of a "hot summer" and a long autumn where the
farmers' unions agreed to take over the demands of the
striking smallholders in mid October. The sitting DNA
government did not give in until the last moment. They
did not agree with the time frame of "within six years"
until the final hours before voting when they realized
that the left socialists would join the conservative and
center opposition and vote for that time schedule.

Another reason for the decision was that the oil wells
in the Norwegian North Sea were opened at this time and
had produced the first oil income for the State. Without
this, it would have been very difficult for the State to
afford the expenditures entailed. The transfers via the
State budgets to agriculture and forestry rose from 1.4
billion N kr. in 1974 to 7 billion in 1980. This means
8,500 US Dollars in transfers per farm in 1980, hardly

possible if the State budgets had not been strengthened with "oil money" during those years. It may explain why the government could meet the demands from extra-parliamentary action and public opinion.

Another result of the political unrest was a system of fair relief service that guarantees a subsidy to animal farmers, proportionate to the labor demand on the farm if he hired a farm relief worker. There were also some other changes, among them new tax rules that were more favorable to the family farmers.

One problem remaining after the policy changes in 1975 was the problem of income differences. Some minor changes were made to give the small farmers and the farmers in less favorable areas a better income. A system of price differentiation according to the size of the farm and the area of the country was developed. These measures, however, did not alter the situation significantly.

We might say that the policy makers of 1975 left a bomb under the new policy, a bomb that today threatens the very foundation of the Norwegian agricultural policy system. The large transfers from the State budget are now being questioned because research shows that much of the subsidies end up in the pockets of large farmers in central areas. At the same time, many farmers in the peripheral areas have had to quit farming and move because there is no alternative employment in their communities.

CONSEQUENCES AND CONCLUSIONS

I have described the development of the Norwegian agricultural policy over almost four decades. In the last decade there was a break in that policy which is remarkable both in a Norwegian and especially an international context. A policy which advocated rising productivity and enlarged production units was exchanged for a policy giving more support to small units and promising income equality between farmers and workers within six years. These changes came about in a fluid political situation where the Social Democratic government was fighting for its life on two fronts. At the same time, the government had been the architect of some important elements of the new social policy. To summarize, the new policy had three main elements:

- an increase in national self-sufficiency in food products,

- an equal standard of living for farmers and industrial workers within six years, and
- a better equalization between smallholders and big farmers and between farmers in central and peripheral areas.

There were political controversies about the last two principles. Traditionally, the smallholders had been in favor of "internal equalization," while the large farmers had been in favor of better incomes through better prices. Because this gives more to the big and less to the small, it has always been difficult to maintain a united farmers front.

The year 1975 is a landmark in Norwegian farm policy. Internationally, some of the elements in the new policy are out of the ordinary. The farm relief service is one example: it guarantees each farmer with an average animal holding 12,000 N kr. (1700 US $) in state support if he hires temporary farm help. This has already provided 4,000–5,000 new full-time jobs and about 30,000 part-time jobs in rural areas. Farm families take holidays as a result, although they do not have as many days free as their urban compatriots.

Other consequences are more negative. The verbal support for the smallholders has not been enough to stem the exodus from farming as some politicians believed it would. On the contrary, it seems that the large transfers have produced a new group of rich farmers. These are not only reproducing themselves, but they are able to enlarge their farms and accumulate capital. Those with big investments just before the 1975 decision have gained from the rising incomes. Without sharing new expenditures, these farmers now find themselves particularly well off now.

These newly rich farmers are also socially visible and are a threat to the political support for the budget transfers to agriculture, as Brox has pointed out. But it is difficult to attack those big farmers politically. They have a strong influence in the farming lobby. They have time and the money to speak their cause, and they represent a political electorate which both the Social Democrats and the Center Party fear losing to the growing Conservative Party.

The smallholders are now in a difficult situation. Many believed that the 1975 decision would mean a future for them in farming. This was commonly believed by all farmers. The result was a rise in production that crowded

the national market. National prices are far above the
world market prices and the farmers are now suffering
collectively for this overproduction.

This shows the limits of the new agricultural policy.
Without a planned transfer of labor force to other sectors
of society, it is not possible to carry out an
equalization policy between farming and other industries.
The development of agricultural technology and animal and
plant production will increase output, given the same
amount of labor force. When there is no income
difference forcing some farmers to leave agriculture, the
logical result will be overproduction. The present
production quotas will probably not solve the problems.
(The quotas are based on the so-called "past deliveries,"
an average of the last three years.) These types of
measures will support the financially strong farmers--the
farmers that have "climbed the ladder"--and the rest will
drop behind as they did before.

As a final conclusion, I would like to summarize the
analysis of family farming and Norwegian agricultural
policy and its consequences. Family farming is the main
mode of organization in modern capitalist agriculture. As
far as there is a consumption fund left to live from
(regardless of what source) when installments and interest
on loans are paid, family farming goes on. Through
increased production, however, markets are overfilled with
farm products. To regulate farm production and secure the
social order, the capitalist State has to intervene in the
agrarian sector. The normal way of intervention is
through stimulation of structure rationalization, i.e.
forcing some farmers (the small) out of business, and
strengthening the survival chances of others (the large).
Through the mobilization of unprivileged agrarian groups,
the state may be pressed to support small farms and
marginal regions. This will soon strengthen the survival
strategies of the small farmers. But markets are again
overfilled with farm products, and the State will have
legitimate reason to intervene with even stronger measures
in market relations. A policy to cut down on farm
production is implemented, which forces the families with
the least consumption fund to leave the business. A new
group of "small farmers" are now created, from which
farmers' demands may emerge. But rather than taking up
militant action, demanding State policy in favor of their
groups, these "small farmers" seek jobs in other
industries (if such jobs are available). Sometime in the
future, part-time family farming might replace full-time

family farming as the main mode of organization in
Norwegian agriculture.

NOTES

1. Most of my data comes from the Agricultural Census,
Central Bureau of Statistics. I also use some
micro-economic data from the Norwegian Institute of
Agriculture Economics in Oslo, which every year collects
accounts from about 1000 farms of different size groups
from all over the country. I also used data from a survey
of 923 farmers and 371 farmers' wives about the health and
working conditions in agriculture. This survey is done by
the Rural Research Group, Institute of Sociology,
University of Trondheim.
2. Family farming, part-time or full-time, is the main
mode of organization in Norwegian agriculture. There are
about 100 cooperative farms (group farms), 310 farms owned
by joint stock companies, and 300 farms owned by
institutions. Corporate and cooperative farms constitute
less than 1% of the total number of farms.

94

REFERENCES

Almas, R. 1977. Norsk jordbruk - det nye hamskiftet.
Oslo: Gyldenal.
Almas, R. 1978. Hitra-aksjonen - smabonder i
skattestreik. Oslo: Oktober.
Almas, R. and J. Odegard. 1983. Women in Rural Norway.
Recent tendencies in the Development of the Division
of Labour in Agriculture and the Participation of
Rural Women on the Labour Market. Paper to the XII
European Congress for Rural Sociology, Budapest 1983.
Brox, O. 1980. Mot et konsolidert bosettingsmonster,
Tidsskrift for samfunnsforsking, vol. 21, no. 3/4.
Brox, O. 1980. Djrfeldt, G. 1981. Agriculture in a
corporative economy. Report to the ECPR-seminar in
Firence, March, 1980.
Djurfeldt, B. 1981. What happened to the Agrarian
Bourgeosie and the Rural Proletariat under Monopoly
Capitalism, Acta Sociologica, vol. 24, no. 3, 167-192.
Havens, E. and H. Newby 1981. Agriculture and the State:
An analytical approach, Paper on to the seminar of
"The political Economy of Food and Agriculture in
Advanced Industrial Societies," Norman Bethune
College, New York University, Toronto, The model also
published in Journal of Agricultural Economics: Vo.
XXXIII (2) 1982, page 140.
Hernes, G. (ed.) 1978. Forhandlingsokonomi og
blandingsadministasion. Bergen: Universiteforlaget.
Marx, K. 1983. Kapitalen. Oslo: Oktober.
Odegard, J. 1983. Landbrukets helseundersokelse 1982-
Kodebok med fordelinger- Brukeren, Report no. 1, 1983,
Department of Sociology, University of Trondheim.

5

A Persistent Culture: Some Reflections on Swedish Family Farming

Ulrich Nitsch

The social, political, economic, and technical context of Swedish farming has changed tremendously since its early beginnings. Nevertheless, family farming has remained the dominant mode of food production. What factors have contributed to family farming's durability? What are its prospects in the future? In the following presentation I will explore these questions. To place family farming in its proper perspective at present, a brief review of the history of family farming is followed by a description of contemporary Swedish agriculture. An analysis of post-war agricultural policies shows how politicians gradually became more interested in economically efficient food production than in maintaining the structure of family farming. Yet family farming has survived.

I think that the family farm's survival is primarily due to the personal commitment of the farming family. Results from some recent empirical studies show that a majority of Swedish farmers still perceive farming as a way of life. In the concluding sections of my presentation I discuss the contributions of family farming to the Swedish society and the prospects for survival of this unique institution.

FROM VILLAGE-DEPENDENT PEASANTS TO GOVERNMENT-DEPENDENT FARMERS

It all started with family farming. The first settlements in Sweden were solitary farms or small hamlets occupied by an extended family. In a recent paper Knut Pipping (1984) presents an overview of Scandinavian farming from its beginning until the 20th century. The following analysis of the structure and political power of the Swedish peasantry is primarily based on Pipping's paper.

The first settlements in Sweden were established at the end of the second or beginning of the first millenium BC. They were established along valleys, shores, and bays, where settlers could find fodder for their cattle. A group of farms or hamlets in a particular area formed a social unit within which individuals cooperated in the construction of primitive ramparts. These ramparts served as refuges for the people and their cattle during times of unrest. The need for and organization of a defense system continued to have a decisive influence on the structure and political power of the peasantry throughout Swedish history.

Already in the Viking Age (850–1050 AD), family farming was protected by law. A yeomen of that time who wanted to sell land which he had inherited had to offer it for sale publicly at the local thing-moot (town meeting) to allow kinsmen an opportunity to excercise their birth-right, i.e. their right of preemption. Only if no kinsmen wanted to purchase it could it be sold to a non-kinsmen.

Later in the 13th century, a similar law was introduced to prevent land from being donated to the church. During this time, many landowners wanted to give land to the church for the benefit of their souls. The law stated that only a certain proportion of land could be used for this purpose in order to protect the rights of the heirs. Thus, Pipping points out, peasants did not own their land unconditionally; they held it in trust from their kin group.

In the Viking Age, a normal holding is assumed to have been a family farm run by an extended family. It was basically a self-sufficient, economic unit covering most of its residents' needs. However, land holding was differentiated both in respect to the size of the farms and the kind of ownership. Many farms were so large that they needed non-family labor; and absentee ownership, as well as leasing, was rather common. Thus, there seems to have been three categories of landholders during the Viking Age—wealthy absentee landowners, common peasants, and tenants.

The landowners of the Viking Age cooperated in an elaborate system of defense. The maintenance of this system implied rules for the assessment of land and the computation of tax contributions. These rules were most likely accepted by the landowners themselves at local thing-moots rather than being imposed by a central authority. The political independence of the peasants is also indicated by their conspicuous yearning for equality as stated in the Provincial Statutes of that time.

Resistance to Feudalistic Tendencies

During the 12th and 13th centuries, when a centralized royal power had been established in Sweden, the king, nobility, and the church acquired much land. The number of independent peasants, however, remained fairly large during this period, and their rights remained protected by law. The nobility was not to be compared with the continental type of vassal. They did not hold their land as fiefs from the king, as did continental vassals, and received their main source of income from their own allods (inherited property).

A period of feudalistic tendencies started during the Reformation (around 1530), when the king confiscated the church's land and the Crown became the wealthiest landowner. During the following decades and up until the middle of the 17th century, vast tracts of land were given to the nobility to assure their support of the king and their contribution to the army. In the middle of the 17th century, only 28% of the land in Sweden was owned by the Crown and independent peasants (Andersson, 1953). However, this period of feudalistic tendencies was a short one. During the last few decades of the 17th century, the king revoked to the Crown most of the land that had been given to the nobility by his predecessors. The status of the peasants thereby changed from tenants of the nobility to tenants of the Crown. Most of them were later offered opportunities to purchase the land they leased.

Even during the most feudalistic period, Swedish peasants did not live as serfs. On several occasions they expressed their discontent and mobilized resistance when their rights were threatened. They retained a certain protection by the law and upheld their traditions of local self-government on the village level (Andersson, 1953). Consequently, they maintained a considerable political influence. They were invited to send representatives to a legislative assembly in 1435 and to later assemblies until they were formally organized as the Fourth Estate. This occurred in 1617.

Towards Dependency on Governmental Policies

By the beginning of the 18th century, the period of royal absolutism in Sweden had ended. Political power had shifted to the Four Estate Diet (legislative assembly) in which the Peasantry, in cooperation with the Clergy and the Burgers, deprived the Nobility of some of its privileges. The peasantry also freed themselves from some of the control exerted on them by the Crown. However, during the same period, a reform in the reallotment of land was initiated that was stiffly resisted by the peasants.

Up until this time, the arable land of a village had been partitioned up in such a way so as to give every landowner a just share of both the good and less fertile fields. This resulted in extremely fragmented ownership patterns. In some villages each family owned as many as 60 to 100 narrow strips of land. All strips in a field had to be plowed, sown, and harvested at the same time under the supervision of the village council. The landed gentry and the rural clergy considered this system of land distribution to be a serious obstacle to the introduction of improved farming practices. Since there was a great need for an increase in food production in the country, they initiated a land reallotment reform.

After implementation was completed, about 150 years later, this reform had completely changed farming conditions. It resulted in a dissolution of the villages and dispersion of the farms that freed the individual peasants from many constraints to which they had earlier been subjected by the village community. However, it also changed the traditional peasant way of life and resulted in a loss of many traditional relationships and forms of cooperation between neighbors. It thereby formed the basis for the transition from traditional village-dependent peasants to modern farmers who control the markets for agricultural production through their strong cooperatives. But simultaneously, as Pipping points out, they have become increasingly dependent on government agricultural policy and the decisions made by their own organizations.

THE CONTEXT AND CHARACTERISTICS OF PRESENT FAMILY FARMING

At the end of World War II there were about 600,000 persons gainfully employed in Swedish farming. There were about 300,000 farm holdings (of two hectares or more) and the arable land on these holdings totaled about 3.6 million hectares. Today, there are only 140,000 persons left on 115,000 farm holdings, representing 2.9 million hectares of arable land. Thus, the number of persons employed in farming and the number of farm holdings decreased by approximately 75% and 60%, respectively. As a consequence of this decline, rural areas have become largely depopulated. Today only 17% of the Swedish population live in the countryside.

The decline in the farming population was the result of a rapid mechanization and a sharp increase in the scale and efficiency of farming. For instance, during the post-war period, the number of tractors increased from 30,000 to 190,000. Almost all small grain is now harvested by combines. The average size of a farm holding has increased from 12 to 26 hectares of arable land, and the average size of a dairy herd from 5 to 17 dairy cows. Average yields have often doubled. Milk production, for example, has increased from 3,600 to 6,400 kilos per cow annually (among recorded dairy cows) and average wheat yields have increased from 2,300 to 4,600 kilos per hectare (Statistics Sweden, 1946, 1951, 1984a).

A Small Industry and Moderate Farm Sizes

At present, farming accounts for only a small part of Swedish industry. Less than 4% of the country's labor force work on farms, and farm production contributes only 2% to the Gross National Product. However, this is enough to allow Sweden to be self-sufficient with respect to basic foods and still produce a surplus of grain that must be exported.

About 70% of the cropland is used to produce small grains and grass for fodder. About one-third of the farmers have dairy production, and animal husbandry is the most important source of farm income. Most Swedish farmers own some woodland that contributes to a considerable part of their income.

From an international perspective, Swedish farms produce relatively high yields and are very efficient. Farming is capital intensive, highly mechanized, and also relies heavily on the use of fertilizers and pesticides.

Almost all of the arable farmland in Sweden is privately owned, about 75% by private individuals and 20% by corporations. An increasing proportion of arable farmland (more than 40%) is leased. About 15% of the farmers lease all of the land that they farm, about 35% lease some of their land, and the remaining 50% own all of the land that they farm.

As mentioned previously, the average Swedish farm is relatively small, with 26 hectares of arable land and 17 cows per dairy herd. A majority of the farmers (60%) cultivate 20 hectares or less and only 3% cultivate more than 100 hectares. One-third of the dairy herds are smaller than 10 cows, and only 3% of the herds contain 50 cows or more (Statistics Sweden, 1984a).

A Heavy Working Load

Most of the labor input on Swedish farms is provided by the family. The farm holders account for about 70% of the labor input, while their spouses and other family members account for about 20%. Only 7% of the labor is provided by employed farm workers.

About 40% of the farm holdings do not provide a full-time job (1,800 hours per year) for one person. Thus, more than half of the farm operators engage in off-farm occupations to supplement their incomes. For 20% of the farmers, the off-farm occupation is full-time. On small farms of 10 hectares or less, more than one-third of the farmers work full-time at another job (Statistics Sweden, 1984b).

Many farmers have a quite heavy workload. One-third of them work more than 2,700 hours per year (off-farm occupation included). Thus, many of them have very little leisure time. According to a statistical survey of Swedish farmers, 40% had not taken any days off during 1976. Only 16% reported that they had had 100 or more days off (Lantbruksekonomiska samarbetsnamnden, 1983). These figures can be compared with blue collar workers, who average 140 days off work per year. Dairy farmers, of course, have the least time off. In an interview study conducted in the Swedish province of Varmland in 1978, I found that half of the dairy farmers had only had a single day or less of free time during the previous year (Nitsch, 1979).

The average age of a Swedish farmer is about 50 years. Most of them, approximately 75%, have entered the farming profession by succession within the family (Brangenfeldt, 1983).

101

A Strong Cooperative Movement

The economic crisis at the end of the 1920s was a
major incentive for Swedish farmers to organize a strong
cooperative movement. Farmers' cooperatives for credit,
processing, and marketing are now an integral part of
Swedish agriculture. By international standards, the
proportion of food processing and marketing controlled by
farmers' cooperatives is very high. Farmers' cooperatives
essentially handle all milk production, 80% of the
slaughter, and 75% of the grain produced in Sweden.
    Almost all Swedish farmers belong to the same trade
union. The trade union and the farm cooperatives are
closely associated in one head organization called the
Federation of Swedish Farmers (LRF). This organization
represents the farmers in all political and economic
negotiations with the government (Federation of Swedish
Farmers, 1982).

FAMILY FARMING AND THE POLITICIANS

The reallotment of land completely changed the social
structure and living conditions of the peasants. This
change was a prerequisite for the mechanization of farming
and depopulation of rural areas that accelerated after
World War II and resulted in a second silent revolution in
farming conditions. At present there are not many farmers
left, and it is uncertain whether the remainder will be
able to retain the way of farming we usually associate
with the concept of "family farming." The meaning of this
concept will be elaborated in a later section of my
chapter. But first, I will describe how family farming
was treated in post-war agricultural policies.

Post-War Agricultural Policies

Agricultural policies in Sweden after World War II
were designed to promote and facilitate the transformation
and decline of the farming sector. This is illustrated by
Per Thullberg in two recent papers based on research
conducted at the Department of History at the University
of Stockholm (Thullberg, 1983a, 1983b). Up until the war,
Sweden had maintained a protectionist agricultural policy
primarily aimed at insuring adequate income for farmers
and securing satisfactory levels of domestic food

production. Thullberg describes how after the War politicians redirected their focus of interest towards improving economic efficiency in food production. Their decisions on agricultural policies were subsequently based on an economic analysis aimed at optimizing the allocation of capital and labor within the society as a whole.

The governmental committee proposing the first agricultural policy after the war suggested that farm production should be regulated by the same demands on economic and technical efficiency as other industries. It recommended measures aimed at promoting economic growth by facilitating the adoption of new technology and shifting labor from farming to other sectors of the economy. The committee argued that this was the best strategy for improving the living conditions of the population as a whole. Economic growth based on technical efficiency was considered synonymous with welfare and social development. However, the Secretary of Agriculture did not altogether accept the technical and economic priorities of the committee. The final proposal approved by Parliment in 1947 stated that family farming should remain the basis of agricultural production. Measures were taken to assure that a farm holding of 10-20 hectares arable land would provide an income equivalent with that earned by an employed farm worker.

Twenty years later, however, economic and technical priorities completely dominated agricultural policy. A new policy enacted in 1967 explicitly stated that the promotion of economic efficiency should be given a higher priority than concerns about the quality of rural life, environmental protection, and preservation of the rural landscape. The policy was prepared by a committee that devoted one and a half pages of a 770 page report to "demographic and social aspects of farming." The social and environmental effects of continued increases in economic efficiency in farming were not considered relevant to agricultural policy. These problems were to be addressed by other departments and agencies. Family farming was no longer given any preferential treatment. Specialization and large-scale farming was considered desirable, whereas part-time farming was regarded as undesirable and was not supported by legislation or financial aid.

To promote efficiency in farming, local governmental agencies, called District Agricultural Boards, were established throughout the country in 1947. The Land Acquisition Act delegated these boards considerable authority in regulating the sale and use of land. According to this act, a prospective land purchaser must acquire permission from the District Agricultural Board to buy the land, unless he or she is a close relative to the seller. When first enacted, the purpose of the act was to protect the interests of family farmers by preventing corporations from buying farmland. During the 1950s and 1960s the emphasis of the act gradually changed to one of consolidating small farms into larger and more efficient enterprises. Consequently, the implementation of the act became very controversial and spawned very negative attitudes towards the District Agricultural Boards among family farmers.

The Contemporary Policy and Debate

There has not been much disagreement among the political parties in Sweden with regard to the post-war agricultural policies. Thullberg points out that they all accepted the basic principles of adjusting farm production to the economic and technical demands of an industrial economy. Up until the 1970s, no real alternative policies to those enacted by the Social Democratic governments in 1947 and 1967 were presented. The political parties differed only in their opinions as to the extent--the means--and the rate at which the basic principles should be implemented. However, according to Thullberg, the Social Democrats have been the strongest supporters of a techno-economic adjustment of farming to market forces. They also were opposed to the re-establishment of the principles of family farming enacted by a liberal-conservative government in 1977. The Social Democrats recognize that family farming will continue to predominate in "the foreseeable future." However, they continue to resist giving preferential treatment to family farming over other forms of efficient farm enterprises (Jordbruksdepartementet, 1983; Thullberg, 1983a, 1983b).

During the 1970s there was a shift toward increasing concern for the social and environmental consequences of farming. In the policy enacted in 1977, the principles of family farming were re-established, and part-time farming was also officially legitimized. The 1977 policy reflects a period of growing public concern for issues such as environmental pollution, pesticide residues in food, the well-being of domestic animals subject to large-scale production, preservation of the landscape, and the depopulation of rural areas. At present, however, this policy is under debate. The present issue is how to handle a growing surplus of small grain in a time characterized by a shortage in public funds and a strong inclination to adjust public policies and services to the commercial forces of a market economy.

According to a recent official investigation, the 30,000 largest farms (i.e., 25% of the total number of farms) produce food enough for our entire nation to be self-sufficient. It has also been argued that in the near future half of the present acreage of tillable land would be enough to produce all the food we need. Such prospects are beginning to initiate a discussion of the fundamental question of what type of agriculture we want.

In this debate one position is the promotion of a continued industrialization of farming with the help of computerization, automation, continued chemicalization, and application of new bio-technology. The aim is to improve the economic efficiency and to refine our control of the ecological system by applying highly technical means. Another position promotes an ecological approach aimed at minimizing the chemical and technological manipulation of biological processes. Others, again, believe that two kinds of agriculture will exist side by side, creating further polarization between large-scale, industrialized farming and small-scale, part-time farming. The discussion has so far focused more on means than on goals. The most important questions about the basic role of agriculture--what values we want it to promote, what needs it should meet, and the analysis of long-term social, ecological and ethical implications of different types of farming--are badly neglected in the public debate.

FARMERS' PERCEPTIONS OF FARMING

The previous examination of agricultural policies in Sweden described how, after the War, politicians adopted a view that farming should essentially be a means for efficient food production. Family farming was thereby subordinated to demands for economic and technical efficiency originating from other sectors of the society. I call this perspective an "instrumental" orientation to farming. But what about the farmers themselves? How do they perceive farming? What implications do their perceptions have on the prospects of family farming?

A Way of Life

Empirical studies conducted at the Department of Agricultural Extension Education at the Swedish University of Agricultural Sciences strongly indicate that most Swedish farmers give priority to personal and family needs over improvement in the economic efficiency of their farm enterprises. They strive primarily to satisfy a complex combination of social needs and environmental concerns, while obtaining personal job satisfaction. Their aspirations have an "organic" rather than "instrumental" orientation, i.e., for most farmers, farming means stewardship and a way of life.

The results of a comprehensive interview study among dairy farmers in the province of Varmland in the middle part of Sweden illustrate what I call the "organic" orientation (Nitsch, 1979). For two-thirds of the dairy farmers in this province, carrying on a family tradition was a strong motivational force. Half of the farmers expected their children or other close relatives to take over their farm, and still more hoped that this would be the case. These results confirm an observation that I often made while working as an agricultural extension agent: "Family" is the most important source of motivation for most farmers. Single farmers often saw little meaning in improving the farm, since they had no family to appreciate their efforts and no family member to inherit the fruits of their labor.

A discomfort with new technology and a strong concern for domestic animals and the environment were reflected in their responses to a set of attitudinal statements. As shown in Table 5.1, a large majority of the farmers expressed a strong "organic" orientation to farming. The statements to which farmers were asked to respond were:

1) We should discontinue our attempts to increase milk yield and consider the cow's well-being.
2) We must reconsider our present farm practices to keep them in better harmony with the laws of nature.
3) The present level of pesticide use in agriculture may result in serious, long-term damages to the environment.

Agreement with these statements was interpreted as an "organic" orientation and disagreement an "instrumental" orientation.

106

Table 5.1. Perceptions of Dairy Farmers as to the Impacts
of Technology on Dairy Cow Well-being and
Environmental Quality (Nitsch, 1979)

	Organic Orientation	Intermediate Orientation	Instrumental Orientation
Well-being of Dairy cows (1)	82%	4%	14%
Environmental Effects of Technology (2)	83%	8%	9%
Environmental Effects of Pesticides (3)	83%	8%	9%

Several other observations in this interview study
also indicated that farmers perceived farming primarily as
a way of life. For instance, even though most of them had
little or no leisure time (half of them had only a single
day or less of free time per year), very few were
interested in changing jobs. They dearly valued their
freedom as farmers, enjoyed working with animals, and
appreciated working outdoors. When asked which
improvements in farming they would most appreciate, they
gave priority to more leisure time and easier working
conditions over an increase in net income.

These observations were confirmed by two later
interview studies. In one study, Landquist and Lundkvist
(1983) concluded that two-thirds of the farmers in the
southern province of Skane did not perceive themselves as
managers of an economic enterprise. They claimed they
were "farmers." They did not usually rely upon economic
calculations as a basis for their decisions about farm
investments. However, their decisions were not made
haphazardly. Landquist and Lundkvist accurately
characterized the farmers' decision-making strategy with
the following words:

Our impression is that farmers usually have clear
goals in their management. Their goal is to make it
possible to continue to be a farmer, with the

traditional chores included in farm work and to
preserve the farm for future generations of the
family. They do not plan by sitting at their desks
doing calculations. Planning issomething, 'that goes
on in my mind continuously in my daily work'...
Decisions are made according to routines originating
from their own farming experiences (Landquist and
Lundkvist, 1983:40).

It should be noted that this conclusion is based on
interviews from a sample of much younger farmers with
considerably larger farms and more formal education than
the average Swedish farmer.
    Lotta Johanson conducted an interview study among
dairy farmers in two other provinces, Dalarna and Halland,
in the middle and southern parts of the country. She
estimated that three-fourths of the farmers in her study
perceived farming as a way of life (Johanson, 1984).
These farmers, she reports,
    ...talked a lot about the advantage of working
    outdoors and being part of nature. They liked to talk
    about how much they loved their dairy cows. They
    would not consider changing to another job, even if
    they wished that they had more free time. I think
    that for many of them, their desire to live close to
    nature is stronger than their need for leisure time
    (Johanson, 1984:59).

WHY FAMILY FARMING?

    With changing conditions in farming, the meaning of
the concept of "family farming" has also changed. Only a
few decades ago, a Swedish family farm occupied the time
of several family members and, in addition, nonfamily
personnel were often employed to work both indoors and
outdoors. A family farm was a social unit producing much
of its own food, and the capital investments in farming
were low. Today, a family farm is mostly a one-man and/or
part-time enterprise, exclusively producing for the
market. The capital investments needed to provide
full-time occupation for one person are very high and far
beyond the means of an ordinary citizen. And thanks to
mechanization, a family now can operate a large-scale
industrialized type of farm enterprise that most people
would find strange to call a "family farm." What do we
actually mean by the term "family farming" today?

108

An Ideological Concept

The term "family farming" does not have any official
definition in Sweden. It is an ideological concept that
is often used as a slogan in political debates. The
participation of family members in the farming activities
is not enough of a criterion. In today's language,
"family farming" also implies a small or moderate scale of
production as opposed to a larger scale, industrialized
mode. Also, many people associate family farming with
diversified production and an "organic" orientation as
opposed to specialization and an "instrumental" orientation. Thus the concept of "family farming" represents a
combination of qualitative farming characteristics.

As described earlier, the tradition of family farming
is now upheld only by a minority of the population,
representing less than 4% of the labor force. It was also
mentioned that since the end of World War II the
principles of family farming have not received much
political support. One might, therefore, ask if and why
family farming is worth maintaining.

The answer to that question depends not only on what
we mean by family farming and know about it, but also
depends on our beliefs and values. The consequences of
farming involve many quantitative and qualitative
aspects: ecological, economic, social, psychological,
political, ethical, as well as aesthetic. They have
long-range as well as short-range implications and
interact in a complex way. Due to the complexities
involved, it is not possible to present a complete and
definite description of the consequences of different
types of farming on the basis of empirical research. To a
large extent, our position on family farming depends on
our beliefs and ultimately rests on our value-priorities.

Long-Range and Qualitative Aspects

My own position is in favor of family farming. By
"family farming," I mean the combination of family
participation in a moderately-sized farm enterprise guided
by an "organic" orientation. My argument is based on the
opinion that farming should serve as more than just an
efficient provider of food. As Schumacher asserts in his
book Small Is Beautiful, farming involves "the whole
relationship between man and nature, the whole life-style
of a society, the health, happiness and harmony of man as
well as the beauty of his habitat" (1975:111-112). A

civilization with a crude, materialistic view of agriculture, Schumacher continues, for which financial matters are the ultimate criteria guiding human action, has little chance of long-term survival. I believe that Schumacher is right. Therefore, to me, the value of family farming is primarily determined by the way it contributes to the long-range, qualitative aspects of society.

There is, of course, no absolute guarantee that a family farm will contribute positively to these aspects. As an agricultural extension agent, I have seen some family farms where the well-being of animals had been neglected and others where polluting farm practices were used. In general, however, there is no doubt that Swedish farm families are very concerned about their animals and take a pride in preserving their farms and the environment for future generations. It also appears from the empirical studies of farmers' attitudes and aspirations referred to above, that family participation in farming on a moderate scale is the best ground for development of an "organic" orientation to farming.

I see this "organic" orientation upheld by most family farmers as a culture that, for several reasons, is urgently needed in our society. By relating to work as a meaningful and creative activity, this culture provides a refreshing alternative to the "instrumental" relationship towards work predominant in most other sectors of our society. In a similar way, I see the kind of family relationship that usually develops on a family farm to be of value in itself. In a society where the role of the family is often reduced to a sanctuary where we eat, sleep, and fulfill our emotional needs, it is important to maintain instances where relationships between family members are based on a sharing of troubles, pleasures, and responsibilities in work. The strong sense of responsibility for carrying on a family tradition and preserving the farm for future generations that tends to emerge from this kind of family relationship provides a valuable contrast to the short-range perspective on production and consumption encouraged in a market economy, largely directed towards satisfying immediate needs.

In recent years, the vulnerability of modern farming productivity to war or other emergencies has become a serious issue in Sweden. Empirical data show that the vulnerability of farm production increases with increasing farm size, specialization, mechanization, and chemical use (Goransson, 1983). This situation calls for the maintenance of moderately-sized, labor-intensive family farms as a means for securing domestic food production. A recent governmental task force also contended that the maintenance of a rural population and rural culture in Sweden are indispensable for preserving fundamental societal values (Industridepartementet, 1984). I am convinced that family farming is an efficacious as well as economically effective method for realizing these values.

Finally, the economic values of the flexibility, creativity, motivation, human energy, and experience characteristic of moderate-scale family farming may be difficult to quantify but nevertheless exist. If our calculations are restricted to comparing the short-term monetary gains of different sized farm enterprises, moderate-scale family farming may often fall short. However, if the positive effects on rural employment and the environment are included, and if the increased productivity due to the personal commitment of farm families could be measured, I think family farming would also prove to be efficient in economic terms.

PROSPECTS FOR SURVIVAL

Since family farming represents a small industry and minority population within the Swedish society, I think its survival will ultimately depend on the strengths and resources of the farming families themselves, including their capacities for adapting to changes in the larger society. It was shown above that the mode of production upheld by family farming provides invaluable contributions to the well-being of our society. However, the problem is that these contributions are largely qualitative, long range, and intangible. Therefore, they often fall short in our present economic and political system.

For analytical purposes, I think it is fruitful to conceive of family farming as a type of counterculture within the techno-economic culture predominating in our society. In the final section of this essay I will elaborate on some of the factors that have helped this culture to survive and discuss its prospects for the future.

Institutional Factors

Legislation regulating land ownership is an

institutional factor that has helped Swedish family
farming survive. As mentioned above, family ownership of
land was protected by law as early as in the Viking Age.
In more recent times, land acquisition legislation has
prevented corporations from purchasing farmland.
Paradoxically, the present land acquisition act also fills
an important function by preventing relatives from taking
over farmland. By stating certain requirements on a
presumptive purchaser's use of the land and on his or her
professional farming qualifications, the act, to some
extent, prevents land from being bought by unqualified
relatives who do not intend to live on the farm and earn
their living from farming. Consequently, more farmland
remains available for actively farming families.
    The strength of farmer organizations is another
institutional factor that has supported family farming in
Sweden. By dominating the processing and marketing of
agricultural products, the farmers' cooperatives have
effectively prevented private food processing corporations
from controlling agricultural production by vertical
integration. The farmers' cooperatives have also helped
family farmers by paying equal prices for their
agricultural products irrespective of the quantity
delivered by a farmer.
    In negotiations with the state, Swedish Farmers' Trade
Union has succeeded in maintaining a strong bargaining
position relative to the powerful consumer organizations
and labor unions. Even if the farmer trade union
executives have, to a large extent, adopted instrumental
values regarding economic and technical efficiency, the
trade union has still had a favorable influence on family
farming conditions by refuting the demands of the consumer
and labor organizations for a large-scale mode of
production.

Motivational Factors

    Ultimately, the survival of family farming depends on
the family's motivation. A farming family receives
motivation by fulfilling one or several human needs.
These needs were depicted earlier as components of the
"organic" orientation to farming. The most important
component was shown to be family itself, i.e. the family
members' concern for each other and their farm. This
seems to reflect a basic human need that, as shown in the
introductory historical review, is deeply rooted in the
history of Swedish farming. It also seems to be a

universal phenomenon already described by Chyanov in his
theory about peasantry as a specific type of economy.
According to this theory, peasant family labor is
primarily directed towards achieving a higher level of
well-being by meeting family needs that are to a large
degree qualitative and cannot be substituted by monetary
gain (Kerblay, 1971).

Recently, Berger (1979) confirmed Chyanov's
observations, reporting on a rural French community. The
determination of the peasant, says Berger (1979:201), "is
to hand on the means of survival (if possible made more
secure, compared to what he inherited) to his children.
His ideals are located in the past; his obligations are to
the future, which he himself will not live to see."
Berger is very pessimistic about the peasant culture's
chances to survive. In my opinion, it has partly survived
as reflected in the "organic" orientation of farming
families. Its future depends mainly on the ability to
maintain shared family commitment to farming. However,
the conditions conducive to such a commitment have
deteriorated.

With few people engaged in farming and living in the
countryside, the probability that a family will consist of
two or more persons well acquainted with farming is small
and diminishing. To survive economically, many family
farmers increase their off-farm activities, expanding
their working loads at the expense of leisure. This
strategy may work if both husband and wife are committed
to the farming enterprise. But what happens if one spouse
works full-time at another occupation and wants to spend
his or her leisure time with the family outside farm work
or away from the farm? How are such conflicts to be
resolved?

The modern capital-intensive family farm that provides
a full-time occupation for one person is also vulnerable
to family occupational conflicts. Under such conditions,
farming is a busy and often very lonely occupation. If
both husband and wife are engaged in demanding
occupations, but only one works on the farm, when will
they have the time and energy to nurture their
relationship?

Divorce rates are high in Sweden, and there are
indications that they are also increasing among farm
families. Divorce is often disastrous for the farming
spouse, economically as well as emotionally. Where is the
motivation to come from when there is no family to

appreciate the lonely efforts involved in farm work?
Social and emotional needs are not satisfied by economic
efficiency.
   I see no easy solution to these problems. As
mentioned previously, in earlier times farming families
exercised local self-government and cooperated in
protecting their common interests. Today, however, the
traditional forms of local cooperation have been replaced
by a dependency on a mass society pursuing a different
culture. In this situation, the only way for family
farming to survive, as I see it, is by reinstituting
traditions of local cooperation. Cooperation is needed
for the use and purchase of farm equipment (including
microcomputers), as well as in the exchange of farm work.
It is needed for economic reasons, since farm equipment
has been getting increasingly expensive, and for safety
reasons, since accidents can occur when working alone.
Cooperation is also needed to increase leisure time; and
last but not least, it is urgently needed for social
reasons. The tradition of family farming can hardly be
maintained by single farmers or families farming in
isolation.

An Informal Activity

   What then are the prospects for family farming in
Sweden? My conclusion is that it will survive. Although
the economic and political environment is not very
supportive, neither is it purposely attempting to replace
family farming with another mode of production. Present
farming conditions place strong pressure on the social
basis for family farming, but I believe that young people
will find new ways of integrating farming and family.
   There are two major reasons for my belief. First,
family farming provides for basic needs deeply rooted in
human nature. Second, industrial work opportunities today
appear to be declining in response to automation and
computerization; and, in addition, the expansion of the
public service sector seems to have passed its peak due to
a common resistance to more bureaucracy and taxation.
There are indications that the informal economy is
presently expanding. By its basic nature, family farming
was always informal.

114

REFERENCES

Andersson, Ingvar. 1953. Sveriges historia. Stockholm:
Natur och Kultur
Berger, John. 1979. Pig Earth. London: Writers and
Readers Publishing Cooperative.
Brangenfeldt, Ulf. 1983. Familjelantbruket i Sverige. In
Familielandbrug- ets framtid, NJF-utredning/rapport No
11. Oslo: 94-119.
Federation of Swedish Farmers. 1982. The Farmers'
Organizations, LRF, Stockholm.
Goransson, Gert. 1983. Jordbrukets sarbarhet -
problem och losningar. In Jordbruket och var miljo.
Stad och land, Report No 22, Swedish University of
Agricultural Sciences, Alnarp: 73-79.
Industridepartementet. 1984. Glesbygden - resurser och
mojligheter, Rapport fran glesbygdsdelegationen, Ds I
1984:20. Stockholm.
Johanson, Lotta. 1984. Intervjuundersokningen. In Gun
Bernes and Lotta Johanson: Bondernas syn pa ledighet
och   trygghet,   Examensarbete   85,   Lantbrukets
informationslara, Swedish University of Agricultural
Sciences.
Jordbruksdepartementet. 1983. Kommittedirektiv for
utformningen av en livsmedelspolitik, Dir 1983:103.
Stockholm.
Kerblay, Basile. 1971. Chyanov and the Theory of
Peasantry as a Specific Type of Economy. In Teodor
Shanin   (ed.):   Peasants   and   Peasant   Societies.
Middlesex: Penguin Education: 150-160.
Landquist, Bengt and Lars-Erik Lundkvist. 1983.
Lantbrukarnas   behov   avservice   och   radgivning   i
foretagsledning,   Examensarbete   74,   Lantbrukets
informationslara.   Uppsala: Swedish   University   of
Agricultural Sciences.
Lantbruksekonomiska samarbetsnamnden. 1983.
Levnadsstandarden   for   jord-brukare.   Stockholm:
Rapport avqiven av levnadsstandardgruppen.
Nitsch, O. Ulrich. 1979. Farmers' Perceptions of and
Preferences   concerning   Agricultural   Extension
Programs. Dissertation in Continuing and Vocational
Education at the University of Wisconsin. In Report
at the Department of Economics and Statistics No.195,
Swedish University of Agricultural Sciences.

Pipping, Knut. 1984. Was - and Is - the Scandinavian
Odalbonde a Peasant? Meddelanden fran Ekonomist-
Statsvetenskapliga fakulteten vid Abo Akademi, Ser.
A:194.
Schumacher, E.F. 1975. Small is Beautiful. New York:
Harper and Row Publishers.
Statistics Sweden. 1946. Statistisk Arsbok.
Stockholm: P.A. Norstedt Och Soner.
Statistics Sweden. 1951. Statistisk Arsbok.
Stockholm: P.A. Norstedt Och Soner.
Statistics Sweden. 1984a. Yearbook for Agricultural
Statistics. Stockholm: Liber.
Statistics Sweden. 1984b. Jordbrukets arbetskraft 1983,
Statistiska Meddelanden, J 1984:12.
Thullberg, Per. 1983a. Hur har driftsformerna inom
jordbruket vuxit fram som endel av
samhallsutvecklingen. In Jordbruket och var miljo,
Stad och land, Report No 22, Swedish University of
Agricultural Sciences, Alnarp, pp. 35-43.
Thullberg, Per. 1983b. Swedish Agricultural Policy during
the Postwar Period. Paper presented at the ECPR Joint
Session in Florence 1983 (Dept of History at the
University Of Stockholm).

6
Postwar Technological and Social Development on Family Farms: The Case of Finland

Nils Westermarck

SHORT BACKGROUND REVIEW

Finnish agriculture is based on family farms. The average size of farms is small, about 12 hectares of arable land. The number of larger farms has not increased very much. In fact, present agricultural policy does not support expansion of farms. Only 10% of the total area of arable land, 2.4 million hectares, is rented.

Forest land is an integral part of the Finnish farm, with the average farm unit including 35 hectares. The regional distribution, however, varies. In general, there is more arable land in the south than in the north, but correspondingly more forest land in the north.

About 99% of farms are privately owned, but a large number of them belong to pensioners or heirs. Thus, only about half of the farms are owned by farmers belonging to the statistically registered active population. This group includes many farmers who are, in fact, part-time farmers. In 1982, about 75,000 farms obtained more than 75% of their income from agriculture and forestry. There are about 200,000 farm units in Finland, but only half of them are real producing farms.

Finnish agricultural production is very intensively based on livestock. Only 15% of the arable land is used for production of cash crops. Milk accounts for 38% of the total value of production and cattle for 53% when beef production is taken into account. The structure of production has changed over the years, with milk's contribution decreasing and meat's contribution increasing. In the past, milk was produced on almost all farms, today only on 3 of 10 farms. About half of the farms had no animals in 1982.

117

118

FARM PEOPLE

The Finnish rural society can be defined as
traditional until the beginning of the 20th century. The
real change from the traditional to modern took place no
earlier than during the first half of the 20th century.
The change from traditional agriculture to modern
agriculture has had its counterpart in the farm families.
The way of life, attitudes, motives, and roles of the
farmers and the farm wives have experienced a huge
change. A peasant farmer has become a farm business
entrepreneur, the farmer's wife is now either an active
partner or she does not take any role in agricultural
production.

The European farm family of today, while living in an
industrialized society, is characterized by a weakening of
the affinity organization and a strengthening of the
actual contribution of the family. However, when compared
to undertakings in other fields of economy, the family
farm still displays a remarkable feature of affinity and
human contact. The individual members feel a joint
responsibility, but, at the same time, they tackle their
individual duties more independently than previously.

The great change in the farming couple's labor input
that has taken place during the last few decades is
reflected in the agricultural labor input statistics. Of
the total labor input in the farm unit (agriculture,
forestry, housekeeping, extras), the farm entrepreneur's
input represented 25% in 1960, and had increased to 39% by
1984. The relative input of the spouse remained more or
less the same, having only decreased from 42% to 39%. The
input of other family members amounted to 18% in 1984; the
corresponding figure for hired labor had gone down to 4%.
The male farm entrepreneur today participates much more
than before in animal husbandry. As a sidelight,
according to the census of 1980, 18.5% of Finnish farm
entrepreneurs were female (Statistical Office, 1985).

TECHNOLOGICAL ACHIEVEMENTS AND HINDRANCES

Starting Point After the War

As a consequence of the defeat in World War II,
Finland was compelled to cede a good tenth of its land and
agricultural area to the Soviet Union and to resettle

40,000 Carelian refugee farm families onto the reduced acreage. Land was expropriated from the State, communities, larger farms, and farms owned by absentee farmers. This resulted in diminished possibilities of rationalization and technological improvements.

Very large capital investments were lost in buildings and equipment that could not be used fully after the acreage of land per farm unit was reduced. The resettlement program after the war was, however, an unavoidable consequence of a war involving the loss of a territory upon which approximately 11% of the population had lived.

Crop Husbandry

Finnish agriculture is characterized by a great diversity in crop husbandry, largely as a consequence of the great range in natural conditions. There is a whole series of transitional stages between the bread grain and sugarbeet farms in the Southwest and the North-Finnish grassland farms on the fringe of the Arctic region. The increase in total crop production during the post-war period from 1945 onwards is partly attributable to clearance of 350,000 hectares of new cultivated ground. During the last two decades, however, land clearance has come to a standstill, with 2.4 million hectares of arable land. The annual increase of the crop expressed in crop units is, therefore, now attributable to technological development only.

During the last three decades the use of commercial fertilizers has doubled. The use of tractors and combines has reduced the stock of horses from 300,000 to 30,000. As a consequence, 400,000 hectares of arable land previously used to produce horse feed were released for other uses. In many technical respects tilling methods have improved. The combines are now responsible for 90% of the grain crop threshing. Also, more sophisticated methods of harvesting grass and hay, particularly in the making of silage, are being used. Chemical soil maps indicating the nutritional state of soils have been popular with the farmers. There has been a very significant increase in the use of insecticides and pesticides, and plant breeding has played an important role in increasing output with new varieties. One technologically weak point is the still common occurrence of fields with open ditches, with a good half of the arable land area in need of underdrainage. Government financial support in recent years has, however, encouraged installation of underdrainage. Although great annual variations in the yields occur, we can say that the average yield per hectare for all crops has risen 30% within three decades.

Considering the above actions to promote the technological standard in crop husbandry, the rise in the average hectare yield appears to be rather modest. This is mainly due to the rigid climatic conditions. We must recall that Finland is the northernmost country in the world where agriculture in a virtual sense is pursued.

Animal Husbandry

Livestock production accounts for the farmers' main source of income from agriculture. The prominence of animal husbandry is partly due to the rigorous climate, a restricting factor for cash cereal crops in large areas of the country. It is also due, in part, to the large number of small family holdings relatively better suited for raising animals than producing cash crops. These two factors imply that the trend of production has been toward animal husbandry, especially dairy cattle husbandry. Finnish cattle breeding has always been concentrated on milk production. The herds are, however, still modest in size, about eight milk cows on average.

Women, to a considerable extent, tend cattle. However, in the last two decades a change in the old pattern appears to have taken place. Men are taking up milking, but 50% of the work in cow-sheds is still carried out by women. The agricultural holiday and replacement assistance program, supported by the State and several municipalities, was intended to promote equality among agricultural producers in relation to other groups. It is estimated that there are currently around 4,000 full-time holiday replacements in Finland. The need for such services is expected to grow substantially in the next few years. Agreement has also been reached on the provision of replacement assistance for farmers' wives to give them a four-month maternity leave.

The technological progress in dairy milk husbandry has been extremely rapid within the recent decades. Today 85% of the cow population is milked by machine while three decades earlier machine milking was practically nonexistent. The artificial insemination breeding method reaches every cattle farm compared with one of ten in 1950. Milk recording associations are dealing with some 40% of the cow population. Furthermore, a shift in the milk cattle stock has taken place. Ayrshire cattle and Frisians have replaced the original native Finnish breed. Also, cattle feeding has improved considerably, due mainly to the increased use of silage fodder. Use of computers to prepare feeding plans is rapidly winning ground. Due to the above mentioned technological changes, the average milk yield per cow is at present 4,800 kilograms. In 1970, this figure was 3,700 kilograms and in 1960, 3,000 kilograms. To some extent beef cattle production has been introduced, as well as cross-bred cattle.

Even in other branches of animal husbandry, especially swine and poultry, significant technological achievements have been attained both in feeding and breeding. As an indication, the production per hen, per year is now 13.5 kilograms of eggs, an increase of 6.5 kilograms in three decades.

HUMAN AND ECONOMIC ASPECTS OF THE ADOPTION ON
NEW TECHNOLOGY

Changes in Energy Consumption

The increase in energy consumption during the last two decades has been as rapid in agriculture as in society at large in Finland just as in the other Nordic countries. This trend has been almost exclusively based on imported sources, mainly oil. Agriculture, as well as the food stuff and engineering industries, has steadily become more dependent on the unstable world market. The weakened position of the domestic sources of energy is clearly reflected by the fact that their proportion of the agricultural energy supply today is less than 20%, whereas in 1950 the corresponding figure was assessed to be 70%. The decreasing role of the national supply is due to increased use of nitrogen fertilizers and radical mechanization. The oil price boom in 1973-1980, in conjunction with rising prices for electricity, led to a renewed interest in research concerning energy production methods based on domestic sources of energy.

In 1978, oil consumed by agriculture and horticulture accounted for over 9% of Finland's total consumption. This figure includes private oil consumption of the farming families. The corresponding figure for electricity was 5%. The energy indirectly required for the manufacture of means of production (fertilizers, forage, machines, etc.) probably exceeds the total direct energy consumption.

Traditionally, firewood has been used to heat the houses of farmers and their animals. Today, however, the proportion of firewood as a source of energy is less than 20%, but is increasing. The role of straw and peat is marginal. The potential to increase use of domestic resources exists. In this connection, the current interest in cultivated energy wood deserves mentioning. At the present time, however, it is difficult to say anything about the prospects for the energy wood projects recently started. Energy wood cultivation is not yet utilized in practice. The statistical data introduced here unfortunately are impaired by defects.

Improvement in Farm Entrepreneurship

Technological achievements are always intimately related to level of human knowledge and skill, degree of enthusiasm, and belief in the future. These factors inspire individuals intellectually as well as help bolster their physical strength. During the last three decades the author has carried out three long series of researches, partly in Finland and partly in Sweden. The purpose of the studies is to find out the influence of the farmer's mental ability, his vocational and theoretical education, and his age on the economic results, as well as the effect of intensified advisory services and individual farm planning (Westermarck, 1974). The results from the Sweden study were, briefly, that in all size groups the net farm income, as well as the total net income, for the subgroup of farmers with at least agricultural vocational secondary school was higher than that of farmers with only formal primary school education.

Later, two research projects were carried out in Finland to elucidate the influence of intensified individual advisory services and farm planning on adoption of improved technology and economic success on Finnish family farms. The researches lasted for 15 years. For reasons of comparison, control farm groups located in the same region and belonging to similar size groups but without the same services, were chosen. An examination of the economic progress, whether on a basis of the total net income, the net farm income, or the so-called coefficient of profitability, revealed that a marked successive improvement of profitability had taken place in the study farm groups but no corresponding development was seen in the control farm groups.

A common phenomenon on family farms is that farm couples operating a larger family farm possess a higher vocational-theoretical level than farm couples on medium sized or small farms. Several investigations and surveys carried out in different countries indicate that a positive correlation exists between making use of advisory services and the farm size expressed in hectares or acres.

Leagans (1979), found that smallholders remain low income producers more because they lack the requisite means of production than because they are unwilling to make technical innovations when they first become available or later profitable.

With regard to vocational education and involvement in farm advisory services, it is obvious that the small family farmers have been in an inferior situation. Disequilibrium regarding educational level and involvement in advisory services must, however, not a priori express differences in inherited mental ability. A chance to obtain education may very well depend simply on, e.g., the existence of some private fortune or be insisted on by parents or other close associates.

Local Clusters of Specialized Farms

As is well known, production organization on individual farms and in different regions depends largely on the law of comparative advantage. However, it can frequently be observed in practice that certain measures of specialization have been executed without natural and economic conditions in any way appearing to render an explanation for such a phenomenon.

Looking at livestock husbandry we find that the Swedish speaking district of Ostro-Bothnia, a very confined area in Finland, which holds only about 4% of the total agricultural population of the country, accounts for 65% of the total farm fur production in Finland. Here and there one meets with counties in which poultry farming is multifold to that of neighboring counties, without economic conditions differing from each other in any way.

Even in crop husbandry similar specialization can be observed. For example, one parish in the aforementioned

124

Swedish speaking Ostro-Bothnia produces 40% of the total
tomato crop in Finland. The location of this area is
fairly remote from any important market center. Patches
of cultivated strawberry growing are located here and
there without any special economic and natural reasons.

In those examples the human factor is obviously the
most important reason for reorganization. Natural and
economic circumstances have not favored certain branches
of production, but the phenomena may be explained by the
fact that the farmers have been in need of extra income.
Some enterprising person has taken the initiative,
succeeded, and others have followed his example. This is
a healthy process because by specializing regionally in
some branch of production, it becomes possible to utilize
many advantages of large-scale production. This concerns
the rationalization of the primary production as well as
marketing products.

ORGANIZED INTER-FARM COOPERATION IN PRIMARY
PRODUCTION ON FAMILY FARMS

Need and Forms of Cooperation

The small size of the farm units is one of the
disadvantages of family farming. This factor acts as a
barrier to structural rationalization and tends to prevent
the application of more efficient methods of production,
thus reducing the farmer's chances of earning a
satisfactory livelihood.

This situation presents reasons for considering all
possible arrangements in which the agricultural and forest
production of family farms can be rationalized despite
slowly growing average size of the units. One alternative
is an organized joint utilization of the means of
production by groups of farms, leaving the private
ownership of the land intact.

It goes without saying that participation in a group
or in a jointly owned enterprise in primary production
means, to some extent, renunciation of the right of
individual decisions. The same is true for any kind of
cooperation within a fixed frame. However, an attitude of
extreme individualism is no longer tenable; it must
definitely be considered as a thing of the past. Modern
family farming is in need of people prepared to give up a
strictly traditional, individual role to assume the role

of a team worker. Above all, mature individuals, capable of cooperation without getting lost in the crowd, are needed. Organized inter-farm utilization of the means of production has to be considered a supplement, too, not a substitute for family farming. In all cases, the land remains private property.

The following models offer examples of inter-farm cooperation:

a) Mutual neighborhood activities without the obligations of organized cooperation.

b) Regular exchange of assistance.

c) Organized inter-farm cooperation involving manpower and/or material means of production, as settled by agreement.

d) A jointly owned enterprise within a certain branch of production.

e) Common management of a group of farms.

All these models have their advantages as well as disadvantages. The crucial questions are not only economic. The approach is to a great extent determined by subjective evaluations and mental qualities.

It is obvious that, at least in Finland, a psychological and ideological resistance to cooperation on the horizontal level in primary production exists among owners of family farms, although they have a very affirmative attitude in the face of cooperation in the marketing sector. The success of organized cooperation in primary production presupposes mutual responsibilities with regard to the use and pricing of inputs.

Findings from Finnish Research in Agriculture Proper

At the Department of Agricultural Economics, Helsinki University, the profitability of certain organizational models has been calculated on a theoretical basis (Westermarck, 1977).

The results showed that inter-farm cooperation was a profitable alternative. Gross margin was used as a measure of profitability. This figure was obtained, as usual, by subtracting variable costs from gross return.

However, even though theoretical models are a first step to action, innovations generally do not become accepted unless they are supported by experience and demonstrable results.

With regard to organized inter-farm use of means of production, a distinction may be made between large groups of farms and small groups, the latter ones accounting for three to ten farms. Among the large groups, mention may be made of machinery banks. Among agricultural projects in the small cooperative groups, production rings and joint dairy barns may be mentioned. Joining a large group involves no major changes in human relationships. In a small group, on the other hand, the working conditions and habits of the individuals influence the lives of all group members, especially where animal husbandry is concerned.

In most cases such a cooperation model, where a certain branch is jointly used and even jointly owned, requires less investment but presupposes good professional skill and high mental ability of the members.

The joint use of farm machinery among neighbors is common in Finland. However, this form of cooperation is usually of an informal or occasional character, which makes it difficult for a farmer to know if, when, from whom, and at what cost he may obtain the machine he needs. Moreover, the liablility for damage to the machines and machine maintenance may be a problem.

Machinery banks seem to offer a solution satisfying the need and eliminating at least some of the problems. A machinery bank may be described as organized renting of machines at fixed rates by the assistance of a middleman between the farmers in a given area. The machines remain in private ownership. The rates are annually fixed by the members of the bank. Interested farmers report the machines they can offer as well as what kind of machines they wish to hire, and the middleman puts all the data on a list.

Investigations have shown that the machinery bank appears to reduce the problems relating to the question, from whom and at what price a machine may be obtained, but not the problems connected with the timing of the arrangement.

Findings from Finnish Research in Farm Forestry

Turning then to the problems of family farm forest ownership and management, one solution is regional cooperation according to a joint management model. In this model, developed at Department of Agricultural Economics, Helsinki University, selling timber, logging, and silvicultural operation are carried out according to a common plan for a whole region. This plan is a combination of the joint management plans and the

individual farm unit plans. The activity is supervised by
a managing board elected by and among the participating
forest owners and regulated by a set of rules. These
rules, however, allow the forest owner the freedom to
decide in each particular case whether or not to
participate in a planned project. The forest units remain
private property.

The idea behind the establishment of joint management
was that the common interest of the group is considered in
planning and performing activities such as silvicultural
operations, planting, cutting, sales, road construction
and maintenance.

The findings from the forest sector on Finnish family
farms clearly show that the establishment of
joint-management forest areas might be the most successful
way of reducing the disadvantages caused by the scattered
ownership of farm forestry in a country such as Finland.
The forest investment needed for an increased timber
production will be implemented because the forest owners
will get better returns for their efforts. The selling
activity could reach the allowable cut by regional
planning and the cooperation of the farm forest owners.
The cooperation group is of a size that guarantees the
forest owner the possibility to make his own decisions
concerning his forest and makes possible a direct contact
between the owners of farm forests. Finally, it may be
mentioned that about half of all privately owned woodland
is now managed based on the joint management model. This
is virtually a remarkable achievement taking into account
that the model was introduced only rather recently.

INCOME DISTRIBUTION AND DISPERSION OF PROFITABILITY

The Conflicting Forces

The main interest here focuses around the problems of
the existence and extent of a trend towards a widening
income gap between better-to-do and lesser-to-do groups of
farmers which has arisen within the decades since the
Second World War. In this respect, two conflicting forces
or phenomena exist. For example, on one hand research and
technological development has favored farmers with better
education, higher mental ability, larger amounts of
economic resources, farmers operating farms situated in
more fortunate natural regions, versus farmers belonging

to opposite categories. On the other hand, governments in many welfare countries have taken measures to level the social and economic differences between the two categories.

Nobel prize winner Schultz (1978) is very resolute in proclaiming his opinion as to the role of government policy measures and the influence of mental ability to deal with disequilibrium in saying: "The value of the ability to deal with disequilibria is high in a dynamic economy. In my opinion, two important inferences can be derived from the economic dynamics of agricultural modernization. First, disequilibria are inevitable. They cannot be prevented by law, by public policy, and surely not by rhetoric. Second, the function of farm entrepreneurs in perceiving, interpreting, and responding to new and better opportunities cannot be performed efficiently by governments."

Public Measures to Smooth Disparities
Within the Farm Population

One of the most relevant public measures of an economic nature is intended to bridge, or at least smooth, the gap between poor and well-to-do farm people and level regional disparities. This policy conforms with the endeavor to produce equity and to warrant a satisfactory standard of living. Such a policy cannot, however, imply parity or equality as to attain a similar income and welfare level for everyone. Such a state of affairs is a utopian one and should certainly completely spoil the enterprising spirit of human beings, especially the entrepreneurs.

Nevertheless, agricultural policy should be shaped so it contributes to the realization of the general aims of the officially announced regional policy. This means that agriculture must deliberately be guided in such a way as to alleviate the task of maintaining settlement, especially in the least favored areas; i.e. districts suffering from stagnation, depopulation, diminishing employment, and with a low income level.

The economic and social policy measures to remedy drawbacks may, for instance, imply subsidies for interest payments on loans for financing investments, transportation subsidies and government supported prices for some products.

Switzerland is a highly developed country with long traditions of policies to level regional income disparities in farming and rural areas including substantial financial and social state supports as a means to maintain settlement in remote mountain areas. The Secretariat of the Swiss Farmers Union has put together numerous valuable empiric figures from Swiss bookkeeping farms for the period of 1946-1979 (Anon. 1979, 1981). These indicate the interesting phenomenon that between farms of various size during the early postwar years, differences strongly grew but later on a tendency to smooth differences has come about. Two main causes for the latter phenomenon are stated, viz.:

- a more intensive line of production on the small farms with an increase of the number of livestock and enlarged cultivation of fruit, vegetables and vineyards; and

- the falling off of numerous low income and less profitable small farms with the survival of only the most progressive and profitable ones.

In order to bridge the income gap between regions or at least reduce the differences, the Federal Swiss Government highly supports agriculture. The fact that the subsidies are spent to the benefit of farming is clear. An investigation in 1976 showed that about 25% of the net farm income of the bookkeeping farms located in the valley districts consisted of subsidies in one form or another. The corresponding figure for the bookkeeping farms in the mountain districts was around 38%. A policy along those lines must produce an effect, but how many countries can afford and are willing to sacrifice so much for agriculture and rural development?

A couple of years ago the author gained corresponding data also from some other developed countries – Austria, Belgium, Japan, Norway, and Finland. Within the scope of findings from the countries referred to, the reports mostly denote that the technological development has been conducive to widening the gap. Public measures have not managed to mitigate the cleft. Only in Switzerland and, to some degree, in Norway have government actions to support family operated small farms and farms in remote regions borne fruit. Such an achievement has, however, been possible only due to the fact that the government has over a long period of time and with virtual single-minded actions supported the less-well-to-do groups of family farms.

What kinds of measures then has the Finnish government executed to level the income gap within the framework of the farming sector? A pervading phenomenon in Finland during the last three decades has been that several public measures to support agriculture have been strengthened, especially on the geographically less favored small farms and farms in remote regions, throughout. National budget calculations show that when all support measures were shared they accounted for 2% of the national gross agricultural return in 1959-61, 4% in 1969-71, 13% in 1980-82, and 10.5% in 1983--85. The majority of the support has been directed to the small farms in the remote regions.

Furthermore, the price policy during the postwar period has favored the livestock producers, who are predominantly small and medium sized farmers. For our purposes it does not appear relevant to take into account sources of earnings outside agriculture or to try to penetrate the influence of technological development in agriculture on incomes from forestry and extras. We may only say that observations from many countries, among them Finland, indicate that small farmers are likely to earn relatively more extras in addition to income from agriculture proper.

Intimation of Farm Records

In many European countries farm records are kept based on bookkeeping. However, we have to recall that figure obtained from bookkeeping farms do not constitute a statistically random sample of farms because farm account activity is carried out by voluntary efforts. Consequently, the participants must be considered, on average, somewhat more alert and prosperous than the great mass of farmers. This is, of course, a weakness which we cannot avoid in a free society. Compulsory records used to keep for taxation purposes will not reproduce the true influence of the farm and nonfarm income sources mentioned above.

In order to illustrate the post-war development in Finland, a rather homogenous and typical Finnish region, Central Finland, was chosen (Westermarck, 1983). Almost all the farms, regardless of size, are family farms, and the principal agricultural income is produced from livestock, mainly milk cattle husbandry.

In comparing the figures for the two groups, the number of small farms during the last period unfortunately had declined considerably. This decline is attributable to several factors, mainly a shift to part-time farming with decreased interest in farm records, or acreage was increased to exceed 10 hectares. This abates to some extent the significance of a comparison in time.

Nevertheless, the tendency for a widened gap between the two groups in favor of the group with larger farms is clear. The concept coefficient of profitability is calculated by dividing the net farm income by a figure calculated by adding together the interest claim of 5% for invested capital and the value of the family labor input calculated at the wage rate for hired labor.

The present-day development of agricultural products in the world market has been characterized by oversupply

Table 6.1. Number and income of Finnish farms

Size group 10 hectares	1959–1961	1969–1971	1977–1979	1980–1982
Number of farms	120	55	22	19
Net farm income, marks(1) per hectare	552	656	2804	4694
Net farm income per lu(2)	2306	3087	14023	24587
Coefficient of profitability	0.72	0.43	0.48	0.62
Size group 30 hectares				
Number of farms	24	19	37	56
Net farm income, marks(1) per hectare	274	495	1618	2455
Net farm income per lu(2)	2158	6886	28253	56733
Coefficient of profitability	0.88	1.14	0.93	1.00

1) One Finnish mark = 20 U.S. cents
2) lu = one labor unit corresponding to 2000 work hours in agriculture per year

and low prices. This has led to increasing difficulty in granting the farm people a reasonable income level. The prices on the domestic market have, therefore, been set apart from those of the international market. This means, in practice, that commercial exports are only possible with the aid of government subsidies. The fact that exports bring in exceedingly low profit returns may be blamed on the difficulties of finding commercial customers. There is no reason to expect that the international prices of farm products will change in any way which would improve Finland's ability to compete favorably on the world market. An export of agricultural products obstructs, therefore, the possibilities of maintaining domestic price levels which would offer a desirable standard of living to the agricultural population.

FAMILY FARMS IN THE TURBULENCE OF SURPLUS AGRICULTURAL PRODUCTION

On a long-term basis an adaptation of the volume of production so that it meets with domestic demands is a necessary stipulation for ensuring a reasonable income for those engaged on agriculture.

Understandably, there are some serious conflicts involved in the prevailing situation. They include sustaining agricultural producers' incomes while keeping the prices of their products competitive, improving efficiency of production while solving the problem of surpluses, and increasing the size of farms while preserving the population base in rural areas.

Although measures to support the less developed areas and the small family farms have been necessary, they have caused a surplus of livestock products. Each medal had its two sides.

Technological development, together with progress in many other respects, has resulted in quantities of products without corresponding outlets to reasonable prices. The subsequent issue is a precarious situation with discrepancy between the individual farmer's goals as an entrepreneur and the public agrarian policy measures to dampen the volume of products. Such a situation has serious repercussions for the farm entrepreneurs.

Overproduction brings about a very serious and regrettable situation, especially for the young, educated farmers who possess the willingness and ability to rationalize their undertaking and enlarge the farm size and the production but are hampered by economic circumstances. Such a situation delays the timely and necessary generation shift. Farmers in general are already older (on average 50 years of age) than other entrepreneurs in modern Finnish society. In order to speed up the generation shift, start-up supports are available for young farmers. It is, however, logical to presume that although this system is well-grounded, it will lead to a tendency to increase the volume of production. Again, we are confronted with a contradictory situation.

Past measures aimed at achieving equilibrium have concentrated upon taking land temporarily out of cultivation, paying dairy cattle slaughter premiums, and following a restrictive policy with respect to imported feed concentrates.

Recent public policy measures designed to restrict milk output imply a fear that such a system will paralyze efforts to raise the efficiency of agricultural production. These measures impose a two-price system with maximum delivery quotas per farm, implying considerably lower prices for quantities exceeding the ceiling. Preservation of a desirable family farm system in many respects also needs public protection against gigantic agribusiness firms producing enormous quantities of eggs, broilers, and pigmeat.

In the effort to achieve equilibrium, the psychological reactions and attitudes of the farming population play an essential part. Traditionally, the progressive farmer is the one who achieves the greatest harvest per hectare and the greatest yield per animal. Nevertheless, an alteration in the way of thinking is required. Attention should be paid to the farmer's entire sphere of action. In other words, the decisive factor in the presentation of the family farm system is an augmented acquisition of income from agriculture, forestry, and other earnings together. This means that, in certain instances at least, it might be relevant to pay more attention to extra earnings in combination with agriculture and farm forestry. Besides this new thinking, we must pay more attention to reducing cost pressures.

In the contemporary situation of turbulence the only acceptable method of balancing production and domestic consumption is to reduce the capacity of agriculture – cultivated agricultual area and the number of livestock. To reduce the already rapidly declining force of family labor would, of course, alleviate the problematic situation, but would also serve to depress formerly viable rural environments.

Although Finnish agriculture is primarily based on small-scale family farms, the most difficult task in agricultural policy is to regulate supply. Overproduction has not yet decreased, despite many measures taken to curtail it. Exports have to be heavily subsidized and

farmers must finance exports which exceed the production
ceilings. The dual price system for milk came into effect
the beginning of 1985. A quota was levied on each farm
for milk production according to previous level of
production. For marketed quantities exceeding the quota,
only world market prices are paid. For the time being, no
final judgments can be made as to the degree to which the
quotas have helped to curtail the production. Of course,
they have prevented production increases on some farms.
However, the already existing bonus system, which pays
milk producers who voluntarily curtail their production,
has also had an effect. No clear picture showing which
effects are due to which system is available.

At the beginning of 1986, an allocation of egg
production which includes a kind of double price system
came into effect. Quotas were levied on every farm
producing eggs.

The dual price program is a system which gives the
administration and legislature much power and possibility
to regulate supply. In the longer perspective, the
program, together with other supply management measures,
prevents farmers from taking advantage of technological
progress or economies of scale.

The use of the land for purposes other than
agriculture and forestry will probably become increasingly
common. As this occurs, activities such as summer cottage
rental, the use of the land for leisure-time activities
and other forms of service would be relevant. The belief
that a farmer can produce only foodstuff and timber ought
to be considered obsolete in today's space age.

REFERENCES

Daw, M.E. 1962. Benefits from Planning. University of
    Nottingham, Dep. of Agr. Econ. Loughborough.
Einkommenunterschiede in der Landwirtschaft. Mim. Brugg,
    1981.
Leagans, P. 1979 Adoption of Modern Agricultural
    Technology   by   Small   Farm   Operators: An
    Interdisciplinary Model for Researchers and Strategy
    Builders.   Cornell   International   Agricultural   Mim.
    New York.
Schultz, T.W. 1978.   Politics versus Economics in Food and
    Agriculture. Princeton.
Schweizerisches Bauernsekreteriat. Die Einkommensdisparitat
    in der Schweizerischen Landwirtschaft. Probleme und
    Losungsmoglichkeiten. Mim. Brugg, 1979.
Westermarck, N. 1974.   The Influence of Certain
    Entrepreneurial   Variables   on   Economic   Success   in
    Farming. Eur. R. Agr. Econ., Vol. 1 No 4.
Westermarck, N. 1983.   Postwar Trends in Income
    Distribution and Dispersion in Profitablility among
    Different   Farm   Groups.   Proceedings   Eighteenth
    International Conference of Agricultural Economics.
    Gower.

7
Family Farming and the Agricultural Crisis in Denmark

Torben Bager

INTRODUCTION

Danish agriculture is known internationally as a success story. It can be ranked among the most advanced in Europe and has an export rate of approximately two-thirds of total production. Usually this success has been attributed to the strength of family farming in Danish agriculture, and generally success has been seen as an illustration of the ability of family farming to adjust to changing conditions. In recent years, however, Danish agriculture has been in its depth of the worst economic crisis since the 1930s. This has created astonishment among observers and social researchers, leading to questions on how to understand the crisis: Is it only a temporary depression, or is it much deeper and broader and possibly a result of family farming reaching its borders?

HISTORICAL OUTLOOK

At the end of the 18th century, a number of agricultural reforms were introduced in Denmark. The feudal structures were broken up, and a class of freeholders was created holding medium-sized farms (typically 10-100 hectares). This class gradually achieved a dominant position in Danish agriculture and historically can be viewed as the backbone of Danish society, both economically and politically.

At the end of the 19th century, Danish agriculture once again experienced important changes. In the 1870s grain prices were falling, and there were problems with

137

138

the exportation of livestock to Germany. Therefore, Danish agriculture shifted to animal husbandry in the 1880s. Dairy farming and pig raising became the dominant activities, accompanied by the foundation of hundreds of cooperative dairies and pig slaughterhouses. Thus the shift led to the establishment of an agro-industrial complex which was dominated and controlled by the powerful class of freeholders. Furthermore, the shift resulted in increased production, and gradually Denmark gained its position as an exporter of high quality food, particularly butter and bacon. Britain provided a rapidly increasing market for such products and became the main importer of Danish food.

The basic structure of Danish agriculture did not change much during the 19th century, but a shift towards the end of the century provided opportunities for small-scale farms to expand, i.e. true family farms, where the owner and his family were able to make a living based on their own work. These farms typically had 5-10 hectares of land, and employed production methods which could be characterized as intensive mixed farming. They combined small-scale advantages in agriculture with large-scale advantages in industry by means of the cooperative industrial plants. This combination provided an economic basis for expansion, but expansion was also influenced by social and political factors. The small-scale farmers' movement gained increasing political influence. In fact, a series of agricultural laws designed to subdivide estates into small-scale farms passed through Parliament between 1899- 1919. The subdivision process was particularly rapid in the 1920s and 1930s, in spite of the agricultural crisis in the 1930s, and resulted in small-scale farms increasing their share of the total cultivated area from 18.7% in 1919 to 25.3% in 1949.

This development contradicted forecasts by Marxists and other theorists that a process of social differentiation would develop in agriculture as it did in industry. In the controversy between Marxists and Socialists at the turn of the century, Socialists claimed that developments in agriculture would differ from that of industry, and they used Danish agriculture as an example. This provoked V.I. Lenin to write an article in 1907 on Denmark which he ironically called "the ideal country." Based on statistics from Danish agriculture, he concluded that a process of social differentiation between a "kulak" class and agricultural laborers could be observed in

Denmark. He predicted that this differentiation would become more marked in the future.

Now we know that this prediction was erroneous. Family farming gained strength in the 20th century in spite of the dramatic changes in production methods and equipment. The first half of the century was characterized by the subdivision process, and the 1950s, 1960s and 1970s were characterized by a dramatic decrease in the number of agricultural laborers. Since the 1960s, approximately 80% of the total input of labor stems from the family, with this share holding fairly constant over a number of years. Only in recent years has it decreased slightly.

Some have, however, raised doubts about the dominance of family farming in the future, arguing that the recent decline in the share of family labor is likely to continue due to the process of industrialization in agriculture itself. Some of the advanced farms in Denmark have production methods almost like assembly plants, and generally the borderline between agriculture and industry has become very diffuse. This may be the fundamental cause of the severe crisis in recent years. Possibly Danish agriculture has been harder hit by the agricultural crisis than other European countries because of its relatively advanced stage of development. Perhaps family farming is only competitive as long as farming is rather simple and mixed, but becomes less competitive in the course of the industrialization process. And perhaps company farms with wage-laborers are finally underway, as Lenin predicted.

In order to verify such assumptions, it is necessary to describe and analyze the crises in Danish agriculture. Only such an analysis enables conclusions on the character and scope of the Danish case. It is important to know whether the crisis is explained mainly by specific national factors which are not likely to occur in other countries, or if it is of a more fundamental character.

THE CAUSES OF THE CRISIS

The crisis of Danish agriculture in the period 1980–1983 is illustrated by an explosive increase in the number of forced sales, low farm incomes, falling farm prices, and a heavy burden of debt.

Foreclosures of farm mortgages and forced sales had been an almost unknown phenomenon in agriculture since the

140

1930s, but as Table 7.1 shows, the number increased
rapidly in the period 1979-1981 and remained at a high
level in 1982 and 1983. Denmark has approximately 100,000
farms, so in the years of crisis more than 1% of the total
number of farms ran into forced sales every year.

Table 7.1. Forced sales, average farm incomes, farm
prices and total agricultural debt in the
period 1979-1985.

	1979	1980	1981	1982	1983	1984	1985
Number of forced sales	169	589	1607	1452	966	839	482
Average farm net incomes (1000s D.Kr.)	35	22	34	68	49	86	65
Farm prices (1970-74=100)	294	249	210	191	231	267	329
Total agricultural debt (mil D.Kr.)	72	78	82	82	83	85	90

Source: Landoekonomisk oversigt, 1983, 1984, and 1986.

Since the middle of the 1970s farm incomes have been
low, particularly in 1980 when they were very low. In
spite of the low incomes, farmers invested heavily in the
1970s and also raised amounts loaned, using loaned funds
for consumption purposes. Furthermore, the rate of
interest increased dramatically in the late 1970s. The
result was a rapidly increasing burden of interest that
forced the agricultural community to its knees.

The background for the significant increase in
agricultural indebtedness was the rapidly increasing price
of land and property. In the 1970s land and property
value increased approximately 20% a year, while the rate
of inflation was only 10% a year. Farmers, farm advisers,
and financial institutions expected this trend to continue
in spite of the low farm incomes. Ever since the 1930s,
prices of land and property had increased, and nobody
expected a decrease. Nevertheless, this was what
happened. In 1982 prices of land and property had fallen
to about two-thirds of the 1979 level, pushing many
farmers into a position where debts exceeded assets.

141

The loans taken out—and thus debts incurred—in the 1970s were used for a variety of purposes. Many were used for investments, especially buildings and modernization of dairy and hog facilities. The amount invested was so high that at the end of the 1970s it exeeded the amount invested in industry. Money was also borrowed to finance young farmers' succession to property. In Denmark, most property is taken over or succeeded to at the current market price, and it is usually only possible for young farmers to finance a limited proportion of the purchase price out of their savings. They must borrow most of it, and at a time of rapidly increasing property values, this form of indebtedness obviously also increases as well.

Although the above capitalization and investment situation is the main reason for the acute crisis in which agriculture found itself, the crisis must not be viewed in isolation from the long-term trends in the evolution of agriculture. Farms have become more specialized in recent decades, while production has gradually become concentrated on a smaller proportion of farms. There is an overall tendency towards farms either becoming industrialized agricultural units, or becoming a part-time or spare-time occupation. This process leads to a state of permanent economic pressure on the small, full-time farms. Consequently, the crisis led to an increase in the number of farm close-downs. During the crisis, the proportion of annual close-downs rose from approximately 1% of the total number of farms to 3%.

The structural process in agriculture is known in all industrialized western countries, but the dramatic indebtedness of the Danish farm community is mainly a specific Danish trait. However, the burden of debt in other countries also seems to be increasing, probably as a consequence of the tendency towards industrialization of agriculture that implicates heavy investments in buildings, machines, and other items. The Danish crisis, therefore, had its specific national causes, but it was also inflicted by factors of a more general nature. In this sense, the Danish crisis may be a first sign of what might happen in other countries in the future.

THE IMPACT OF THE CRISIS

When we compare the present crisis with the agricultural depression Denmark suffered in the 1930s, we find that the current crisis has had much less uniform

142

effects: Certain categories of farms and farmers were
very badly affected and others were hardly touched.
As evidence of this, differences in agricultural
income increased considerably during the crisis.
If the Danish farms are divided into 10 income groups,
the gap between the highest and the lowest income was
288,000 D.Kr. in 1978-1979, 343,000 D.Kr. in 1979-1980,
383,000 D.Kr. in 1980-1981, and 391.000 D.Kr. in
1981-1982. The cause of the widening gap over this period
was decreasing incomes in the lowest income group.
Incomes in the highest income group remained at the same
level.   Another interesting phenomenon is that both of
these income groups are characterized by farmers who are
relatively young and farms having relatively large lands
and many animals, while other income groups are
characterized by older farmers, small lands, and few
animals.
The most important reason for the nonuniform effects
of the crisis is the unequal distribution of the burden of
interest payments. These payments were particularly heavy
in respect to young farmers heavily involved in animal
production. This category typically owes large amounts of
money as a result of the cost of establishment and heavy
investment. This explains why the lowest income group was
dominated by young farmers with many animals. But it does
not explain why the highest income group has the same
composition. The explanation is partly due to the fact
that some young farmers bought their farms in the
beginning of the 1970s when prices were fairly low, while
others bought their farms in the late 1970s when prices on
land and property peaked and the interest rate was high.
Another explanation is the "personal factor" which seems
to become increasingly important during the process of
specialization and industrialization.
The reason for the foreclosure of mortgages among
older, full-time farmers of low-acreage property and more
or less all around production, is the structural pressure
more than the burden of investment. Some full-time
agricultural smallholders also with fairly all around
production exploited the favorable loan market in the
1970s without investing much in production. On this kind
of farm, the burden of interest payments increased without
any corresponding significant change in the level of
production.
The above categories of farmers have sought a wide
variety of ways out of these problems. Young farmers with
a high level of animal production have typically tried to

produce more in order to overcome the crisis, particularly
by increasing work on the farm and off of it. In many
cases, however, the problems were so extensive that they
were forced to borrow more money, which of course merely
increased their difficulties. Typically, the only
solution to this problem is to get some of the debt
written off. Some have succeeded in this, as a result of
both emergency government legislation and creditors'
willingness to accept compromises. One widespread course
of action was to allow the farm to be sold and then buy it
back at a reduced price in the wife's name.

Courses of action adopted by small, mixed production
farms differed from this pattern. These farmers are
frequently older and unable to significantly increase the
amount of work on the farm. On the contrary, older
farmers typically are forced to cut down on their animal
husbandry in order to lighten their burden of labor. It
is also difficult for them to decrease their debts by
means of compromises with banks and other lenders, partly
because official legislation is aimed at the younger
farmer and partly because creditors frequently have very
little confidence in them. The courses of action
typically adopted by these farmers thus comprise: going
out to work for wages, reducing their consumption, dipping
into their savings, or selling out.

As a result of the unemployment situation, it is much
harder to find paid work today, especially for the older
farmers. In addition, there are natural lower limits to
one's reductions in spending and drainage of reserves.
Selling out is the only course remaining open for an
increasing number. But even this way out was in the years
of crisis severely restricted, especially for farms
situated far from towns. Available options have, by and
large, become fewer and more painful. There are
increasing numbers of farmers looking toward a less
well-off old age than in the past when the sale of one's
farm usually resulted in a comparatively comfortable
existence for the pensioned farmer.

The crisis also brought about a dramatic reduction in
the amount invested in agriculture, especially in the
construction of byres, sties and other structures. This
factor has caused a slowdown of the industrialization of
animal production which is on the way in agriculture.
This does not, however, imply that the brake has been put
on structural evolution, just that it has changed in
character, since the crisis also results in the
abandonment of more farms. In 1983, 1984 and 1985,

investments have increased once again; but investments are still far below the level of the late 1970s.

The crisis has had no obvious effects on the evolution of agricultural production. Although a questionnaire sent to farmers hit by forced sales (Bager, 1983) indicated that their production frequently was temporarily affected, with a change of ownership the effects did not seem to be permanent. Most highly productive property has been taken over by efficient young farmers.

The questionnaire also revealed that many farmers forced to sell out were bitter and angry, particularly as a result of two factors. 1) The effects of the crisis were distributed very unequally among the various categories of farmers, not merely shaking out the least efficient ones. 2) It has been very much a matter of chance whether a particular farm in financial difficulty has been able to obtain partial remission of debt. One reason for this is there has been no comprehensive political solution to the problem of the agricultural debt. It has largely been up to the individual farmer to attempt to establish a compromise with his creditors.

The wrath of those forced off of their land has been primarily directed towards the politicians, the banks, the farmers' unions, and towards the financial consultants associated with the agricultural organizations. It is particularly interesting to note farmers' dissatisfaction with their own agricultural organizations. They had previously enjoyed a very high degree of confidence among the rural population. Farmers realized that their organizations were quite unprepared for the crisis, even putting the solution to the problem of indebtedness quite low on their list of priorities. In particular, the younger farmers with a high level of animal production felt let down, betrayed; some of them started new organizations to better guard and advance their own interests. The most significant movement, "LR 80", began a series of noteworthy actions in 1979 and 1980 in order to direct the attention of the agricultural organizations and the politicians to the problem.

The crisis highlighted the fact that the structure and activities of the agricultural organizations and farmers' unions were out of step with developments. The tendency towards industrialization and specialization in one sector of agriculture has emphasized the divergencies of interest in agriculture, and the agricultural organizations have shown very little response to this fact in their structure and activities.

The questionnaire also disclosed the difficulty farmers who had been forced to sell out had in maintaining their liberal ideological convictions when faced with the harsh realities of the crisis. In reply to the questionnaire, only 32% stated that they agreed that foreclosure and forced sale were phenomena which a liberal profession had to live with in times of crisis. Generally, the replies to the questionnaire showed a high degree of idealogical uncertainty.

One may presume that these ideological doubts have increased during the crisis, but it was possible to discern them before the crisis broke out. This particularly applies to the question of governmental intervention vis-a-vis the agricultural sector, but it also applies to structural developments in agriculture. Many farmers are hesitant to accept the idea of governmental regulation and direction of structural evolution, despite the fact that there is a broad spectrum of opinion in agriculture which feels that the trends towards specialization and industrialization are not durable in the long run.

The crisis can, therefore, be regarded as one among many expressions of a basic ideological dilemma in the rural population: the conflict between what the farming community, based on its liberalistic ideology, finds desirable and what actually happens. In reality, the rural population in the period since 1960 has witnessed the gradual dissolution of most of the things it believed in and regarded as being of true value—such as the closely-knit community, with its many small competitive units. The closely-knit agricultural community has been heading toward dissolution for a long time (Friedland, 1982). Trends towards concentration and centralization have meant the rise of the great units, e.g. in the dairy sector; and State regulation of agriculture has gradually become more intensive. A proportion of the agricultural population has cooperated actively in this process, not because they found the development desirable, but because they felt it was unavoidable. An illustration of this is the enormous process of concentration and centralization seen in the agricultural sector's own cooperative undertakings.

The crisis has also furthered changes in the family pattern on the farm which have been developing for a very long time. In the past, every member of the family took some part in running the farm. Today, often only one person—usually the husband—runs the farm while the rest

146

of the family is occupied off the farm. During the crisis, more and more women have found employment off the farm. This has been based both on economic necessity and on the woman's wish to have an outside job, especially among younger farmers' wives who have a higher educational qualification.

Thus, the crisis can be said to have accelerated a dissolution of the family and the sociocultural pattern in the rural areas which has been developing for a long time. This indicates that the crisis must be viewed as more than a mere temporary financial problem. The crisis has noneconomic aspects, and the acute depression is intimately associated with longer term changes in agriculture.

HOW TO OVERCOME THE CRISIS

Since there are both short-term and long-term aspects to the crisis, the means required to overcome it need to be both short-term and long-term in character.

The crisis peaked during the course of 1982, at least as far as modernized farms were concerned. Incomes rose and the burden of interest payments was reduced for a fair proportion of farms. In addition, the decline in farm and property prices bottomed out.

The prospects, however, are still dark; and the fundamental problems remain unsolved. The burden of debt has not been relieved. In fact, it seems as if Danish agriculture will run into a new period of crisis in the years to come. One of the signs of such a development is a rapidly increasing number of forced sales in 1986 compared to 1985.

The present agricultural policy is based mainly on the assumption that the crisis is best defeated by a simple increase in the level of earnings and investment. At this juncture, it is worth making one point very clear: Certain problems cannot be solved, but are, in fact, aggravated by developments of this nature. If developmental tendencies of the past continue, we can expect the trend towards a dissolution of the old family and sociocultural structure to continue. The problems associated with handing down economically top-heavy farms from one generation to the next are bound to increase. We must expect that as the tendencies towards specialization and industrialization are permitted to evolve, it will become more and more difficult for young farmers to take

property over on reasonable terms. Under the current
system of change of ownership and generation, one would
expect the degree of self-financing to tend to drop, a
factor which, taken together with specialization, implies
a greater degree of vulnerability.

The picture thus develops of a future agriculture
where most production takes place on factory-like
agro-technical farms which are highly vulnerable. This is
scarcely a tenable situation, from either the individual
farmer's point of view nor that of society as a whole. We
can, therefore, anticipate increased pressure for
legislation permitting farms to be owned by companies,
unless an alternative path of development is followed in
the future.

If the present tendencies of development of Danish
agriculture continue in the future, the prospects are
bleak. The markets for the typical Danish products, like
butter and bacon, do not look promising in the future. In
particular, dairy farming is likely to face increasing
problems. In 1984 an EEC agreement led to a major cut in
the Danish milk production and a further 3% cut is likely
in 1987. The countries within the EEC will hardly provide
an expanding market for Danish dairy products, so the
world market will probably be the decisive factor. If
Danish agriculture continues to rely on dairy products and
bacon, incomes in agriculture are likely to fall in real
terms, and this probably will mean the closing of
thousands of farms. Furthermore, the labor force in
agriculture will be significantly reduced, thereby
increasing the problems of unemployment in Denmark. Also,
environmental problems are likely to increase if the
process of industrialization proceeds. Therefore, we must
look for alternatives to a continuation of the present
tendencies of development.

All of the above points stress the need to include
noneconomic aspects and longer-term prospects when
planning agricultural policy. It seems necessary to work
out a policy for structural development, probably in
association with innovation in the sphere of production,
as well as a policy which considers the standards of
living, the quality of life, and sociocultural factors.

One of the main obstacles to the elaboration of
alternative development strategies is probably the
narrow-minded economic thinking that increasingly
dominates the politicians, farm advisers, and farmers
themselves. They tend to forget that farming not only is a
matter of economy and business, but also a matter of

ecology and a way of life. Therefore, the narrow-minded economic thinking is problematic. It is likely to produce self-fulfilling prophecies.

Research results show that farmers are split between a narrow-minded view on farming and a broader view that includes ecological and social aspects. For example, a Danish study of amalgamation of cooperative dairies (Michelson, 1984) has shown that farmers are influenced both by their economic interests vis-a-vis amalgamation and by their general attitudes towards farming and their locality. Accordingly, it is possible to categorize farmers into two principal categories: instrumental farmers and expressive farmers, the former being characterized by a narrow business view, and the latter being characterized by a broader view (Nitsch, 1982). Often these two categories are looked upon merely as a matter of the level of modernization. Instrumental farmers are seen as the modern type of farmers, while the expressive farmers are looked upon as old-fashioned. The views of the expressive farmers are typically judged with sympathy, but rejected as old-fashioned and unrealistic.

This view of the two categories is problematic. It is based on the assumption that economic considerations and considerations on noneconomic aspects cannot be combined. The Danish case shows that this assumption is untenable. The agricultural crisis in Denmark is not only one of economics, but includes a number of noneconomic aspects. Furthermore, it affects instrumental farmers with modernized farms more seriously than expressive farmers.

We must improve the understanding of how economic perspectives are influenced by changes of the social and ecological pattern. As long as the social and ecological conditions are viewed as a kind of luxury that necessarily will implicate decreasing farm incomes, if they are to be improved, alternative development strategies are not likely to gain sufficient political support.

One of the effects of the Danish crisis has been numerous experiments with social and ecological innovation. Farmers in quite great numbers have experimented with alternative methods of production, alternative products, and social innovation. Collectives and group farms have been formed and new products introduced, such as nonhomogenized milk, goat cheese, organically grown vegetables, and other products. Some of these experiments have been quite successful, and the markets for such products seem to be growing both in Denmark and internationally because of the growing concern among consumers about chemicals in food, the treatment of animals, and other issues. Recently some of the large dairies have resumed production of nonhomogenized milk, as a result of its commercial success. Generally, however, the support by cooperative industries, farmers' organizations, research institutes, and the government has been very limited, and this seems to be an obstacle to further progress. A shift in the methods of production and introduction of new products requires support from powerful organizations and the government in order to be tested thoroughly.

The social innovation needed is still very unclear, but certainly the crisis has questioned the values of family farming. It has become evident that family farming today often is a very lonesome occupation. Furthermore, the crisis has revealed the vulnerability that follows in the footsteps of specialization and industrialization. What is needed, therefore, seems to be some kind of reform in the present family farm system.

To some extent it is possible to learn how to deal with these matters from Danish history. The crisis at the end of the 19th century was overcome by a shift in production to quality food and by social innovation through formation of cooperatives. Probably the basic means to overcome the present crisis are the same. Production must once again be shifted or at least supplemented with new products and new methods of production. But innovation in the sphere of production must be followed by changes in the social system, i.e. some kind of reform of the family farm system that preserves the advantages of family farming, particularly the high motivation of the farmers, but cuts off the problematic traits. Organizational reforms in the agro-industrial complex also seem important, particularly since the present structure is rather hostile towards innovation. Finally, it seems imperative to change the dominant way of thinking that tends to exclude noneconomic considerations. An alternative path for agriculture to follow, therefore, requires a process of social, economic, organization, and ecologic innovation that encompasses the whole food chain.

THEORETICAL IMPLICATIONS

A study of the crisis in Danish agriculture raises certain theoretical questions, especially when it is looked at more from the long-term point of view. The crisis would seem to herald fundamental changes in agriculture, but it is not clear what their nature and depth will be; and the corpus of concepts which would enable us to capture these changes appears to be weak.

First, let us look at a few conceptual considerations. The concept of "the family farm," applied by many field workers and research scientists, is not particularly appropriate or useful in any analysis of the fundamental changes in agriculture because, among other reasons, the family farm has gradually been squeezed out by the one-man farm, (i.e. farms run largely by one person, the remaining members of the family having their primary occupations off the farm). The concept of "the peasant farm" is more applicable, since this term would cover both family farms and one-man units, as well as contrasting them with the company-owned farm. But even the term "peasant farm" seems inadequate to cover the fundamental changes in agriculture which appear to be on their way. We seem to need a concept covering the old type of peasant farm, characterized by stability, freedom of action, and loose market relationships with its environment as well as the new type of peasant farm characterized by a high rate of change, a high degree of vulnerability, and rigid ties to the supply, sales and finance elements of the structure. Thus, we need to distinguish between "old style" and "new style" peasant farms and between peasant farms as such and company-owned farms. A conceptual corpus will have to be built up which can encompass these distinctions.

Both before the crisis and during it there was an increase in the importance of the "new style" peasant farms, and probably there will also be an increase in the importance of company-owned farms in the future. The old style peasant farm, with its high degree of stability and flexibility, will probably gradually die out, possibly via a transition to part-time farms with a low volume of production.

The consequence of the increase in the importance of "new style" farms is that the true extent of the freeholder's much vaunted freedom has been severely limited, so that it is little more than a caricature of what it once was. The low proportion of the farmer's own capital put into the property and the high degree of vulnerability have resulted in the exchange of freedom for a state of dependence and restraint - particularly vis-a-vis the banks, but also in regard to a series of

other external factors. The degree of constraint has been
so extreme during the present crisis that many farms hit
by the depression have more or less been placed under
outside administration. The only degree of freedom left
to the freeholder in such cases is his chance of making a
future profit from increased land and property values.
However, developments in Denmark in recent decades show
all too clearly that this is no tenable solution in the
long run, because increases in the value of property act
against the interest of future generations of farmers who
are forced into debt in order to finance the previous
generation's capital gains.

The spread of "new style" peasant farms and perhaps
company-owned farms can be regarded as a gradual sloughing
off of the specifically agricultural and petit bourgeois
characteristics of farming. The borderline between
industry and farming would thus vanish at the same time at
which it becomes questionable whether one can maintain the
posture of regarding the farmer as a member of the petit
bourgeois class. One sign of departure from petit
bourgeois characteristics of "old style" peasant farming
during this crisis has been the difficulty of the
modernized farm to economize its way out of the crisis.
Private consumption constitutes so small a fraction of the
budget of a modernized farm that cutting it down hardly
helps at all. In the 1930s, when the "old style" peasant
farms were still predominant, it was possible for most
farms to beat the crisis by cutting spending. This is
just one example of the way in which "new style" peasant
farms are less flexible than the "old style" ones were.
Flexibility is the main reason for the success of the
peasant farm in the 20th century (Djurfeldt, 1981).
Therefore, the evolution of inflexible, "new style" farms
increases the likelihood of a transition to company-owned
farms, i.e. farms without petit bourgeois features.

The "new style" peasant farms must be regarded as
being on a parallel with the majority of small businesses
in an advanced capitalist society, such as small-scale
industrial, trading, and manufacturing enterprises.
Small-scale undertakings of this sort are still very
extensively represented in Denmark, and there are no signs
of their being defeated in competition with large-scale
enterprises. This may be due to large-scale business'
clear and manifest interest in the continued existence of
small-scale ones.

Small-scale undertakings must, therefore, be regarded
as a permanent feature of the scene in an advanced

capitalist society. They must be looked at in association with the tendency towards the evolution of a monopolistic sector and a nonmonopolistic one in such societies. In every branch of trade and industry, there appears to be a tendency towards "old style," petit bourgeois, small-scale undertakings gradually evolving into "new style," small-scale undertakings. It is an evolutionary process of this sort which agriculture is currently undergoing.

Many people in the farming community today appear worried about the prospect of future developments, in particular the likelihood of the future extent of limited liability company ownership of farms. At the same time, it seems to be dawning on people that the day of the "old style" peasant farm is about over. Thus, during the recent crisis, a number of farmers announced their intention to prepare to surrender the concept of the freehold title to their property and with it the possibility of increases in capital gain if they could be guaranteed more reasonable living conditions in return. In general, however, farmers and their organizations have not yet acknowledged the fact that fundamental changes are on the way. Consequently, they have shown very little willingness to enter into any discussion of alternatives to the current developmental or evolutionary prospects.

Agricultural sociologists and economists would appear to have a significant part to play in the years to come – clarifying the nature and depth of these changes and outlining alternatives to the developments we see before us.

REFERENCES

Bager, Torben. 1983. Tvangsauktionerne i landbruget – et bondeslutspil? Esbjerg: Sydjysk Universitetsforlag.
Djulfeldt, G. 1981. "What happened to the Agrarian Bourgeoisie and Rural Proletariat under Monopoly Capitalism?" Acta Sociologica, Vol. 24: 167-191.
Friedland, W.H. 1982. "The End of Rural Society and the Future of Rural Sociology" Rural Sociology, Vol. 47: 589-608.
Lenin, V.I. 1907. The Agrarian Question and the Critics of Marxism, coll. works, Vol. 13.
Michelsen, J. 1984. Hvad mener andelshaverne? Esbjerg: Sydjysk Universitetsforlag.
Nitsch, U. 1982. Farmers' Perceptions of and Preferences concerning Agricultural Extension Programs. Uppsala: Svriges Landbruksuniversitet, rapport nr. 195.

8
The Family Farm in the Federal Republic of Germany

Ulrich Planck
translated by Max J. Pfeffer

THE POSITION OF THE FAMILY FARM IN THE SOCIAL AND ECONOMIC ORDER

The Federal Republic of Germany came into being in 1949 after consolidation of the British, American, and French occupation zones. It encompasses 53% of the area of the former German Reich (based on the boundaries of 1937) and includes the characteristically small-scale farming of much of northwestern and southern Germany. The east-Elbian agriculture of the former German Reich, having had a high proportion of farms employing wage laborers, today lies within the boundaries of the German Democratic Republic, Poland, and the Soviet Union.

After much discussion of the guiding principle of agricultural policy, the preservation and promotion of the family farm has emerged as the declared goal. The Agriculture Act (Landwirtschaftsgesetz) of September 5, 1955, requires the federal government to submit an annual agricultural report "which states the average production conditions that guarantee the sustained existence of a family, given proper management of the farm."

This guiding principle of German agricultural policy entered into the stated goals of the Common Agricultural Policy (CAP) of the European Economic Community (EEC). Family farm promotion was not explicitly mentioned in the agreement founding the EEC (Treaty of Rome, March 25, 1957). But at the conference of agricultural experts at Stresa in 1958, the Treaty of Rome was interpreted to state that, "given the significance of the structure of European agriculture, which is characterized by the family farm, and given the unanimous desire to maintain this specific characteristic, all means should be applied to

155

156

raise the efficiency and competitiveness of the family farm."

The German-French Agriculture Board advocated the preservation of the family farm even more decisively. In its 1958 report the Board states, "The farm population has always been a factor of social and political stability and has been a basic element of the intellectual attitude of Europe." The report goes on to say, "Preservation of farm families with their independence at work and their human values is more important than ever to keep modern society, with its rapid development, in equilibrium. The work of the farm family and farm property has assured care for the soil, the maintenance of soil productivity, and a high level of productivity through centuries." The European Association of Agriculture (CEA-Confederacion European de L'Agriculture) repeated its declaration of support for the family farm.

Farm organizations declare their support for the principle of the family farm. The German government has also repeatedly stated unambiguously that its aims are the preservation and continued development of the family organization of farm production. The government's preference clearly lies with the modern version of the family farm. According to Josef Ertl, Minister of Nutrition, Agriculture, and Forestry from 1969-1982, "The family farm (has) a clear priority" (1980:492) under the goals of agricultural policy in the 1980s. And Georg Gallus, Undersecretary of Agriculture, believes that the future of German agriculture lies, as far as one can tell, with the family farm (1982:491).

DEFINITION OF TERMS

Measures introduced in the 1950s to improve farm structure were designed to generate and reinforce healthy family farms. The Board for the Improvement of Farm Structure ("Ausschuss zur Verbesserung der Agrarstruktur") first had the task of defining the term "family farm" more precisely. Its definition included the family organization of labor, farm production as the main source of family income, and farm income. According to this definition, "Family farms are enterprises that are capable of offering a family full employment and an adequate income solely from agriculture." The EEC Commission adds freedom of economic decision making on the part of the farmer to this definition.

The acreage or herd size of the family farm can vary
greatly, depending on how favorable natural and economic
conditions are. The labor capacity of one to two fully
employed male workers, varying as the family structure
changes with the generational cycle, is assumed. The
lower boundary of the size of the family farm is based on
the criterion that it should earn "an adequate (parity)
income per fully employed male worker relative to
comparable professional groups." The upper size boundary
is fixed on the basis of the labor capacity of two fully
employed male workers. Upper and lower limits are not
stable within a geographic area across time. Advances
that raise productivity decrease the lower size
boundaries, while labor saving advances raise the upper
boundaries.

Recently it has been argued that, "the limits of a
family farm are exceeded when the land and/or livestock
held by a farm:
- exceeds the size in hectares or in number of
  animals necessary to realize economies of scale, or
- is excessive given the work load for the amount of
  labor available on a typical family farm, or
- exceeds the realization of returns required to
  satisfy the income demands of a typical farm
  family" (Neander 1983:72).

It is assumed that the work on the family farm is, "in
effect exclusively, or at least regularly," (Ries 1947)
carried out by family members. Those farms that employ
nonfamily labor as one of the family or occasionally make
use of wage workers, private contractors, or assistance
from cooperatives or neighbors are included in this
definition. Farms based primarily on the employment of
wage labor are excluded from this definition.

The income criteria is the most controversial.
Without a doubt, there are farms that, on the one hand,
are too small or have yields too poor to generate a
sufficient income or parity wage. On the other hand,
there are farms too large or located in an area too
remote to permit the operator to take up off-farm
employment. In either case they are family farms. The
majority of farms in mountainous areas fall into the
latter category. The criterion that a family farm should
earn its entire income from farming has been attacked even
more strongly. On the basis of this criterion, part-time
farms and, in principle, also farms with supplementary
income, are denied classification as family farms. This
stands opposed to reality. Part-time farms are defined as

farms whose operator and spouse earn more than half of the
family income off of the farm or whose operator commits
the majority of his labor time to his off-farm job. Farms
with supplementary income are defined as farms whose
operator or spouse works off the farm but earns less than
one-half of family income off the farm and whose operator
commits the majority of his time to the farm. The
sociological character of the family farm lies neither in
its capacity to "offer a family full employment and an
income solely from farming" (Leitbilder fur baeuerliche
Familienbetriebe, 1960), nor to fully employ one to two
full-time man units (AK or Arbeitskrafte, EEC
definition). Rather, family positions should be connected
to roles in the farm enterprise and vice versa.

The most important criterion is the family
organization of labor. The number of nuclear families
involved is, therefore, irrelevant. The familial role
structure is decisive. Thus, the extended family in the
form of a multi-generation family farm falls within the
sociological definition of the family farm, while the
multi-family enterprise without close family connections,
such as group farming (the merger of less than seven
farmers), the agricultural production cooperative
(Kolchos), and communal farming (Kibbutz), does not.

The organizational form of the family farm is not
limited by property relations. A farm is a family farm
even when land and inventory are rented or allotted on a
limited term basis, as long as the familial criteria
stated above are met.

The income earning nature of the farm is of as great a
significance for agricultural policy as for sociology.
The German agricultural statistics distinguish between
full-time (Haupterwerb) and part-time (Nebenerwerb)
farms. Full-time farms are differentiated into exclusive
income (Vollerwerb) and supplementary income (Zuerwerb)
farms. All farms for which the farm operator's labor time
is at least 0.5 AK and the off-farm income of the farm
operator and spouse is less than 50% of the total earned
income are classified as full-time farms. Exclusive
income farms are full-time farms where the off-farm earned
income of the farm operator and spouse amounts to less
than 10% of total family income. Supplementary income
farms are full-time farms and the off-farm earned income
of the farm operator and spouse is at least 10% but less
than 50% of total family income. Part-time farms have
operators who commit less than 0.5 AK of labor to the farm
or the off-farm income of the farm operator and spouse

amounts to at least 50% of earned income. Exclusive income farms are the focus of agricultural policy regarding family farms and of economic support for farms. Workers employed on farms and in farm households are classified as family workers and nonfamily workers. Those designated as family workers include farm operators and family members. The two main categories of workers are made up of full- and part-time employed family workers. Work on the farm is measured in units of AK (Arbeitskraftein- heiten). One AK corresponds to the capacity of a fully employed man. This indicator is used as a measure of the development of employment in the farm sector.

THE DISTRIBUTION OF FAMILY FARMS

By means of a representative sample, the proportion of family farms within the entire EEC was more accurately determined in 1967. According to the study, 70.3% of all German farms operated exclusively with family workers and 27.0% operated predominantly with family workers. Only 2.7% of German farms were operated predominantly with nonfamily workers. Thus, accounting for only about 5% (1979) of the total, farms regularly employing wage labor are even less significant in the Federal Republic of Germany than in other EEC countries. About one-third (34%) of German farms made use of the services of private contractors; this figure is also below the EEC average. In general, the "pure" family farms are relatively small and exhibit relatively low labor productivity. The larger farms are found primarily in the category "predominantly family workers, with simultaneous and regular employment of nonfamily workers."

Of 720,800 farms in 1985 (excluding farms of less than 1 hectare of farmland), 50% were operated as exclusive income farms, 10% as supplementary income farms, and 40% as part- time farms. In comparison with 1965, the decline in the number of supplementary income farms was stronger than either of the other categories. The rate of decrease between 1965 and 1985 was 78% for supplementary income farms, while in the same time period the number of exclusive income and part-time farms declined at a rate of 30%.

Farms with less than 1 hectare of farmland were comprised of 10,055 exclusive income farms, 2,933 supplementary income farms, and 28,909 part-time farms. A

portion of the exclusive income farms with little land are
nurseries, nonland based livestock operations, and timber
producing operations.

The mix of exclusive income, supplementary income, and
part-time farms, as well as large, middle, and small
farms, varies by region. Regionally differentiated size

Table 8.1. Number of Farms by Farm Type, 1965 - 1983

Year	Total Farms (1000)	Exclusive Income Farms (1000)	%	Supplementary Income Farms (1000)	%	Part-Time Farms (1000)	%
1965	1,252	512	40.9	323	25.8	418	33.3
1970	1,083	466	43.1	234	21.6	383	35.3
1975	905	409	45.2	139	15.3	357	39.5
1980	797	397	49.8	86	10.9	314	39.3
1985	724	357	49.5	70	9.7	296	40.7

Source: Agrarbericht der Bundesregiernng 1986,
         Materialband, Tab. 15

structure is, above all, the result of historical
development, particularly inheritance customs. The custom
of partible inheritance (Realteilung, i.e. equal division
of the inherited farm property among the heirs) promoted
small farms, while the custom of nonpartible inheritance
(Anerbenrecht, i.e. the inheritance of farm property by
usually one heir who then compensates siblings for their
share of the inheritance) led to the maintenance of a
middle and large farm size structure.

In the Federal Republic of Germany there are three
zones of traditionally dominant inheritance customs
(Figure 8.2). They are: the North German nonpartible
inheritance region, the Southeast German nonpartible
inheritance region, and the Southwest German partible
inheritance region. Inheritance customs, as well as farm
sizes have been subject to a swift transformation for two
decades. Nevertheless, the influences of various forms of
inheritance which have been effective for centuries are
still clearly reflected in regional farm size structures.
This is true in spite of the fact that partible
inheritance is increasingly being displaced by forms of
nonpartible inheritance of landed property.

Almost two-thirds of the Federal Republic consists of

mountainous and highland areas which establish natural
barriers to the spread of large farms into those areas.
Half of all family farms are situated within villages
and small towns, about one-third at the perimeter of
villages and small towns, barely one-tenth in hamlets, and
only one in every eight in the open country (Figure 8.3).

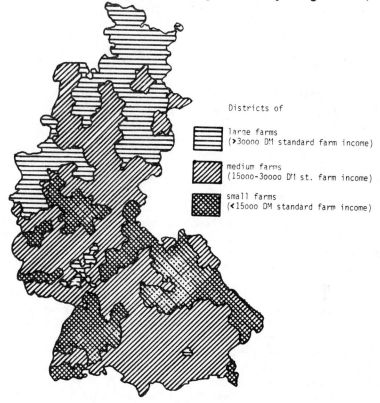

Districts of

large farms
(>3oooo DM standard farm income)

medium farms
(15ooo-3oooo DM st. farm income)

small farms
(<15ooo DM standard farm income)

Figure 8.1. Average Size of Farms in the Federal Republic
of Germany (Source: Agricultural Census,
1979)

In the period 1956 to 1973 about 23,437 farms were
relocated from crowded villages into the open country
where they could better expand. The greater the farm
size, the more frequently farms locate in the open
country. The social surroundings in villages and small
towns are distinctively urban and commercial. Only
hamlets and farms in the open country have to some extent
preserved their agrarian character, but they also are
subject to strong urban influences.

162

CHARACTERISTICS

Family farms are living social units comprised of the following components: family, household, management, and enterprise.

Family

Family structure is an essential element of farm organization. The organization of personnel on the family farm is determined by the size and composition of the family. As a rule, older and younger generations operate the farm jointly. Most farms are generally passed on to the successor when the farm operator reaches the age of 65. The child best suited to operate the farm is chosen as successor. The succeeding generation is recruited primarily from farm families; 98% in the case of men and 85% in the case of women. On the average, farm families have more children than nonfarm families.

However, the declining "usefulness" of the child and relatively weak personal ties to children also reduce the willingness of farm families to parent a larger number of children. The reproductive model is dominated by the two- to three-child family. Despite a decreasing age of marriage (in 1980 the average age of marriage was 26 for rural men and 22 for rural women), the interval between generations has decreased minimally because parenthood has simultaneously been delayed. The socialization of children follows a rather traditional pattern. The persistence of this traditional pattern is favored by many siblings and the participation of grandparents in child rearing. Sex-based patterns in occupational training are increasingly being dismantled. The frequently observed coresidence of generations has a primarily economic basis. The element that binds family members together now and in the past is joint interest in the farm.

The once solidly structured labor and living association of the farm family has, nevertheless, been undermined by a variety of circumstances. The functional dislocation of the existential domain divides members of the farm family to a considerable extent. School attendance, shopping, occupational training, recreational activity, and off-farm employment frequently take place in neighboring locations. Specialty services and goods and varied jobs and occupational training opportunities generally are found in locations with a population of more than 5000.

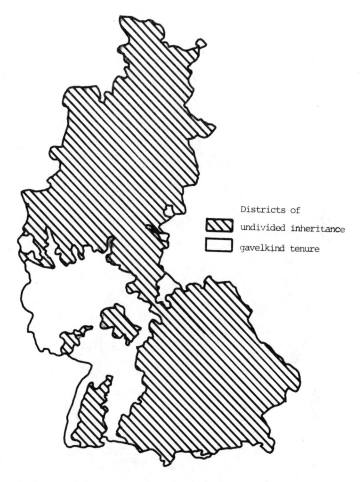

Districts of
undivided inheritance
gavelkind tenure

Figure 8.2. Primary Forms of Hereditary Transmission of
Landed Property in the Federal Republic of
Germany (Source: H. Roehm, 1964).

Family ties are an essential aspect of the family
farm. Claims and privileges based on family arrangements
that include unlimited, unremunerated work on the farm and
in the household largely take the place of labor
relations. On one hand, the binding power of family ties
releases energy and secures high levels of labor input.
On the other hand, inner familial tensions can cripple the
willingness to contribute labor and consume energy. The
efficiency of the family farm is, thus, closely connected
to the internal state of the family. In general, both the
family and farm atmosphere is good. In approximately 5%

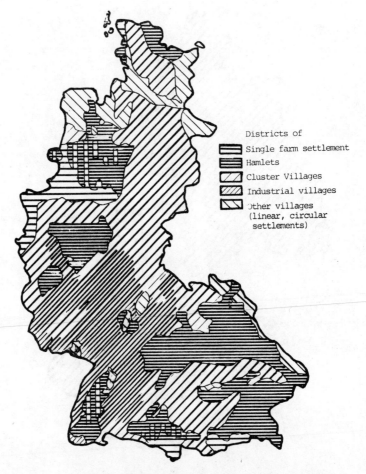

Districts of
- Single farm settlement
- Hamlets
- Cluster Villages
- Industrial villages
- Other villages
  (linear, circular
  settlements)

Figure 8.3. Forms of Rural Settlement on the Federal
Republic of Germany (Source: W. Kuhn).

of all families, serious tensions and conflicts are
evident. Generational conflicts are more frequent than
marital conflicts. Conflicts between the generations are
primarily ignited over questions of farm organization,
transfer of the farm, and personal life styles.
Nevertheless, authoritarian structures have, in general,
been transformed into relations of partnership between the
sexes and the generations. Of course, under pressure of
public opinion, the role of the patriarch is frequently
feigned, even though he plays a minor role in the domestic
life of today's farm family.
The stability of marriages is far above average.

Divorces, separations, and desertions are rare. Sometimes positions on the farm are doubly occupied. The presence of two fully productive couples may lead to special problems on the farm. Farms on which there are no children present or those children present are not interested or capable of taking over their parents' farm may also be problematic because the older generation, lacking a sufficient pension, must rely on the farm's output.

Family events are decisive and critical occurrences on the family farm. Birth and death, marriage and divorce, sickness and physical handicap all influence the productivity, profitability, and continuity of family farms.

Social security is no longer solely centered on the solidarity of the family association, but rather is shared by a collective insurance system which is legally based upon the Agricultural Accident Insurance Act (landwirtschaft- liches Unfallversicherungsgesetz, 1886), the Old Age Security Act (Altershilfegesetz, 1957), and the Health Insurance Act (Krankenversicherungsgesetz, 1972). It is a security system for farmers and under the control of farmers and includes provisions for income and structural policy. It is financed with contributions from members (1985: 2.9 billion DM) and with public funds provided by the federal government (1985: 3.5 billion DM). "The steadily rising costs of agricultural social policy has hit small and middle exclusive income farms particularly hard. These farms must contribute, on the average, almost 26% of the profits to social security. In isolated instances it is significantly more." (Gallus 1982: 487)

The Household

The average size of farm households is 4.1 persons. Despite a downward tendency, this is above the national average of 2.4 persons. This fact is the result of 1) the small proportion of one-person households, 2) the higher number of children, and 3) coresidence with the older generation. According to the official statistics of 1966, 10% of farm households were made up of one generation, 43% of two generations, 28% of three or more generations, and 19% were multigenerational "extended" households. In the meantime, it is likely that the proportion of "extended" households based on the presence of domestic servants has declined drastically, mostly in favor of two generation

166

households. In 1982 only 13,000 nonfamily workers with room and board in the farm household were counted.

Despite the relatively low income in farming, the technical and hygienic outfitting of farms is generally very good. General equipment includes connections to public electrical and water supplies and telephone, as well as possession of a washing machine, sewing machine, vacuum cleaner, freezer, refrigerator, electric range, car, radio, and television. Although a large proportion of farm families live in very old structures--almost half of all housing units are 120 years old or older--most are equipped with a bathroom and toilet, and more than half have central heating and central hot water. Hidden by the averages are, of course, structurally determined and associated regional differences. With increasing farm size, the farm households are better equipped. Therefore, in North German regions with above average farm size, the living standards are also better than those in southern Germany. On the other hand, one often finds very comfortable living arrangements on part-time farms.

The relatively high degree of self-sufficiency in fruits, vegetables, grains for bread, milk, eggs, meat, as well as wood for heating or for lumber is part of the distinctiveness of the farm household. Practically all farm households have a kitchen garden from which they provide practically all their fruits and vegetables and preserve considerable amounts for consumption in winter and spring. Although there is a downward trend, the majority of farm households butcher their own animals for home consumption. About half of farm women bake bread. Household production of textiles and clothes, common three generations ago, is done as a hobby today. For example, one out of seven farm women tailor their own clothes.

Farm Management and the Farm Operator

Family farms are, above all, characterized by the fact that the farm's operator, as owner or renter of the land that he farms, also manages the farm's operation (i.e. the farm operator, alone or with the help of his family, completes the majority of the farm work). On the average, exclusive income farms operate 26.1 hectares, supplementary income farms operate 15.4 hectares, and part-time farms operate 5.2 hectares of farmland. Table 8.2 shows the distribution of various farm characteristics by farm type.

167

Table 8.2. Distribution of Farmer Characteristics by Farm
            Type

Selected Characteristics	Exclusive Income	Supplementary Income	Part Time
		(percent)	
Full time man units	63.7	9.8	26.5
Total farmland	78.7	9.4	12.8
Tilled land	80.3	7.9	11.8
Permanent pasture	75.7	10.9	13.4
Dairy cattle	83.0	9.0	8.0
Hogs (except suckling pigs)	82.7	9.9	7.4
Laying hens	79.0	6.3	14.7
Total Market share	80.9	9.5	9.6

Source: Agrarbericht 1985 der Bundesregierung, p. 11

    Diverse, regionally dispersed availability of
professional and technical schools, courses, educational
programs, and farm media provide basic and continuing
education for farm people. Occupational education begins
with the requirement to attend a vocational agriculture
school for three years. This program is accompanied by
practical training on the student's parents' farm   or
another farm. The education of the farm operator is
continued with attendance at a technical college (for two
winter semesters) and supplemented with attendance at
agricultural education programs. University education in
agriculture is not common; university graduates as a
proportion of total farm operators is 1.5%. The level of
education has been steadily increasing. The younger the
farm operator and the larger and more specialized the
farm, the higher the level of education. The proportion
of farmers with any agricultural education whatsoever
rises from 52% of the operators of small farms with less
than 5,000 DM of (standard) farm income to 88% of the
operators of large farms with more than 50,000 DM of
(standard) farm income.
    According to a 1979 government survey, 12% of all farm
operators had completed basic agricultural education with
a journeyman accreditation (Gehilfenpruefung); 3% were
accredited as masters (Meisterpruefung); 50% had attended
a vocational agriculture school, and 30% had attended a

168

Table 8.3. Education of Farm Operators by Age, 1979

Type of Education	Total Farm Operators	35	Age 35-44	45-54	55-64	65+
			(percent)			
Agricultural						
On the job	13.3		25.0	14.3	13.3	8.5	3.3
Institutional	50.6		63.4	61.6	50.9	38.6	20.8
Nonagricultural	20.4		27.4	21.8	18.9	16.8	19.1
Any professional	66.5		82.9	77.4	65.9	52.9	38.2
TOTAL	100		100	100	100	100	100

Source: Stat. Jahrbuecher ueber Ernaehrung,
          Landwirtschaft und Forsten, 1983:57.

technical agriculture college. Noteworthy is the 20%
ofall farm operators who completed nonagricultural
training. A representative survey in 1980 showed that the
average level of education of farm youth lies markedly
above the average reported in the government survey cited
above. A generation ago the working knowledge of farming
was based on occupational experience, passed from father
to son and from mother to daughter. Today the majority of
farm youth receive an institutional education. About 70%
of farm youth, following four years of elementary and five
years of middle school, complete their general education
and enter a combined (practical and institutional)
occupational training (Berufsausbildung). Before they
began their professional training, 30% furthered their
education at secondary schools (Realschule or Gymnasium).
     The significance of the age structure of farm
operators is revealed by the interrelationship between age
and educational level. According to the government survey
of 1983, 15% of all farm operators were less than 35, 20%
were age 35 to 44, 35% were age 45 to 54, 23% were age 55
to 64, and 7% were 65 years of age and older. In 1949,
18% of all farm operators were women -- a consequence of
the war. Since 1956 this proportion has steadily fallen.
In 1983 only 8% of all farms were operated by women. As

an aside, expectations of a farm wife include not only
support of the husband in the barn and in the field, but
also the ability to be able to replace him in the event of
an emergency. Tending the household and garden, caring
for small animals, raising young animals, and bookkeeping
are the most frequent responsibilities of the farm wife.

The Farm Enterprise

Most family farms are operated as an independent
business. Therefore, the farm enterprise is a part of the
assets of the owner with no legal independence. The farm
operator, with all of his assets, is liable for business
debts. Farms engaged in the production of wine and
specialty crops or with high sales levels are frequently
incorporated (Gesellschaft des Buergerlichen Rechtes).
Other forms of incorporation are seldom or perhaps never
suited to the family farm for tax-related or other
reasons. Also, cooperative forms of farming have not been
successful in Western Germany. For the most part, the
basic conditions for advanced forms of business
organization are absent. For example, in 1983 only 13% of
all farms kept books; even in the farm size class of more
than 50,000 DM of (standard) farm income, only 55% kept
books.
    The entrepreneurial component does not function as
well as the traditional component of the family
farm--family, household, and the management of farm
activities. Frequently entrepreneurial functions are
delegated to nonfarm organizations, because farm operators
lack time, education, or the ability to perform
entrepreneurial tasks. Thus, cooperatives, producer
organizations, and accounting agencies often provide
support for these tasks.
    Characteristic of modern family farms are ties with
other farm units, whether these ties are with neighbors,
cooperatives, or firms through a contract. These ties
take the form of cooperation between individual farms in
carrying out farm operations (horizontal integration),
ties with farm cooperatives or contractual ties with
private firms for the purchase of inputs and the sale of
outputs (vertical integration), and other ties to the
"technological and administrative task environment" (see
Planck and Ziche 1979:279)
    Farmers have come together to form 252 machine sharing
groups (134,000 members with 3.6 million hectares of

farmland), 1,200 producer organizations, and 8,610 cooperatives (10.9 million members, 86 billion DM in annual sales). The German Farmers' Union (Deutscher Bauernverband) and its state affiliates, of which over 90% of all farmers are members, look after the economic policy interests of farmers. Almost half of all farm wives are members of at least one of the 12,000 farm women's organizations which offer a rich cultural program. Youth groups for farm children, sponsored by farmers' organizations and catholic and protestant churches, are open to all. The German Agricultural Society (Deutsche Landwirtschaftsgesellschaft) brings together farmers, their wives, and others with an interest in agriculture. It arranges agricultural fairs and professional exhibitions; tests tractors, farm implements, and food processing machinery; and awards prizes to the best products of German agriculture.

Every farmer and farm wife can take advantage of extension services at no cost. About 5,000 extension agents as well as 2,000 staff personnel are employed by government agricultural agencies. Besides this, there are 320 private consulting and producer groups with their own advisory staff. Finally, farm input and output industries, as well as trade organizations and cooperatives, retain their own farm consultants. Advisory services offer family farmers aid in decision making in the areas of production technology, farm and household management, and marketing. Recent advisory emphases are nutritional guidance and the provision of socioeconomic information. Farmer organizations offer specialized advising in the social and legal areas (e.g. help with questions about rent, farm transfer, inheritance settlements, and old age security). Tax consulting takes place at private agencies. Traditional information reaches farmers through the farm media. At least one agricultural journal or magazine is read on every full-time farm and on half of all part-time farms. Many regularly tune into farm radio programs.

SOCIAL CONDITIONS

Work and Recreation

An additional important characteristic of the family farm is the allocation of time between work and recreation. Basically, the work time of family members is

not measured. This characteristic results not only in a
work day of far above average length, but also in frequent
work on Sundays and holidays and no annual vacation from
work. Government statistics from 1983 report the
following average weekly hours of work:

Table 8.4. Weekly Hours of Work for Employed Persons,
1983[a]

Occupational Status	Agriculture and Forestry	Manufacturing
	(Hours per week)	
Men		
Self-employed	66.0	51.4
Family workers	43.0	33.6
Wage workers	43.9	39.0
Women		
Self-employed	52.0	38.9
Family workers	44.7	32.9
Wage workers	38.6	33.9

Source: Agrarbericht 1985 der Bundesregierung,
Materialband, Tabelle 6.
a: Week of June 6-12, 1983

The comparison of workers in agriculture with those in
industry and artisanal production shows significantly
longer hours of work in agriculture, above all for family
workers. While wage workers have progressively struggled
for shorter working hours, work hours of family workers on
the farm have remained at about the same level since
1970. Female family workers, as a rule the wife of the
farm operator, occupy the equivalent of more than a
full-time position on the farm. Three-fourths of all farm
wives are responsible for the farm household without any
outside assistance. She works an average of 70 hours a
week which amounts to 3,640 hours per year. Empirical
studies have uncovered individual cases in which the farm
wife works even more than 4,000 hours per year. A survey
showed that 81% of all farm wives in villages remote from
industry had never taken a vacation, and only 4% took a

172

vacation of a least two weeks in length annually (van
Deenen and Kossen-Knirim, 1981). The main reason for this
abstinence from taking a vacation is their actual or
perceived indispensability on the farm. Additionally,
vacation is not yet a part of the general behavioral
pattern within villages.

The Income Situation

The income of the family farm is based primarily on
returns to labor to which, aside from the farm operator,
the farm wife regularly contributes and other family
members frequently contribute. The contribution of farm
wives to returns to labor amounts to about half on small
farms, a third on middle-sized farms, and about one-fifth
on larger family farms. The older generation, in as far
as they live on the farm or nearby and are able, regularly
provide assistance with farm work. On the other hand, the
contribution of children and nonfamily youth has declined
sharply. Today children constitute a cost rather than an
asset. Children's contribution to farm work was expected
as a matter of course one generation ago. Now their
portion of farm work has been reduced to an occasional
contribution or disappeared altogether. Also, nonfamily
youth cannot be employed as in earlier times because
continuing school attendance, out of town occupational
training, and recreational interests take precedence. In
the past, farmers' sons and daughters worked on the farm
at least until the end of mandatory schooling at the age
of 14 or 15. Now they seldom pay for room and board at
home from their off-farm income. Nevertheless, it is
commonplace that young people employed off the farm help
with farm work when necessary as long as they live with
their parents. Some do this out of a sense of duty and
others simply because they enjoy it.

Both real and nominal farm incomes have risen
considerably, but have remained at about one-third or more
below the level of comparable occupational groups since
the Agricultural Report (Agrarbericht) of the federal
government began official publication of farm income in
1956-1957. The "parity wage" (Vergleichslohn) in
1983/1984 amounted to 34,303 DM per industrial worker. In
contrast, a family farm worker earned only an average of
21,508 DM. The majority of farmers find the shortfall in
farm income relative to the overall increase in incomes
unjust and consider this situation to be a reflection of
their disadvantaged position in economic policy. For the

operators of many small- and middle-sized farms, the gap in incomes within the farm sector is even more significant than the gap between farm and nonfarm incomes overall. Average returns per family worker in 1983-1984 were 49,104 DM in the top quarter of exclusive income farms, while average returns per family worker were minus 567 DM in the bottom quarter of all exclusive income farms. Particularly distressing is the continuous widening of this gap within the farm sector. One study of intersectoral income differences shows that the efficient use of the factors of production, which is largely dependent upon the farm operator's ability and the farm's productive capacity per worker, has the greatest causal influence upon these differences. Less significant, but influential all the same, are the natural conditions of a specific area and the personal preferences of the farm operator.

Overall, the factors of production in farming are not utilized optimally, as the persistent income disparity experienced by family farms demonstrates. From this situation the need for structural change emerges. This change obviously took place in the past in the form of expansion of small farms, down scaling of supplementary income farms to part-time farms, and last but not least, the abandonment of numerous farms as they were passed from one generation to the next. The structural change judged economically necessary was delayed by legal, social, and economic impediments and was also blocked through the persistence of mature structures. Not to be forgotten is the notion of the family farm, anchored in the thinking of agricultural professionals, which served to retard structural change.

Given saturated markets for farm products in the EEC, the farm income disparity could only to a limited extent be relieved by increased sales of farm products. This situation forced the adoption of measures to rationalize farm production, especially the reduction of the number of workers engaged in farming and securing supplementary income from off the farm. Labor input was reduced from 29 AK (1950-1951) to 5.8 AK (1983-1984) per 100 hectares of farmland as production levels increased. More than half of all farms complement farm income with earnings from off-farm work, as well as with pension and investment income. To some extent, off-farm incomes outweigh farm incomes. According to the Agricultural Report (Agrarbericht) of 1981, farm operators and their wives obtained the following proportions and respective amounts

of off-farm income: 33%, less than 10,000 DM; 45%, 10,000
to 20,000 DM; 18%, 20,000 to 30,000 DM; 4%, 30,000 DM and
more. In 1983 almost 30% of all family workers (including
the farm operator) worked off the farm and 43% of all farm
operators worked off the farm. On about 61% of all farms
either the farm operator or some family member worked off
the farm. This proportion was 75% for farms under 10
hectares; and on farms with more than 50 hectares, the
proportion still reached 23%. In the period 1970 to 1982,
off-farm work on the part of farm operators increased
considerably, particularly in the 5 to 20 hectares
category. The income of full- and part-time farms is
compared in Table 8.5.

Table 8.5. Income of Full- and Part-Time Farms 1982-1983
(DM/Family)

Type of Income	Exclusive Income Farms	Supplementary Income Farms	Part Time Farms
Returns to farming	33,791	19,107	4,195
Off farm employment	58	16,893	32,436
Other income	1,362	1,289	--
TOTAL	35,211	37,289	36,631

Source: Agrarbericht 1984, Uebersicht 21.

DEVELOPMENTAL TENDENCIES

Overview

Structural change in farming took place parallel to
overall economic cycles. It accelerated in periods of
prosperity and decelerated in phases of recession.
Further structural development is essentially dependent
upon future economic and sociopolitical structural
conditions. The developments which most affect family
farms can be summarized in ten points:
1. The amount of land available for farming is
shrinking (a reduction from 13.3 million hectares in 1949
to 12.0 million hectares in 1984) because of retirement

of marginal land from farm production and increasing demand for land. Unfortunately, much farmland considered good and excellent is used for the construction of homes, roads, industrial facilities, and for other nonfarm uses.

2. The total number of farms is declining (from 1,791,815 in 1949 to 771,527 in 1984, or by 57%). Most of the farms that disappeared are under 20 hectares. At the same time, increases in the number of farms larger than 20 hectares are observed and are to be expected in the future (Figure 8.4). Marginal full-time farms are continuously being down scaled or completely given up. Their land goes to the expansion of full-time farms, the creation of part-time farms, and to rural residential property.

3. The trend is from smaller to larger farms. The average land held per farm rose from 8.1 hectares in 1949 to 16.2 hectares in 1984. Herd size also increased.

4. Both the work force employed in agriculture and animals used for traction have fallen continuously (Figure 8.5). In contrast, tractor horsepower and capital investment is rising. Capital investment per "fully employed male worker" (or AK) climbed from 30,000 DM (1956-1957) to 300,000 DM (1981-1982).

5. Worker productivity is rising. In 1900 one German farmer provided food for four people, in 1950 this figure increased to 10 people, and today 40 people are fed with food produced by one farmer. The amount of farmland operated per person engaged in agriculture has steadily grown (in 1950-1951 this figure was 3.6 hectares, in 1984 it rose to 16.7 hectares).

6. Yields per hectare and per animal are rising in all branches of production because of technological progress.

7. Farm income and wages of farm workers display an upward tendency. Nominal returns on exclusive income farms increased by a factor of 10, from 2,680 DM per family worker in 1956-1957 to 26,282 DM in 1982-1983. Hourly wages of farm workers were increased from 1.24 DM to 11.11 DM in the same period of time.

8. Streamlined farm organization based upon a few marketable products or specialization in one main product has taken the place of the diversified farm.

9. There is increasing dependence on nonfarm factors. This dependence is evident in:

   a)   Increasing significance of rented land; 94% of all farmers cultivated their own land, but 58% rented additional land in 1983. Rented land as a proportion of all farmland grew from 12% in 1949 to 33% in 1983. The necessary expansion of the amount of land farmed can, in general, only be achieved by means of land rental, since no one will sell land except out of necessity. Annually only 0.2% to 0.3% of farmland is sold, and it is usually sold at prices far above the value of the land based on productivity.

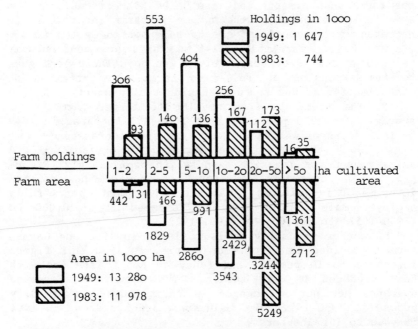

Figure 8.4. Development of Farms According to Size of Farms (Agrarbericht, 1984).

b) Increasing use of borrowed money. Farm debt climbed from 3.1 billion DM in 1949 to 47.8 billion DM in 1984. Farm sales, by comparison, amounted to 58.0 billion DM in 1983-84.

c) Increasing integration with the nonfarm sector. This integration is expressed in the value of farm inputs, which rose from 17.7 billion DM in 1972-1973 to 34.8 billion DM in 1982-1983. In constant prices this rise constitutes an increase of 20% within one decade.

10. The familial character of West German farming is being consolidated in two ways:

a) More and more farmland is being concentrated in family farms, especially in exclusive income farms (an increase of 9.13 million hectares in 1973 to

177

9.34 million hectares in 1984, or from 72% to 78% of total farmland).

b) Farm work is increasingly carried out by family workers: a rise from 77% of total AK in 1950-1951 to 89% in 1983.

Labour units in Mill.
Animal power units in Mill.

Tractor kw
in 1o ooo Mill.

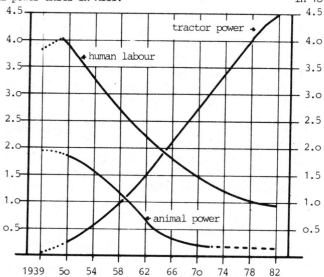

Figure 8.5.   Labor and Traction Power in Agriculture (Agricultural Statistics).

Point 10 requires a bit more detailed explanation. In 1949, 446,274 farms with permanently (i.e. non-seasonally) employed nonfamily workers were counted. In 1982 permanent wage workers were still employed on only about 39,000 farms. The number of permanent nonfamily workers (wage workers) declined from 1,104,363 in 1949 to 83,300 in 1985. The number of seasonal wage workers did not decline as rapidly (479,502 in 1949, 84,000 in 1983). Nonfamily workers decreased from 18.2% (1949) to 5.2% (1985) of total permanent agricultural laborers.

The Concentration of Land Holding

The Reich Settlement Act (Reichssiedlungsgesetz, 1919), the Land Reform Act (Bodenreformgesetz, 1946-1947), the Refugee Settlement Act (Fluechtlingssiedlungsgesetz, 1949), the Federal Act Concerning Exiles (Bundesvertriebenengesetz, 1953), and the act concerning measures to improve farm structure and safeguard farm and forest operations (1961) all contributed to the concentration of land in family farms. The last act mentioned specifies that plots of farmland over a particular size are, in principal, to be sold only to farmers. Between 1949 and 1961 alone, farmland held by family farms increased by about 780,000 hectares. Land is sold or rented out mostly by small farms operated part time or by farms employing wage labor. The land reform carried out after World War II under pressure from the military government of the occupation forces contributed only 210,000 hectares to family farms in the decade of 1945 to 1954. Another 450,000 were made available by the end of 1964 under the Land Reform Act and Reich Settlement Act, which benefited 53,000 family farms with an allotment of land.

The policy of reintegrating refugee and exile farmers also contributed to the increased number of family farms. About 440,000 farm families that had owned or would have inherited a farm in their area of origin were part of the 10.7 million exiles from the former Prussian provinces east of the Oder-Neisse-Line, from earlier German settlement areas in eastern and southeastern Europe, or from the 3.4 million refugees from the German Democratic Republic. The damages incurred as a result of the loss of these farmlands was estimated at 9.5 billion Reichsmark--based on standard tax assessments. Those suffering losses had to build a new existence in West Germany. They took over a total of 219,375 farms from 1949 until 1982, which accounted for a total of 826,671 hectares. About 40,000 were exclusive income farms, 48,000 were part-time farms, and 132,000 were smallholdings under 0.5 hectares.

A total of 12,214 million DM were spent for this resettlement from 1949 to 1976. This total was made up of 7,983 million DM from federal and state budgets, 2,332 million DM from the Compensation Fund (Ausgleichsfond), and 1,909 million DM from other sources, which included borrowed money. Under this program of integration, 126,718 homesteads were created on 145,593 hectares, 63,048 farms were purchased, 18,772 were rented, and in 10,837 cases, exile or refugee farmers married into existing farms. The integrated "new farmers" were not subjected to contraction of the farm sector to the extent that indigenous farmers were, but not all of them could retain their farms. An inventory at the end of 1976 showed that in place of the 440,000 farms lost in the East, 23,000 exclusive income farms, 49,000 part-time farms, and 120,000 smallholdings under 0.5 hectares were still operated by exile or refugee farmers in West Germany.

The Concentration of Livestock Production

The concentration of livestock production currently underway is particularly important for family farms. It signifies both opportunity and danger.

Family farms reacted to changed price and cost relationships by considerably expanding livestock production, especially dairy production, for the following reasons. Even with a decline in the number of nonfamily workers, the family work force remains almost twice as large, in terms of total AK, as that in larger than family farms. Thus, the family farm must above all be concerned with realizing a larger production volume with the available family work force by intensifying production. In contrast to farms employing wage labor, family farms have no alternative but real growth. This growth is possible only by means of an increase in livestock production which demands labor input throughout the year.

The average size of livestock holdings has risen in the case of cattle, hogs, and poultry mostly due to the disappearance of small operations and the expansion of those remaining, as well as the emergence of industrial livestock production. The concentration of livestock holdings is increasing in dairy farming, cattle feeding, pig breeding and feeding, and egg and broiler production.

While the expansion of holdings in dairy farming, cattle feeding, and pig breeding generally remained within the size parameters of the family farm, the concentration of pig feeding is jeopardizing many family farms. Because pig feeding is, in principle, possible without extensive land holdings, concentration in the form of industrial animal production on a massive scale is feared. Nonetheless, until now family farms have also expanded their operations in this branch of production. Presently, industrial pig feeding encompasses about 6% of production, which is still relatively insignificant.

Egg production is completely different. It is shifting extensively from family farms to large industrial enterprises. The number of operators with more than 10,000 hens is an insignificant 0.2%, but approximately 600 operators account for more than half of all laying

hens. Eight massive operations with an average of 950,000
laying hens accounted for 16.4% of all laying hens in
1980. Broiler production is even more concentrated. More
than 90% of all broilers come from holdings of more than
10,000 chickens. Operators with the capacity to hold more
than 200,000 chickens at a time increased their share of
total stock from 17.5% in 1977 to 29.4% in 1980.
Industrial operations account for more than 70% of total
stock.

   Since animal production constitutes the backbone of
many family farms, maximum size limits to protect the
nonindustrial production of certain animals have been more
forcefully promoted since 1981. Until now these proposals
have had little success, which led Vogel to conclude: "If
we wanted to, we could; but one must seriously doubt if we
want to" (1982:357). Vogel produces a list of critics who
have doubts about the seriousness of agricultural policy
makers in creating a policy favoring the family farm.

   The concentration of animal production in fewer but
larger operations runs parallel to an increase in the
number of farms holding no animals. The latter rose from
about 5% of all farms in 1961, to 11% in 1971, and to 16%
in 1981.

EVALUATION

   Because of its relative superiority, the family farm
is favored in the agricultural policy of both the Federal
Republic of Germany and the EEC. Individual support of
family farms that are rationally operated and capable of
surviving in the long run was justified by Minister of
Agriculture Josef Ertl as follows, "This form of
production is best suited to accomplishing social policy
functions expected of agriculture and rural areas on
account of its efficiency and adaptability" (1980:492).
Undersecretary in the Ministry of Agriculture Georg Gallus
expanded on the social policy line of argumentation by
referring to the personal freedom, flexibility, and
adaptability of the family farm: "This organization of
farm production makes possible individual freedom within
the family, but also demands a high level of
responsibility vis-a-vis other family members. Family
farms are flexible not only in terms of labor allocation,
but also more adaptable with respect to the income
situation" (1982:490).

   In a penetrating analysis of the goals of agricultural

181

policy, Hans Guenther Schlotter (1969) challenged the
relative superiority of the family farm precisely in terms
of its much vaunted adaptability. In his opinion, "The
family farm in comparison to the farm employing wage labor
has a principally narrow range of adaptability which can
underlie total blockage (of adjustment) and conceivably
higher adjustment costs on the average." From this he
concludes that the family farm meets social policy norms
to a lesser extent than both farms employing wage labor
and part-time farms, and that the latter forms of
organization better correspond to the goals of
agricultural policy. The Commission of the European
Community also arrived at a similar conclusion in
1968.

    The superiority of the large-scale farm, first imputed
by the French socialist Louis Le Blanc, is unable to
withstand empirical scrutiny. Stated Le Blanc: "The
well-being of agriculture consists of the adoption of the
large-scale farm" (1839). Nevertheless, Karl Marx and
Friedrich Engels adopted the opinion of Le Blanc. Karl
Ballod concretely stated the Marxian agricultural utopia
in his book, Der Zukunftsstaat; Produktion und Konsum im
Sozialstaat (1898). Based on the reading of Der
Zukunftsstaat, Karl Kautsky, a noted Marxian theoretician,
claimed to foresee the death of the family farm (1899).
Nevertheless, just four years later Eduard David (1903)
initiated a reexamination of the agrarian question on the
part of the Social Democrats. The planned establishment
of large-scale farms has not been a part of the social
democratic agricultural policy since the Kiel convention
in 1927.

    According to the well-founded view of A. Weber, "There
can be no economically compelling need to wish to realize
large-scale farms through a concentration of workers"
(1974:58). Also, Georg Blohm, a farm management expert,
is certain "that the large-scale farm is in no way
demanded in order to take advantage of modern
technological advance" (1977:16). The electric motor and
tractor broke the monopoly of large-scale farms in the
mechanization (motorization) of agriculture. Of course,
mobile sources of energy can only share to a limited
extent in the performance of individual farm tasks. But
small farms can partake of the advantages of large
machines by means of shared use of machinery. Biological
and chemical technologies are readily shared; and all
mechanical technologies, in as far as they are not bound
to an immobile energy source, can be shared as well.

Thus, modern technologies can also be utilized efficiently
on family farms.

If the preconditions of adequate specialization of
production (i.e. utilization of machine sharing
possibilities and mastering of production technology) are
met, the productive capacity of a farm family with an
average of one to two AK is generally sufficient to
realize potential economies of scale in labor and capital
costs in most branches of plant and animal production.

The notion that large-scale industrial farming offers
certain cost advantages is not disputed. But the most
modern technologies cannot solve all of the problems of
agriculture, rather they create additional problems of
environmental stress, loss of species (through land
clearing and monoculture), and the elimination of jobs.
Large-scale livestock production leads to problems of the
removal of excrement, disease control, and residues from
preventative medicines. Thus, Gallus, upon weighing all
the factors, sees no advantage in large-scale industrial
farm production.

"Embedded in such production are much higher risks
with respect to protection of the environment, nature,
and consumers. Industrial farm production also
provides no increase in security regarding an adequate
food supply and does little to solve the problems of
agricultural policy. The family farm can make use of
progress in biotechnologies as well. The close
physical and psychic ties to the land and animals
permit the family farm operator to exercise special
care and responsibility for the goods he is in charge
of. But this form of agriculture should also be
encouraged in order to maintain a broad distribution
of property, help as many people as possible live
self-sufficiently, and maintain a sufficient
population density in rural areas" (Gallus 1982:491).

Without a doubt, family farms have caused less
environmental damage than large-scale farms, especially
nonland based mass livestock holdings. A main concern of
the family farmer always was to improve the productive
base of the farm and to preserve it for future
generations. However, we have moved away from the notion
that the family farm, in particular, contributes to the
preservation of the land and to an ecological balance.
Modern farming consumes nonrenewable energy in substantial
quantities and, above all, pollutes water with phosphates

and nitrates. The latter is the result of runoff from fertilization. Family farms also take part in energy consumption and environmental pollution in as far as they operate conventionally. Presently, less than 1% of all farms are operated alternatively, i.e. organic farming. Despite the fact that the demand for alternatively produced products currently cannot be met with domestic production, the expansion possibilities for alternative production are estimated at less than 3%. In any case, discontent with the excessive use of chemicals is noticeable within family farming. Under the influence of alternative cultivation practices and the pressure of public opinion, the application of chemical fertilizers and pesticides is being curbed, and possibilities for reduced chemical usage through better cultivation, crop rotation, and integrated pest management are being investigated.

PROBLEMS

Under constantly changing price-cost relationships, technological progress and the market situation prove to be the most important factors in development of the farm sector. This development is accelerated or retarded by the wage structure and the conditions of the labor market. Development of the farm sector is characterized by growth in the size of farm units and specialization and concentration of production. The opinion of Lothar Richter (1970:458) is increasingly being adopted, even in agriculture. He believes that economic growth can only be realized in new, more productive forms of organization of production. However, precisely this precondition for economic growth is generally not found in family farming. Specialization and concentration are not very compatible with the independence of the family farm. This requires cooperation and integration at higher levels and, therefore, conflicts with property rights which are of such marked importance to the farm population. Herbert Koetter has repeatedly pointed out that higher social status and more personal freedom in private life are purchased with greater interdependence and contraction of decision making authority at the farm level.
The weaknesses of the family farm include:
1. the dependence of farm organization upon family composition and development,
2. almost total dependence on family personnel,

184

3. the tendency for the self-exploitation of family workers,
4. the compulsion to accept the drudgery of work if the needs of the family are to be met,
5. the difficulty to gain qualified successors, and
6. the insufficient supply of land and/or capital.

The problems which place the family farm in question may be described as problems of technological development, capital, growth, parity, replacement labor, and succession.

The Problem of Technological Development

Technological progress affects the development of the farm sector in various ways. Progress in biotechnology raises yields and simultaneously lowers marginal costs of production. This causes increasing application of production inputs which enhance and stabilize yields. The consequence of such practices is to reduce land as an input and to increase its productivity. In this respect, such technology meets the needs of family farms with a limited supply of land. However, it harbors the danger of surplus production which eventually leads to restrictive market policy measures (production quotas). These measures enhance such difficulties, because family farmers generally seek to compensate reduced income with increased production.

Progress in machine technology has, above all, a labor saving effect. Mechanization replaces, eases, and speeds up manual labor and results in increased labor productivity. Of course, the labor saving effect cannot result in cost reductions through the displacement of workers on the family farm. To utilize the labor capacity of the family, production must be intensified (e.g. year-round indoor animal production or milk production) or labor intensive branches of production (e.g. specialty crops) must be established. Progress in machine technology favors larger farms, especially farms employing wage labor. Technologies are constantly improved, but with increasing capacities, they simultaneously become more expensive. Their profitability is largely bound to their level of utilization. An optimum level is often reached only on those farms which are larger than family farms. Therefore, family farms frequently make use of modern technologies through contractors or machine sharing. Family farms cannot fully make use of the

possibility of replacing expensive manual labor with
relatively cheap machine labor, as is the case with farms
employing wage labor.
The application of mechanical-technical developments,
as a rule, ties up capital, i.e. high fixed costs arise.
The pressure to specialize and a loss of organizational
flexibility result. Therefore, the highly mechanized farm
must fix its field of production as well as its financial
arrangements.

As wages and income demands climb, labor processes
employing capital-intensive, high-level technology with
little manual labor become more significant. This pattern
is even more pronounced when economies of scale can be
exploited. Because of their relatively small size, this
sort of investment is only possible on family farms under
certain conditions. The adoption of such technologies in
an effort to utilize the available work force causes
increased production on family farms. Under certain
circumstances this may lead to surplus production and
falling prices. Such conditions, in turn, especially
impact upon small farms that have low liquidity.
Therefore, continued investment becomes the fate of the
family farm.

Capitalization Problems

Paul Meimberg (1970:15) feels that increasing pressure
to capitalize in order to raise labor productivity to
industrial levels exceeds the parameters of the
conventional family farm. Farm investments compete with
the demands of private consumption for the available
income. While around one-half of gross income (controlled
for inflation) was taken as family income in 1950, the
proportion was only about one-fourth by the end of the
1960s. Larger farms had income advantages based on the
fact that they could more easily raise and accumulate
capital with which to improve their farm operations.
Enlargement of livestock or land holdings was reserved for
those who had access to sufficient capital, either from
their income or from the sale of land. Most farmers saw
no possibility of accumulating capital. Many go so far as
to draw on the substance of their property or from their
off-farm income to invest in their farm.

The Problem of Growth

In the past, family farms possessed equipment corresponding to the labor capacity of the family. At a higher level of technology, the system of the family farm goes into disequilibrium, which steadily grows as a consequence of technological progress. Further rationalization demands that labor supply and land and animal holdings be adapted to the most cost effective technologies. Only those farms that constantly expand the size of their production units have chances for survival. The exclusive income farm is condemned to focus only on growth. Growth of individual farms through expansion of the area operated is only possible if other farms give up land, since there no longer are land reserves in Germany. The condition for further development of exclusive income farms is a corresponding supply of suitable land. However, the supply is far from sufficient. Therefore, competition is expressed in land purchase price and rent that is largely out of proportion to its productivity. Government programs promoting land transfer have until now been unable to initiate land sales. Land transfer is decisively limited by both concerns for economic security and the expectation of future increases in value. There is generally little occasion to give up one's own land (except, e.g. to finance the building of a house), especially in areas where many farmers supplement their incomes or farm part time. People stick to their land even more in those areas where there are no income and employment alternatives to farming.

The struggle to survive takes the form of competition for the means of production and market shares and has led to very dubious manifestations which appear capable of destroying farmers' morale and solidarity from within. Interaction between farmers has, in part, taken on brutal forms; hatred and jealousy destroy solidarity between farmers; inconsiderate outbidding in the rental and purchasing of land create discord; and mutual distrust drives farm families apart and into isolation. Due to economic pressures, cooperatives and machine sharing groups, originally created as self-help organizations addressing economic and social weaknesses, are drawn into the process of weeding out less productive farms.

In terms of farm policy, competition among farms is supported to the advantage of those farms considered "capable of development" ("entwicklungsfaehige Betriebe") by the "individual farm assistance program" (einzelbetrieb-

liches Foerderprogramm"). This program limits grants of
government funds to farms larger than a designated minimum
size.

The Parity Problem

The parity problem results from the fact that the
normal standard of living of comparable occupational
groups in Germany apparently cannot be reached by the
majority of family farms. This disparity is, above all,
associated with income and work time. The income
disparity has its source in the limited demand for farm
products, which cannot be expanded at will, and the
consequent pressure on producer prices. If the individual
farmer wants to earn more, the number of farmers must be
reduced. If the number of farms is not reduced, then the
income expectations of farmers must be lowered. However,
it is very likely that possibilities for the
rationalization of production have not been fully
exploited on every farm. "The structural and social
dilemma of most family farms consists, as always, in the
fact that they produce with inefficient machines at too
high a cost, have no market power, and offer working
conditions (with respect to recreation and vacation, and
in times of illness and old age) that do not conform to
social norms. More cooperation would help, because it
makes structural, intellectual, and social advantages
possible" (Vogel 1982:357). But as long as farmers are
unprepared to give up their independence in favor of
agricultural cooperatives, social claims for work time
equivalent to that in industry, time off on weekends, and
vacations of several weeks in length border on the
impossible. Neither present nor future claims can be
fulfilled through retention of the organizational form of
the family farm (see Kommission der EG 1968).

The Problem of Replacement Labor

The wage and income gradient, as well as shorter work
time in other occupations, has contributed to the exodus
of workers from agriculture. First nonfamily workers
left, but in the 1960s family members and frequently the
farm operators themselves left farming. In many cases the
workforce available on the farm was reduced to the farm
operator and his wife. Currently, exclusive income farms

have, on the average, less than 1.3 family AK. Farms that
employ less than 1.5 AK fall beneath the farm size level
considered critical for earning an acceptable income, yet
they are still too large to be operated part time. These
so called "one man farms" run into problems of labor
availability if the farm operator cannot complete his farm
work because of illness or accident. Also, the wish to
take a vacation, participate in an educational program for
several days, or take a professionally related field trip
leads to problems on these farms. Pregnancy, motherhood,
or a case of infirmity in the family can also lead to
problems of labor supply. Every loss of a family member,
either fully or partially involved in operation of the
farm, poses the problem of labor replacement. In earlier
times, help could be found relatively easily within the
family itself, within the kin network, or within the
neighborhood. There was generally someone around who
could fill in. Today there is simply a lack of helpers,
all the more so as highly professional qualifications are
required.

The Problem of Succession

The problem of succession is composed of two parts:
the successor and the problem of farm wives.
Traditionally, the family farm was passed from father
to son, and where no son was present, to the daughter,
adopted son, or nephew. In the past, a strong moral and
social pressure to accept the role of successor existed.
It was even a privilege to be the successor. Today
potential successors examine very carefully whether the
family farm will provide a life which meets their
preconceptions of a standard of living, social prestige,
and self-fulfillment. The result is frequently negative.
With an eye toward the uncertain future, many parents
provide their children with a nonfarm education. In doing
so, they eliminate a succeeding generation that is trained
in farming. As a result, there is a lack of farm
successors. Based on a survey of the Agrarsozialen
Gesellschaft, 20% to 30% of all farm operators age 55 and
over in the Federal Republic of Germany have no successor
(ASG-Materialsammlung Nr. 137). If no successors are
available who are capable and willing to take over the
farm, the farm is given up. There is no doubt that the
number of potential successors and their preparedness to
continue to operate the farm is declining.

Even more serious is the degree of difficulty of the young farmer's experience in finding a suitable wife. The extent of this problem is illuminated by the results of a survey conducted in Bavaria which showed that about one-fifth of all farm operators are single. The exodus of young women from rural areas far exceeds that of men of equivalent age. The farm "marriage market" is severely reduced, and relatively few young women, because of their constitution, attitude, and education are suited to the occupation of farm wife. Only a small proportion would even consider marriage to a farmer. According to a survey conducted in 1980, only 4% of all young rural women would most like to marry a farmer, 53% would marry a farmer given particular conditions (attraction, personal characteristics of the partner, working conditions on the farm, etc.), and 41% would under no circumstances marry a farmer. The continued existence of the family farm will, in the final analysis, depend upon whether or not enough qualified young women are prepared to take over the duties of a farm wife at the side of a farmer.

REFERENCES

Agrarberichte der Bundesregierung. Bonn. Ballod, Karl
    (Pseudonym: Atlanticus). 1898. Produktion und Konsum
    im Sozialstaat. Stuttgart. (Unter dem Titel "Der
    Zukunftsstaat" 1919 in (Auflage).
Blanc, Louis. 1839. Organisation du travail. Paris.
Blohm, Georg. 1977. Die Entwicklung der Landwirtschaft,
    in: Berichte ueber Landwirtschaft 1: 1-18.
David, Eduard. 1903. Socialismus und Landwirtschaft.
    Berlin.
Deenen, Bernd van und Christa Kossen-Knirim. 1981.
    Landfrauen in Betrieb, Haushalt und Familie.
    (=Forschungsellschaft fue Agrarpolitik und
    Agrarsoziologie H. 260.).
Ertl, Josef. 1980. Agrarpolitik seit 1969 - Rueckblick
    und Ausblick, in: Berichte ueber Landwirtschaft: 58
    480-501.
Frank, Walter. 1972. Ueber die Strukter der
    landwirtschaftlichen Betriebe in der Europaeischen
    Gemeinschaft. Agrarwirtschaft (Hannover), Jg. 21, H.
    4, 110-119.
Gallus, Georg. 1982. Agrapolitik am Scheideweg zwischen
    Familienbetrieb und industrieller Agraraproduktion, in
    Berichte ueber Landwirtschaft 60, 4: 481-193.
Gruener Bericht 1956 der Bundesregierung. Bonn,
    Bundestagsdrucksache 2100.
Kautsky, Karl. 1899. Die Agrarfrage. Stuttgart.
Knirim, Christa. 1976. Familienfunktionen in
    Abhaengigkeit von familialen Strukturen in Stadt und
    Land, in: Berichte ueber Landwirtschaft 54, 4:
    549-562.
Kommission der Europaeischen Gemeinschaften. 1968.
    Memorandum zur Reform der Landwirtshcaft in der
    Europaeischen Wirtschaftsgemeinschaft (MANSHOLT-Plan).
    Bruessel.
Lueckemeyer, Manfred. 1982. Landwirtschaftliche
    Viehhaltung oder "Agrarfabriken"?, in: Berichte ueber
    Landwirtschaft, 60, 3: 403-419.
Meimberg, Paul. 1970. Die Konzentration in der
    Landwirtschaft: Konsequenzen fur die Strukturpolitik.
    Wiesbaden.
Neander, Eckhart. 1983. Zur Abgrenzung, Charakterisierung
    und Bewertung baeuerlicher Landwirtschaft, in Berichte
    ueber Landwirtschaft, 61, 1: 67-78.

Neander, Eckhart. 1984. AuBerbetriebliche Einkommen von
    Inhabern landwirtschaftlicher Betriebe und ihren
    Angehoerigen in der Bundesrepublik Deutschland.
    Braunsweig: Institut fur Strukturforschung,
    Bundesforchungsanstalt fue Landwirtschhaft.
    Arbeitsbericht.
Planck, Ulrich. 1964. Der baeuerliche Familienbetrieb
    zwischen Patriarchat und Partnerschaft. Stuttgart
    (-soziologische Gegenwartsfragen, Neue Folge, Heft 20).
Planck, Ulrich and Joachim Ziche. 1979. Land und
    Agrarsoziologie. Stuttgart.
Reichling, G. 1978. Die Wiedereingliederung der
    vertriebenen und gefluechteten Landwirte in der
    Landwirtschaft der Bundesrepublik Deutschland, in
    Berichte ueber Landwirtschaft: 56, 4 618-648.
Richter, Lothar. 1970. Betriebsgroesse und
    Betriebsentwicklung in der Landwirtschaft, in:
    Berichte ueber Landwirtschaft 48,3:450-468.
Ries, Ludwig Wilhelm. 1947. Betriebslehre der deutschen
    baeuerlichen Familienlandwirtschaft. Stuttgart.
Roehm, Helmut. 1964. Die westdeutsche Landwirtschaft.
    Agrarstruktur, Agrarwirtschaft, landwirtschaftliche
    Anpassung. Muechen.
Schlotter, Hans-Guenther. 1969. Raumordnungs - und
    agrarpolitische Ziele in der landwirtschaftlichen
    Raumplanung, in: Akademie fue Raumforschung und
    Landesplanung (Hrsg.): Grundlagen und Methoden der
    landwirtschaftlichen Raumplanung. Hannover: 33-52.
Statistiches Jahrbuch ueber Ernehrung. Landwirtschaft
    und Forsten, 1983. Hamburg.
Vogel, Gisbert. 1982. Solidaritae und Konkurrenz in der
    Landwirtschaft, in: Berichte ueber Landwirtschaft:
    350-361.
Weber, Adolf. 1974. Der landwirtschaftliche
    Grossetrieb mit vielen Arbeitskraeften in historischer
    und international vergleichender Sicht, in Berichte
    ueber Landwirtschaft 52, 1:57-80.

9
Family Farming in France: Crisis and Revival

Hugues Lamarche
translated by Jacques Marre and Keith M. Moore

In France, agricultural production relies entirely on the family farm. This aspect of French agriculture is basically the same today as it was more than a century ago. However, this historic permanence does not mean that its reproduction is always the same. Today's family farm has been profoundly modified over the course of time to the point where it is not possible to discuss or understand it in the same terms. When comparing family farming in different periods, we might even ask if we are observing the same thing. The answer to this question depends on the breadth of the meaning given to "family farm." A definition is, therefore, necessary.

In Europe, and France specifically, the family farm is compared to the peasant or agricultural production unit. This has created confusion that must be cleared up at this point. Louis Chevalier (1947) offers the following definition of family farming which, while classical, remains incomplete:

> One can define family farm as a rural farm of a size that a family can cultivate by its own means or aided, as frequently happens, by one or two hired workers.

If all the essential elements of family farming are present in this definition, they must be interpreted in a broad sense. The family farm is a unit of production where capital and labor are intimately linked to the family. The interdependence of these three factors in the functioning of the family farm engenders very complex and abstract notions, such as patrimony and the reproduction of patrimony.

The family farm was present under the "ancien régime," then developed and became largely dominant around the second half of the 19th century. Despite a deep crisis which has brewed since the beginning of the century, the family farm has adapted, with some difficulty, to the requirements of an industrializing French society.

THE PEASANT FARM AND ITS MODE OF FUNCTIONING

We will not describe in detail the peasant society and the farms which compose it. Many others have already done so with precision and in very poetic terms. Recall, however, the unique components of this system which even today determine the behavior of many small farmers.

The peasant value system rests, before all else, on the land and the family, let us say on the patrimony. The land is not only the site of production, it is also the source of "nourishment." This nourishment is alimentary, but it is also cultural and symbolic. With such intangible values placed on the land, it cannot be considered exclusively as a commodity. To acquire land is the goal of a farmer's life; to lose or sell it is generally considered a degradation. The land is the foundation of the patrimony, that is to say, it holds all of its value in all its dimensions when analyzed in the family context and in the perspective of social reproduction.

That is why the French peasants continued to acquire ownership of the land which they worked throughout the 19th century. This is more a display of the instinct of conservation (property is security, stability) than of a will to capitalize. At the beginning of the 20th century, most of the peasants were proprietors of a part, if not all, of their farms. But acquiring land was expensive and detrimental to other investments. This problem still exists today for the child who takes over the farm from his father and must rebuild it after purchasing his brothers' and sisters' inherited part of the farm.

The mode of production is also based on the family and is designed to meet its essential needs. It is semi-autonomous because of a double objective: to nourish family members and sell surplus production on the market. These surplus sales enable the family to buy items the farm cannot produce (very few things in that period) and to save money to acquire parcels of land if the opportunity arises. The labor force consists of family labor. In 1906, one farm in two did not have a hired worker, one of four employed only a single hired worker (Desert, 1977).

All peasants adhered to this system of values and had the same relationship to the land, family, and money. They all thought about space and time in nearly an identical fashion. However, they did not all belong to the same social class. A great social division existed with possession of land the essential factor.

This peculiar structure of production was also the object of a peculiar agricultural policy whose most illustrative advocate was Jules Meline, Minister of Agriculture from 1883 to 1885 and from 1915 to 1916. The policy can be summarized as the implementation of a desperate protectionism. The results of this policy were not expected. It caused stagnation of the structures and techniques of production and the brutal arrest of the agricultural "revolution" underway in France which lagged behind other European countries.

Since this period, the French peasantry has had a very distinctive character. It can be described as reactionary, traditionalist, archaic, and obscurantist. And as one would expect, peasants were politically conservative. However, the national voting of 1869 allows us to catch a glimpse of certain differences in peasant political behavior. This without doubt explains why the protectionist agricultural policy was developed by France up to and between the two wars. It was designed to create political adhesion among the very numerous peasant masses.

THE NECESSITY OF A CHANGE

The acquisition of property by all classes; a protectionist agricultural policy; successive crises in silk, olive oil, and grape production; along with a climate of declining agricultural prices, all contributed to a decline of agriculture and its place in the national economy. France was lulled to sleep by the prosperity of the second half of the 19th century. Its peasantry was content to have acquired the "Agricultural Revolution" in a period where agriculture was organizing, modernizing, and industrializing in other countries. In 1852, the farms of less than 10 hectares represented 68% of all agricultural land; in 1908 they represented 84%. In certain regions, Rhone-Alpes, Poitou, Limousin and Pays de la Garonne, for example, wheat yields declined several times between 1892 and 1912. In 1912, France experienced a net agricultural deficit in the production of cereals, meat, vegetables, and eggs (Desert, 1977). This situation persisted throughout the first half of the 20th century, as shown in the Table 9.1.

Table 9.1. National Production as a Percentage of National Consumption for Selected Categories of Agricultural Production

	1905-1914	1920-1924	1935-1938
Cereals	90.3	85.8	93.3
Potatoes	100.0	100.0	99.0
Wine	91.0	92.0	82.0
Meat	100.0	93.0	98.0
Butter and Cheese	101.0	98.0	100.0

Source: J.C. Toutain, Histoire quantitative de l'economie francaise, 1961. Cited by Gervais, Jollivet and Tavernier, in l'Histoire de la France Rurale, Volume IV.

Thus, at the beginning of this century, the French peasantry had finally become owners of their means of production. However, their farming methods remained archaic and totally incapable of meeting the requirements of a modern economy, and, therefore, incapable of satisfying the essential food needs of a global society in the midst of industrial development. As a result of this profound crisis (which first materialized as an accelerated decrease in the active agricultural population, followed by a decrease in the number of family farms), the poorest and least organized peasants could no longer reproduce themselves. Many family farms were abandoned, freeing the land for those who could remain; 1,700,000 farms, of which four-fifths were less than 5 hectares, disappeared between 1929 and 1955.

A profound transformation of agriculture seemed necessary to enable the State, agricultural industries and the peasants to overcome the crisis. This modernization radically transformed peasant society and was realized thanks to the existence of a "consensus" between the global capitalist "will" and the precarious local peasant situation. On one hand, society as a whole wanted to transform the semi-autonomous, traditional agriculture into a sector of dynamic production, consuming and exporting. On the other hand, the peasantry experienced total confusion when faced with the powerful urban industrial development and the resulting new values which progressively penetrated even the most remote countryside. In a general sense, the peasantry felt excluded from the development. Parents could reconcile themselves to this situation but their children refused. The younger generation viewed the change as a means to escape from marginal means of existence under the present conditions.

At this point several questions were yet to be answered: Which socioeconomic base would this development operate under? Which structures of production would be best suited to assume the change--the family farm or the large farms such as those found in the Parisian Basin with its salaried workers? These questions remained unanswered. Only the adventurous would have taken a stand as to the ideal methods of agricultural production.

FROM THE FAMILY FARM TO THE FAMILY FIRM

The "true" revolution of French agriculture really began in the 1950s. It is the true revolution because it was not only technical, as that of the 18th and 19th centuries, it completely changed how the peasant world functioned--economically and socially as well as culturally. Whether one liked it or not, this revolution rapidly created a new race of family farmers: the agricultural holders.

The Great Upheaval

The agricultural revolution was due to an enormous effort to educate the peasantry combined with powerful technical advances that enabled information to reach even the most isolated communes. This change can also be attributed to a profound will of certain peasant social strata to take charge of their future. Examples include

the strong role played by the C.E.T.A. (Centre d'Etude
Technique Agricole), the Jeunesse Agricole Catholique, and
much later, the Federation Nationale des Syndicats
d'Exploitants Agricoles (F.N.S.E.A.) and the Centre
National des Jeunes Agriculteurs (C.N.J.A.). Thus,
beginning in the 1950s, a cantonal level of agricultural
advisers began to develop into a complete network,
establishing a true professional agricultural education.
The presence of such an environment played an essential
role in transforming the agricultural world. This helped
develop innovations in the countryside, the acknowledgment
by all that "the craft of the agriculturalist can and must
be learned like all other crafts," and that in order to be
a good agriculturalist it is no longer sufficient to be
born a peasant (Une France sans paysan, p.49). In fact,
getting an education and professional training made
hereditary transmission of knowledge, the only mode of
education practiced and recognized by the French peasantry
until now, less desirable.

The effort asked of the peasants was enormous, and the
list of improvements needed was very long. But the
peasantry as a whole responded positively. And this
group, once thought to be generally conservative,
traditional, impermeable to all changes, and opposed to
progress, showed a formidable capacity to ingest and
digest technical and social progress. Although there were
many transformations in each sector of production, we will
cite only those most important and representative of the
upheaval which had been taking place in the social
relations of agricultural production since 1950.

Modernization is, first of all, agricultural
mechanization which became increasingly necessary because
of the loss of the agricultural labor force and because it
was indispensable for rehabilitating the craft. To the
peasant, the tractor represented both a tool of work and
an essential element for the revalorization of his labor.
It is estimated that in large-scale agriculture,
mechanization has reduced labor demand six to seven times,
while at the same time appreciably improving yields.

The number of tractors used in agricultural production
increased ten-fold between 1950 and 1979, representing an
annual average increase of 33%. The tractor has held, and
still holds, a special place in the hearts of farmers,
especially young farmers, a place identical to that of the
car in French society during the 1960s. In the beginning,
the farmer's goal was to own a tractor, then it was to
have a more powerful tractor. Next he wanted a more

Table 9.2.   Changes in the Number of Tractors (in
             thousands)

	1950	1960	1967	1973	1979
Less than 35 horsepower	--	--	718	--	392
More than 50 horsepower	--	--	29	--	510
Total	137	680	1155	1330	1485

comfortable tractor with a cabin and heating. Today the
desired tractor has four-wheel drive and a heated,
sound-proofed cabin with a stereo. Many farmers are ready
to pay the price for this "deluxe model," even though, for
most of them, it surpasses both their needs and their
means.
        Along with the tractor, farmers began using new
implements to work the soil (ploughs with 2, 3 or 4 plough
shares). The authors of Une France sans Paysans (1965)
estimate that the utilization of 200,000 tractors has
reduced the draft animal population by 2,000,000 and has
allowed agriculture to reclaim 2,500,000 hectares, an
eighth of the arable land. Other agricultural machines,
e.g. the combine harvester and the press, were also
readily adopted, at an average annual rate of 30% and 12%,
respectively.
        Modernization has also involved the utilization of new
cultivating techniques: regular and appropriate use of
chemical fertilizers; adoption of new plant varieties, in
particular, higher yielding hybrid corn which permits
production north of the Loire and up to the Parisian Basin
(Mendras, 1967). Fodder production, usually considered a
product to be gathered, became a cultivated crop requiring
its special growing techniques. Artificial prairies are
developing and forage cultivation is diversifying. In the
area of animal production, dairying in particular, some
important efforts in breed selection are being made. Most
of the traditional breeds have lost ground to more
productive breeds like the French Frisian Black Foot
(F.F.P.N.) in the mid-1960s and, most recently, the
Holstein. We must also note the development of intensive
production techniques in the areas of poultry, pork, and
beef production. Their requirement for highly technical
methods of production, was a main reason for the

200

transformation of the peasant and for his total integration into the market economy (Lamarche, 1977).

Another consequence of modernization is an accumulation of financial burdens to the degree that the farmer can no longer assume them all himself. He must relinquish his financial autonomy, for, as Table 9.3 shows, his level of indebtedness has increased considerably since 1950. Note the slackening growth rate of indebtedness since 1972 which is in marked contrast to the period 1922-1972.

Table 9.3. Change in the Level of Loans to Farmers
(in millions of new francs)

	1922	1930	1950	1965	1972	1981
Short-term loans	1.26	7.84	1,175	8,040	--	--
Medium-term loans	1.50	6.08	351	14,591	90,000	190,000
Long-term loans	1.73	6.68	76	3,131		

Modernization tends to affect farms whose structures change slowly enough. The record shows a growth in the number of medium-sized farms, a large decrease of small farms, and a slight decrease in large farms (Table 9.4).

It appears that agricultural development in France has occurred most on the medium-sized farms. On the other hand, hired labor has diminished considerably during the same period. There were 2,320,000 hired laborers in 1921, 1,210,000 in 1950, and not more than 190,000 in 1981. Thus, the "industrialization" of agriculture is based on an exclusively family labor force; it has not needed a working class as did nonagricultural and quasi-agricultural industrialization. G. Postel Vinay (1974) has studied the evolution of capitalist agriculture in the Soissonnais (north of the Parisian Basin). He clearly shows that even on large farms the number of hired laborers declined as it did elsewhere in agriculture. For example, between 1927 and 1931 for every 100 hectares, there were 12.2 man work units (M.W.U.); this figure dropped to 10 M.W.U. between 1936 and 1950 and 4.2 M.W.U. in 1967 and 1968.

Table 9.4.   Distribution of Farms According to Their
             Hectares of Usable Agricultural Surface
             (S.A.U.)

	1892	1955	1970	% Change 1892-1970
Less than 5 hectares	4,064,000	800,000	422,000	-90
5 to 20 hectares	1,217,000	1,013,000	606,000	-50
20 to 50 hectares	335,000	377,000	394,000	18
50 to 100 hectares	52,000	75,000	101,000	94
More than 100 hectares	33,000	20,000	30,000	-10

Source: Annuaire statistique de la France, 1975.

In spite of all of these transformations, the farmer's relation to the land changed little. Between 1955 and 1970, the percentage of cultivated land owned did not change, representing a little over half of the usable agricultural surface. In contrast, the number of farmers who directly owned their holdings declined by 12% and the number of tenants decreased 6% between 1955 and 1970. The tendency seems to be oriented toward the practice of combined ownership and tenancy where the farmer is proprietor on a portion of his farm and a tenant manages the other portion. This slow evolution reveals the farmer's strong attachment to ownership of the land. Despite the financial restrictions it represents, he always attempts to preserve and reproduce this right to property that he has struggled for over a century to achieve.

The "Success"

The primary consequence of all of the technological transformations that we have mentioned is the agricultural yields and their substantial growth in every sector of production. In half a century, the average yields of wheat quadrupled, those of corn and milk tripled.

Agricultural production began to grow in the 1930s, but the real growth began after 1950. Cereal production increased at an annual rate of 8%, meat at 7%, and milk at 5% between 1949 and 1974.

This change in agricultural production, generally very positive, has permitted a large growth in the agro-food industry (I.A.A.). Although unevenly distributed across sectors, the growth of I.A.A., nevertheless, achieved record rates. The production of livestock foods grew an average of 132% between 1949 and 1973, while pasta production increased only 2%, sugar industry 9%, and canned goods 300% per year. For example, consider the case of a food processor of Morbihan (Lamarche, 1977): a small miller in 1950, he concentrated his efforts on manufacturing animal foods and based his development on intensive techniques of poultry production which were very common at the time in this region. Starting with nearly no turnover in 1950, this industrialist achieved an annual turnover of 400 million Francs in 1970 and found himself at the head of a small multinational corporation with factories throughout France, Belgium, Spain, North Africa, and South America.

Despite this growth, France has only begun to balance her agricultural trade since the 1970s. French society was in full expansion, the standard of living improved considerably, and agriculture had to first satisfy the new

Table 9.5. Change in Average Yields

	1937	1950	1960	1970	1982
Wheat (Quintals/hectare)*	15	15	22	35	53
Corn (Quintals/hectare)	15	12.4	34	51	52
Milk (Liters/Cow)	1600	1800	2100	3098	4731

* One quintal is equivalent to 100 kilograms.
Source: Ministere de l'Agriculture, Statistique Agricole.

Table 9.6. Change in production of meat and cereals (in hundred millions of kilograms)

	1905-1914	1920-1924	1935-1938	1949	1955	1974
Cereals	154	130	139	136	180	405
Meat	15	14	17	18	25	51

Source: Ministere de l'Agriculture, Statistique agricole.

internal food needs. The real leap forward only began in 1975 when France became a producer of surplus agricultural products and entered the group of agricultural exporting countries.

The "success" can also be observed at the level of family farms. Considered as a whole, the peasants have become agriculturalists for which the principle objective is to produce, sell, and acquire the best income from their farm. This availability of a monetary income, as for all French households, has allowed full access of agricultural households to the consumption society. Table 9.7 shows that agricultural households have very quickly made up for their delay in the consumption of durable goods.

This evolution signifies profound transformations which had disrupted the peasantry from 1950 to 1970. The traditional system of values has been overturned; the former values are questioned, and others appear.

First of all, the change concerns the relation to the land which represents the coordinated system of values. The land, this "beneficent being," fertile foster-mother and reservoir of knowledge, cradle of peasant traditions, progressively becomes a tool of labor, a simple site of production. The mere fact that the idea of the G.A.E.C.[1] is accepted (the idea that a farm may not always be solely a family enterprise), and acceptance of the idea that ownership of the land can be collective (G.F.A.),[2] shows that the relation to the land is in the process of changing.[3] Likewise, the acceptance of consolidation, modifying the landscape, the arrangement of holdings, and exchanging plots of land for commercial reasons, implies a certain detachment with respect to the landed family patrimony.

Table 9.7. Percent of Households with Selected Durable
Consumption Goods

	Agricultural Households				All Households			
	1953	1957	1970	1981	1953	1957	1970	1981
Auto	29	--	73	89	21	--	58	70
Refrigerator	--	6	75	95	--	17	80	95
Washing Machine	--	11	63	92	--	18	57	81
Television	--	1	57	90	--	6	70	91
Dishwasher	--	--	1	19	--	--	2	17
Freezer	--	--	32	74	--	--	7	29

This evolutionary trend in the relationship to the
land is accompanied by many other transformations, all
just as important and in very diverse areas, such as:
agricultural production, the family, the relation to
money, social and cultural life and the notions of space
and time.

Regular participation at local fairs and markets, the
legendary ritual of the sale of a product between the
peasant and his merchant, were frequent factors of local
sociability. Their disappearance testifies to the change
in the relationship between the peasant and his
production. The finished product is no more than
standardized merchandise with a fixed price, often already
established by collective agreement. To valorize his
product in order to obtain the best price, or to be proud,
as the artisan before his masterpiece, no longer has any
meaning. Of what importance is quality if one has the
quantity?

The peasant's complete participation in the market
economy and his mutation into a producer/consumer also
modifies his relationship to money. This latter aspect
takes an essential place in the new system of values. It
is necessary to earn money, more and more money, in order
to buy--to buy for the farm, but also for the house and

the family. Money becomes the necessary bias that each farmer must accept if he wants to improve his social condition or just simply maintain it. It then plays a determining role in the decisions and behavior of farmers and, therefore, in the possibilities for the reproduction of various social strata.

From the family's point of view, their transformations are equally important. Without taking into account family migration, which is occuring and even accelerating in certain regions, many changes are bringing about new forms of family realtions - separation of generations under the same roof and eating from the same pot, cohabitation of young couples, emancipation of farm women from their situation as "slaves" as they generally were in the traditional family farm, and abandoning the old family house for a new house without history. It is also necessary to mention the accentuation of father-son conflicts. Certainly these conflicts have always been in existence and they will continue in the future. However, during this period, conflict between generations took on a completely new dimension. It is also a reflection of the opposition between two systems of values - one which remains traditional and turns in on itself, the other requires a much greater openness to the entire society.

The result of all of these changes is a substantial transformation in the traditional notions of space and time which typified the peasant way of life. The farmer "no longer has the time" (strict schedules of production, increasing technical constraints, diversification of tasks and responsibilities). He runs without stop from his farm to the cooperative, from the cooperative to the D.D.A. (Direction Departmentale de l'Agriculture), from the D.D.A. to the credit office, etc. He must be everywhere as well as on his farm. The wise peasant with a slow gait becomes an "active" man, a man under pressure and anxious. Furthermore, traditional space expands with the development of the personal automobile and the popularization of the media (radios, television, and the press).

A new system of representation is put in place composed of values which are not at all inherited and do not come from local cultural traditions. Instead, they are values which come "from above," from the broader society. Adherence by the majority of peasants to this new system of values will help them adapt more easily because the image of the peasantry at the societal level is denigrated. The peasant is a "plouc," a "cul terreux," a

206

"pecnot," a "ventr'a-choux," a "bouseux."[4] We are very far from the eternal order of the fields. All this ended in a profound transformation of relationships to the work, to another way of conceiving "the craft." These workers of the land, still called "peasants," are becoming or are trying to become "agriculturists." They could also be labeled true small family entrepreneurs. Presented in this way, the balance of these 20 years of agricultural development appears largely positive. The industrialists have benefitted from it. The peasants are satisfied with becoming technicians and true businessmen and they feel themselves, as such, somewhat rehabilitated in the eyes of the urban and industrial world. Finally, the State has attained its objective: not only does agriculture feed France, but it clearly contributes by its exports to decreasing the deficit in foreign trade. But any new scene has its other side, and here the "success" is not achieved without pains and without resulting in a different social strata of family farms.

The Consequences of the Success

Since the end of the 1950s, crises of overproduction constantly appeared. Poultry, milk, pork, wine, fruits, and vegetables became each in their turn the sectors in crisis. Thanks to the modernization that we have noted, production very rapidly surpassed needs. And even more importantly than for all other products, agricultural production must be planned and the market controlled because demand is not elastic as it is for the majority of manufactured products. One can eat better and eat a variety of foods but it is very difficult to eat more. The only solution then is to sell elsewhere, to export. This poses the problems of competition. Let us note that the crisis of overproduction concerns, above all, the family farms, which are for the most part in diversified farming. The "large" cereal and beet growers quickly learned to organize themselves, to be in control of production (establishing quotas for production), and create organizations to regulate the market.

The direct consequence of overproduction is that market prices are unstable and, in a general way, have tended to decline. At a time when agriculture was making enormous efforts to restructure itself, and must continue to do so if it wishes to remain competitive, the uncertainty of agricultural prices began to create a malaise and to contribute to growing doubt among many farm families. Their situation began to progressively deteriorate as the costs of production continued to increase.

Table 9.8. Change in Agricultural Production, Agricultural Inputs and Income to Labor, 1955-1971 (in millions of constant Francs)

	1955	1971	Percent Change
Agricultural Production	24,500	37,183	51.8
Industrial Consumption by Agriculture	4,800	16,455	242.8
Remuneration of Labor	19,640	20,728	5.0

The remuneration of labor in agriculture hasn't grown more than 0.3% per year between 1955 and 1971. The result is a regular decline in agricultural incomes at a time when incomes in all other sectors clearly grew. The agricultural income declined despite constant and growing State budgetary support. This support has grown by 240% between 1960 and 1968. Elsewhere the expenditures did not grow more than 120% and the national product increased only 100%. Despite this, the price of steak remains expensive for the average Frenchman. However, if one were to calculate its exact costs of production, including remuneration of the labor of the farmer at the rate of the S.M.I.G. (Guaranteed Interprofessional Minimum Salary), its price would be at least twice as high. Only a structure like the family farm, in which one counts neither effort nor time, is capable of accepting such overexploitation of labor. Any laborer, any other trade association would not accept these conditions of labor during this period of full growth.

There have been many reactions and at times very dramatic ones. Numerous demonstrations and revolts have periodically succeeded one another since 1960: dumping cauliflower in the courtyard of the local courthouse; emptying tanks of wine or milk on the highway; throwing tons of apples into the public dump, etc. A tension, growing more and more serious, appears in the relations between the producers, the industrialists and the State. For various reasons, including the fact that agriculture must be protected because its votes count and it contributes to maintaining the current power structure,[5] this situation of permanent crisis could not continue. It was necessary to find solutions.

Two complementary actions were taken together. The first occurred at the international market level. It was a question of having a competitive agriculture, in order to avoid foreign competition on the national market,[6] and to conquer new international markets. It involved a standardization of production (quality and consistency) and production requirements even more constraining for the financial and technical structure.[7] This entailed the establishment of more rigid production norms, putting a strong hand in family farmer's business, either by practicing differential calculus of prices or by imposing production contracts. Some people cried out at the scandal of these practices, considering them an attack on their freedom as independent producers; they also spoke of the proletarianization of the farmers. Certainly, this phase in the development of capitalism in agriculture profoundly modified the nature of the agricultural craft. Nevertheless, it did not challenge the elements essential to the family farm; namely, family ownership of the means of production and family labor. It was on this very characteristic aspect of the family farm, this very strong attachment to individual ownership and to the family enterprise, that a second action was based.

Since the second half of the 1960s, a clear movement toward the concentration of the means of production emerged throughout France. This concentration was approved by all: the public powers and the firms which saw this movement as the best way of maintaining the farmer's income and, thus, avoid a crisis; by the professional agricultural organizations which advocated formation of dynamic, competitive farmers at the head of small, viable agricultural production enterprises; by the farmers themselves who sought to integrate themselves into French society as businessmen and to improve their status. This consensus brought about, on the one hand, the creation of an elite group of producers still made up of family farmers; and, on the other hand, encouraged the marginalization of other farmers, all those who were at the head of archaic production structures and poorly adapted to the new requirements of production.

This elite proved to be completely capable, thanks to

the use of increasingly sophisticated technology, and responding to the needs of the society. Gunther Thiede (1976), made several predictions based on a study which he conducted in various European centers for agronomic research. He promised, "that the agricultural revolution is going to continue at a brisk pace" and that "by tomorrow, five or ten years, a cow will produce three times more milk, a field will give two times more grain, a pig or a calf will grow two times more quickly, etc..." What good is it to maintain so many farmers who cost more and more? In 1970, the growth in agricultural production no longer required a large mass of farmers as was the case 20 years earlier. And wouldn't it be better to have a few farmers well provided for than to have many unhappy farmers? Such are the reasons for the concentration. In 1963, 74% of all farmers produced 60.5% of all agricultural production; in 1970, they produced no more than 35%.

Besides, the marginalization of the least well-structured farmers (their nonreproduction – disappearance at the end of the current farmer's activity), did not pose problems. It was also necessary for the industrial development of the larger society, which still needed labor power. Between 1955 and 1963, the rate of disappearance of family farms averaged 2.28% per year; it increased to 2.89% from 1963-67 and to 3% between 1967 and 1975.

This evolution was also the result of a national and European agricultural policy[8] tied to a realization that European agriculture had reached a socioeconomic impasse. In 1968, Sicco Mansholt, responsible for the Agricultural Common Market, submitted a brutal plan of reform to the different governments. Observing a stabilization in food consumption and a growth of expenditures designed to support agriculture, he proposed that measures that would force one of every two farmers[9] to leave the profession. The land, thus freed, would permit those who remained to acquire viable structures of production (120 hectares for cereal production, 40 to 60 milking cows and 150 to 200 head of cattle) and to produce competitive merchandise. The Mansholt Plan was coldly received by the French government. But some months later, the report of the Vedel Commission[10] was made public and aroused strong feelings in professional circles because the measures that it proposed went further than those advanced by Sicco Mansholt. This report confirmed the necessity of a massive decrease in the number of farms (2 of 3); it recommended, moreover, the "freezing" of 11 million hectares (a third of the agricultural area is use) made available by the departure of a million farmers. The recommendations of this report were very quickly rejected because this report was published in a pre-electoral period.[11] The authorities tried to reassure the professional milieu, and oppose any measures that ran counter to established ideas of land tenure (stabilization and not concentration). One observes here the difficulty in French society to establish a coherent agricultural policy on the economic, social, and political levels all at the same time.

Despite resistance and reticence, linked to the specific place of agriculture in French society, it is necessary to accept that the recent change tends to destroy the group of family farmers, to break them up in order to preserve only the "best," which will be 300,000 family farmers representing between 3-4% of the active French population. Thus, in order to assure its development, the industrialization of French agriculture was based on a large mass of small- and medium-sized family farmers, while logically the capitalist system required the concentration of the means of production and the formation of a new social strata of family farmers, more businessman than peasant.

THE FAMILY FARM: 1984

Since the mid-1970s, agriculture can no longer be analyzed in the same terms. There are various reasons, but three appear to stand out because they significantly modify the framework in which the future of the family farm must be considered.

1. The development of rural industry. This development generally comes from the growth of industrial agriculture, sometimes from artisanal enterprises. It involves the appearance of new social groups in local society, made up of officials, workers, and employees. One witnesses a rediversification of the local social structure and with it a notable decline of farmer "hegemony" in rural societies. Therefore, the place and the role of the family farm can no longer be considered only within the framework of its relationship to agricultural production, but must be considered in a much broader framework.

2. The dominant neo-ruralist ideology. This ideology

revalues nature, country life and farming as being of
urban origin, in tune with the ideas voiced in May, 1968.
After a delay of some years, it penetrated the countryside
and sensitized everyone, particularly the young farmers.
We will not enlarge upon the nature of this ideology (Avec
nos sabots ... La campagne revee et convoitee, 1978). We
should remember, nevertheless, that it again challenges
"productivism" and the system of representation which
accompanies it, the consumption society and its waste, and
that it rejects the large, the gigantic, the modern, and
advocates the rediscovery of the small, the local, and the
traditional. Such a change of views may not completely
overturn the modern value system of the farmers, but will
cause breaches and new horizons in the previous method of
functioning.

3. The crisis and the unemployment which results. In
the preceding period, we have shown that the global
system's logic of functioning brought with it the creation
of an agricultural elite and the disappearance (exodus) of
the majority of family farmers. Today, the growth of
industrial unemployment makes the exodus toward the city a
great deal more difficult. In fact, it is no longer
conceivable for the State to defend a policy of
development based on the permanent exodus of a part of the
population. Furthermore, the parents, small marginalized
farmers, are no longer looking for ways to build their
children's future social identity outside of agriculture.

Considering this new environment, we observe an
unquestionable challenge to the dominant model of
"productivist" functioning and new possibilities of
development for marginalized farmers.

A Challenge to the "Productivist" Logic

Some of the most structured farmers, the elite,
challenge the systematic modernization and giantism in
agricultural production. This challenge does not imply
their rejection of the capitalist economic system and its
way of life. These farmers are very skilled in modern
bookkeeping as well as production techniques. They
calculate the "quality-price" relationship - the quality
of their income in relation to its cost. They deduce that
beyond a certain threshold, this relationship becomes
negative. At that point it is, therefore, no longer
necessary for them to expand, but simply to maintain
themselves. Some of these farmers extend their

challenge. They not only consider the economic perspective; above that, they dispute the system of values constructed on modernist and productivist ideology. They reject the nature of the work, the rhythms, the noise, the worries, for the benefits related to quality of life. Of course, the majority of modern farmers remain faithful to the productivist ideology and continue efforts to restructure their enterprises.

The problem differs for marginalized farmers. As we have already mentioned, they must find solutions to their agricultural marginalization and to obtain an "acceptable income." It is a question of their survival. In contrast to the preceding group who concern themselves with choices surrounding their way of life, this group struggles for its preservation and maintenance.

The solutions are very diverse and always imply a more or less profound transformation of the value system. Some farmers have found solutions within the framework of agricultural production relations. Here they are "organic" or "biological" farmers, and farmers who produce for very special markets: quality products, plants for medicinal or perfume purposes, and other special commodities. The most common solution is multiple job holding or part-time farming (Lamarche, 1984). Its importance varies according to the possibilities for local employment. The agro-food industry, nearby industry, and tourism are all potential sources of employment.

We now find peasant workers, peasant-artisans or shopkeepers, and peasant innkeepers. Another segment of small farmers maintain themselves through their "handiwork." This system of "making ends meet" permits these farmers with few material requirements to live. They generally combine agricultural production centered on family self-sufficiency with more renumerative activities which vary by what the region has to offer. This may include gathering and selling of mushrooms or whortleberries, selling big game (wild boar and deer), irregular part-time employment (upkeep of roads, paths and forests), or occasional small jobs for large agriculturalists, artisans, or for small local entrepreneurs.

All of these "solutions" yield results which the latest national statistics verify. They point to a slowdown in the rate of disappearance of family farms. This rate was 2% per year between 1975 and 1981 and averaged 3% between 1965 and 1975.

Establishing an Agriculture with Two Gears
===

In making an effort at synthesis, one observes that two models are functioning in French agriculture today. One is productivist. It has dominated the rural world since the war up until the 1970s. It has permitted the agricultural economy to develop for the past 30 years and continues to assure the necessary growth of the national economy. The other model participates in production, but is not productivist. In spite of a clear revival of certain values from the past and the locality, this model is not a return to traditional agriculture. It is based on a system of totally different values and actually opposes the productivist model. The values advocated by the productivist model (profit, consumption, "careerism"), are opposed to the nonproductivist model (time for living, an economy of the necessary and of the indispensable, the search for a certain quality of life). Farmers who adhere to this nonproductivist model do not systematically reject all material values, but they do not live solely for them.

This statement brings us to the thesis advanced by J. Huber (1979) on the dual economy. Like him, we observe the birth of another socioeconomic model. Also like him, we provide a similar explanation for it: the reaction to the dominant system. But the real question is: What is the significance of this movement? Here we cannot associate ourselves with the visions of the author which foresee the establishment of a self-managed system in reaction to the centralizing system.

One can offer many meanings for this movement which remain mere working hypotheses in current research.

1. This movement is only a phenomenon of regulation of the crisis. We are forced to accept the fact that a new model of functioning has developed just in time to satisfy the current crisis. It stabilizes the population with less expense. But nothing at the moment permits us to prove this hypothesis and to claim that it is only an epiphenomenon which will disappear when the crisis is past. If all of the new social strata defined by the various models are capable of reproducing and if the multiple job holding farmers, for example, are organized and determined to be a true social strata, then we can consider the current movement more than a simple regulating phenomenon.

2. This movement is the sign of a new phase in the development of capitalism. This will be the case if the alternative model moves into a preponderant place and

questions the domination of the productivist model. We do not believe the "dual society" will be an outcome; rather, it is only a necessary stage between two phases of development.

The fact remains that whatever the significance of this movement, the family farm will play an essential role, either as the ideal structure for the regulation of the crisis, or as the privileged place for the elaboration of new models of development.

NOTES

1. Agricultural Group for Communal Farming. This structure of production was created in 1962 in order to encourage the reorganization of small- and medium-sized farms and thus improve the structures of production. In 1970, there were 2,190 G.A.E.C. in France, in 1982 there were 24,500. It should be noted that 63 % of the cultivated land in G.A.E.C. are in tenant farming. (Source: Ministere de l'Agriculture, Graph Agri 84).
2. Agricultural Land Group. It was created in 1971 as an alternative to individual agricultural land ownership. In 1979, there were 4,080 G.F.A. on 150,000 hectares (0.5% of the useable agricultural surface).
3. Nevertheless, it changes very slowly because all of these measures of reorganization of the land tenure structure have been salvaged and used within the family structure. A good number of G.A.E.C. are father-son associations and nearly all of the G.F.A. (4,000 of 4,080) are family.
4. Translator's note: These stereotypic terms are not directly translatable, but are similar to hick, hillbilly, sodbuster, yokel, country bumpkin, etc.
5. The majority of farmers vote for the right and the results of elections between the right and the left are very close. Therefore, farmers have an important role.
6. The objective was to avoid crises like that of 1963 provoked by the invasion of American poultry production on the European market.
7. Let us note that France profited from the creation of the Common Market which can be considered as a protected market with respect to nonmember countries of the E.E.C.
8. Numerous measures were being established in order to foster farm restructuring through concentration: obtaining credits and subsidies for structures with

215

certain minimums of production, compensation for early
retirement from the land at two rates according to whether
the pensioner yields his land to a small or medium-sized
farmer, etc.
9. France, given the state of its production structures,
was particularly threatened by the measures of the
Mansholt Plan. It was estimated that about 500,000
farmers were all that was necessary and therefore two out
of three must disappear.
10. This commission was established in 1967 by Mr. Edgar
Faure, then Minister of Agriculture.
11. Presidential elections of 1969.

REFERENCES

"Avec nos sabots ... la campagne revee et convoitee", Revue
Autrement, dossier no. 14, 1978, p. 244.

Chevalier, Louis. 1947. Les Paysans, Ed. Denoel, Paris.

Desert, G. 1977. l'Histoire de la France Rurale, Vol.
III, Ed. du Senil, Paris.

Gervais, M. and M. Tavernier. 1977. L'Histoire de la
France Rurale, Vol. IV, ed. duc Seuil, Paris.

Huber, J. 1979. "Autogestion et economie duale" in
Futuribles, No. 24, Juin, p. 53.

Lamarche, H. 1984. "La pluriactivite agricole: une
solution pour les agriculteurs marginalises?" in La
pluriactivite dans les familles agricoles, Ed. A.R.F.,
p. 343.

Lamarche, H. 1977. "Les paysans face au marche", in
Sociologie du Travail, Ed. du seuil, No. 2/77, pp.
138-159.

Mendras, H. 1967. "La fin des Paysans", Ed. Actes Sud,
Arles, 1st Ed. in 1967, aux Ed. Paris.

Thiede, Gunther. 1976. "Capacite de l'agriculture
europeenne et son avenir", in Economie Rurale, No.
116, Paris.

Une France sans paysans. 1965. Aux edit. du Seuil, Paris.

Vinay, G. Postel. 1974. "La rente fonciere dans le
capitalisme agricole", Ed. Maspero, Paris.

10
Family Farming in Poland

Boguslaw Galeski

Polish agriculture accounted for about 15% of the Gross National Product and engaged 28% of the total labor force (16.5 million) in 1980. This proportion is higher than in any other European country with the exception of Albania, Yugoslavia, Turkey, Greece, and Rumania. The conditions of agricultural production are relatively unfavorable in Poland compared to other European countries. The growing season is short (about 180 days), most of the arable soils are sandy, and 60% of them are acidic. Yields[1] of major crops are lower than the average for Europe (Poland's wheat yield is 2.96 metric tons per ha. while the average for Europe is 3.60) and lower than other Eastern European countries (3.48 metric tons per ha.). Only for potato production (18.85 metric tons per ha.) and sugar beet production (33.79 metric tons per ha.) does Poland show higher Yields than other Eastern European countries (corresponding figures: 16.38 and 30.05). Average yields in Europe for these two crops are 20.38 metric tons per ha. and 42.41 metric tons per ha.

For pork production yields per animal are higher in Poland (85 kg. per animal) than the average for Europe (81 kg.). Beef and veal production is lower in Poland than in Europe (130 kg. in Poland, 220 kg. in Europe, and 185 kg. in other Eastern European countries). This is also the case with milk production (in Poland 2.662 per cow, in Europe 3.512, and in other East European countries 2.660). Poland has good results producing mutton and lamb, and poultry and chicken eggs, showing higher yields than Europe and other East European countries. Lower yields of major crops could be explained, besides unfavorable natural conditions, by insufficient use of chemical fertilizers (in Poland 192.0 kg. nitrogen, phosphorus, and potassium per ha. while the German Democratic Republic, with similar natural conditions used 272.2 kg. per ha.).

Poland is fairly self-sufficient in production of some basic food commodities like roots and tubers, meat, milk, eggs, vegetables, fruits and poultry, even exporting small quantities of surplus meat and poultry, ham, bacon, eggs, fruits, fish, and sugar. Export of food (products of agriculture and of the food industry as a whole) has been an important part of total exports, ranging from nearly 20% in 1960 (in current prices), to 15% in 1970, but only 7.7% in 1980. This decline is not only relative, indicating the increasing role of industry (exports go mostly to the Soviet Union and developing countries) and coal mining, it is also evident in absolute figures. In 1985 Poland exported 121,000 tons of meat and poultry and 84,600 tons of ham and bacon. In 1980 the corresponding figures were 80,300 tons and 77,600 tons. Imports of processed food and agricultural products declined also from 23.7% of the total imports in 1960 (in current prices) to 12.5% in 1970; but in 1980 this percentage rose to 15%. Since 1960 Poland has been importing increasing quantities of wheat, barley and corn. In 1960 Poland imported nearly 2 million tons of these grains, 2.5 million tons in 1970 and more than 7 million tons in 1980 (Statistical Yearbook, 1981). The reason for this increase is the low productivity of Polish agriculture, particularly socialized agriculture, which is not corresponding to a fast growing urban population. If the yields of Poland's major crops increased to the level of yields in the German Democratic Republic, Poland would not have to import cereals. After 1981, because of a financial crisis and U.S. embargo, imports of cereals declined about 40%. Consequently, livestock production went down about 15% between 1980 and 1982 (in the poultry industry the decline was 56%). Very good yields in 1983 and 1984 helped improve the situation. In fact, Poland raised its traditional export of ham and bacon; but the shortages in the internal consumer market did not diminish, and basic food is still rationed.

THE STRUCTURE OF POLISH AGRICULTURE

Polish agriculture, being predominantly private, is an exception within the Soviet block. Table 10.1 indicates the relative weight of different sectors. The organizational forms of agricultural production in Poland need some explanation.

The category of State farms includes all farms operated by State agencies. Most of them are run by the Ministry of Agriculture (84% of land cultivated by all State farms), but some are under management of other governmental agencies i.e., the army, industrial plants, etc. The area cultivated by State farms is smaller than the total cultivated area owned by the State. Each year the State increases its land holdings an average of 800,000-900,000 ha. This land is partly composed of private farms which had no successors or of land given to the State Land Fund in exchange for pension. Each year the State disposes of some land for nonfarm uses, and some land is rented. In the past, particularly after 1974, the land was often given to agricultural circles (more precisely to "cooperatives of agricultural circles"). In 1980, as a consequence of the emergence of the "Solidarity" movement and its pressure on government, private farms received most of this land for temporary use. In the way of structure of ownership, private farms owned 68.4% of cultivated land in 1980; the remaining land was owned by State farms, collective farms, and agricultural circles or was rented by the State to different users.

State farms are organized into 947 main units or enterprises comprising 2099 smaller units or farms. The average size of an enterprise is 4452 ha. and 2011 ha. on the smaller units. The personnel on State farms numbers 490,300 employees, which breaks down to 13.3 persons per 100 ha. For comparison, East German agriculture employs 12.4 persons per ha.; in West Germany the figure is 8.5). The majority of State farm personnel are land workers (365,600), technicians (27,000), and administrators (25,000). Another large portion is permanently engaged in construction and repairs (47,600).

As an organizational unit, the State farm is similar to any industrial organization. There are managers, specialists, and skilled and unskilled workers. Members of the same family may be employed by the same state farm, but in contrast to private farms and collective farms, the family is not the basic unit of work. State farms receive production and other economic tasks (orders) from the Ministry of Agriculture. Their input also comes from the State and the output belongs to the State. Until 1980 the units (enterprises/farms) had no basic decision making responsibility. Decisions about what to produce,

Table 10.1 The Structure of Polish Agriculture in 1980

Share in %	State Farms	Collective Farms	Agricultural Circles	Socialized Agriculture Together	Private
Cultivated land[a]	19.5	4.0	1.4	25.5	74.5
Gross fixed assets	22.6	4.9	5.5	40.2[b]	59.8
buildings total	21.2	4.6	2.4	35.7[c]	64.3
dwellings	11.5	1.5	0.4	14.0[d]	86.0
mechanical equipment	28.8	6.1	18.0	57.9[e]	42.1
Fertilizers supply in NPK per ha	323.2	280.1	280.0	--	154.2
Fodder supply in metric tons/animal	0.6	1.7	1.9	--	0.4
Labor force in ag.	12.0	4.4	5.1	26.4[f]	73.6
Total ag production	17.9	4.4	1.0	23.3	76.7
value per ha in zl	27849	33404	19837	28273	31223
value per 1 th zl of input	1069	1077	685	1047	1569

a. Total agricultural land 19,101, 8th ha
   18,946, 9th ha
   Cultivated land
b. Includes state agencies for productive services 7.8%
c. Includes state agencies for productive services 7.5%
d. Includes state agencies for productive services 0.6%
e. Includes state agencies for productive services 5.0%
f. Includes state agencies for productive services 4.9%

Source: Statistical Yearbook, 1981 Warszawa

what inputs to use, how much labor to hire, where to sell the output, were all made by the higher authorities in the Ministry of Agriculture, not by farm management. The manager's task was simply to organize and supervise personnel for fulfillment of the plan. Several incentives were introduced -- rewards for fulfilling working quotas or for fulfilling the plan. Low productivity and efficiency, using any meaning of these terms, on the State farms must be attributed to the system of centrally planned and administered economy. The resources --land (soil quality is usually better than average), assets, and labor -- could hardly be used in an optimal way by decision makers not familiar with local conditions. Also, there are no economic criteria to assess the productive activity since all prices are decided by the State and there is no relation to the market.

In a market economy some of the State farms would probably go bankrupt, particularly those operating in unfavorable conditions, such as an area divided into hundreds of small plots because of the irrigation system, for example. Other State farms, if operating within a discipline imposed by the market, would use their resources more thoughtfully and efficiently. Since 1982 the changes in the organizational system of State farming are moving in this direction, and the farm management is becoming more independent in production decision making.

General conditions are, however, not favorable. The market is still administratively restricted (food is rationed) and partially speculative as a result. There are not incentives in this case to increase production or to reduce the costs of production.

Collective farms play a marginal role in Poland. After the failure of collectivization of agriculture in 1956, the number of collective farms in Poland dropped from 10,000 to 1,100 and later fluctuated between 1,000 and 2,500. In 1980 there were 2,399 collective farms with 172,000 members (about 72 members per farm). An average farm cultivates 364.2 ha. Usually two or more members of the same family are engaged in the same collective farm. Between 20 and 30 families are usually associated with an average collective farm. The collective farm may be regarded as a symbiosis of family farming and large-scale, nonfamily farming. Each family cultivates its own small plot (about 0.5 ha.) and raises some livestock (sows, piglets, hogs, cows, calves, poultry, etc.). The collective farm, therefore, may be regarded as a multifamily farm. Families use part of their land to cultivate crops which can later be used as fodder for animals raised on individual plots. But collective farms can also take a form similar to State farms if they produce cash crops or raise animals for market. From this point of view collective farms are fairly differentiated. Within them are opposing tendencies -- one to diminish the role of individual plots and in this way make members more dependent on collective farms for their income; a second tendency is to subordinate the collective farm to the need of private plots, for instance producing fodder to feed animals on private plots. The first tendency is represented by specialists and managers on collective farms and opposes the tendency of members to subordinate the collective farm to the interest of families and their mini-family farms.

These oppositions are not strong in Poland, however. The majority of members of collective farms did not get their start as independent farmers, but were former laborers on large manorial estates. After land reform they had much difficulty starting individual farming, due to lack of capital and experience, and often preferred to keep the estate in one unit as it was. Specialists who joined them as managers also wanted to keep the farm together as one organizational unit. During the political crisis in 1956, members of some collective farms were either unable or didn't want to start individual farming when this opportunity again arose. This marginal group is very particular in its social and cultural characteristics. Socially they will not identify themselves as peasants or farmers at all, but rather as workers.

Relative to State farms, collective farms in Poland have much more independence in productive decision making. The plan of production is prepared by their managers or specialists and not by central authorities in the Ministry of Agriculture. They are also more independent in selling products to markets other than to the State. Production per hectare on collective farms is higher than either State or private farms, and average income of members is much higher than that of State farm workers or private farmers. They are also granted more privileges than private farmers -- better supply of inputs, credit or subsidy terms, more lenient and lower taxes, higher pensions, and free medical insurance. The standard of living on collective farms is higher and the working conditions better. The production, however, is much lower than on private farms if measured by value of production per unit of input. In other words, they do not use resources as efficiently as private farmers.

The so-called "cooperatives of agricultural circles" are completely different organizational forms, even much more marginal than collective farms and characterized by extremely inefficient farming. This type of farm was created in 1974 as a result of political decisions to accelerate socialized farming. Agricultural circles had been established earlier in the attempt to introduce collectivization by way of the back door after its failure in 1956. Cooperatives of agricultural circles shared the use of agricultural equipment, tractors, and other machinery. In 1956 tractors were not sold to private farmers. Only agricultural circles could buy them with the help of state subvention, in which funds came from the differences between prices paid to farmers in obligatory deliveries and prices paid to them in so called "free purchase" where prices were by no means established by any market mechanism but were set by the State. The government expected the joint use of tractors under close supervision by State agencies would convince private farmers of the advantages of collective farming. The expected results did not materialize. In 1974 the State (Party) decided to concentrate all mechanized equipment in agricultural circles into a smaller number of localities (approximately on the county level) and organize so-called "cooperatives" of agricultural circles. These cooperatives were strongly subordinated to the State, and farmers lost any influence over the use of tractors. In effect, agricultural circles, deprived of their basic function, lost all significance, although they officially still exist. The new "cooperatives" are free of producer control, whom they are supposed to serve, and are largely engaged in nonagricultural activities (i.e. construction and transportation).

Since 1975 the State Land Fund has been increasingly giving its land to cooperatives of agricultural circles for cultivation. The economic results of this activity are extremely bad, even when compared to State farms. However, political reasons prevent the government from dissolving these "cooperatives" or freeing them from the tasks of cultivating land.

In 1980 there were 1,844 cooperatives of this kind, 889 of them engaged in farming, disposing of about 100,000 tractors which were only partly used for agricultural production. There is no point in speaking about membership, because organization members are officially not farms and members have almost nothing to say in respect to the way it operates. The cooperatives employ a staff of 220,000. Their production is shown in Table 10.1. As private farming in Poland is predominantly family farming, it will be discussed in detail later. It is necessary to say at this point that the term "private" farming may be misleading. Legally, farm families are owners of their land and of other assets used in agricultural production. They are restricted, however, in their rights of ownership and subjected to many regulations. They are not allowed, for instance, to sell land unless given special permission, and the state as priority for buying it. Dividing land among children is restricted, and the inheritor must have prescribed qualities and live on and cultivate the land. They must exchange seed for seed distributed by state agencies, often of poor quality, and are obliged to buy an ascribed amount of fertilizer from the State, usually not corresponding to particular requirements of the farm or it may be delivered in an inappropriate season. The farmer could be expropriated at any time if the authorities decide that the farm is "inefficient."

The State has a nearly total monopoly on markets. The processors and purchasing agencies are part of the State administration or are controlled by it. The prices paid to farmers for their products are decided by the State. The supply and distribution of inputs is controlled by the State as well as prices farmers must pay for inputs and cost of production services. The only products which can be sold also on the free market are vegetables, fruits, and eggs, but a large part of these must be sold to the State, as there is no private wholesale.

Until 1972 there was a system of compulsory deliveries. All farms over 2 ha. had to sell to the State ascribed quantities of crops and livestock (before 1956, also potatoes). After 1972 this system was abolished and replaced by contract production. Farmers cannot refuse to undertake contract production because there is no other organized buyer for their products. Most agricultural inputs (construction material, coal, industrial fodder, fertilizers, plant protection, media) are sold to farmers only if they engage in contract production. In this way, production on private farms and the farmer's level of income is fully controlled by the State, and farmers have a reason to say, "we are not private farmers at all, we are State peasants."

TYPES OF PRIVATE FARMING AND SOCIAL CATEGORIES
OF RURAL POPULATION

There are several reasons why the process of socioeconomic polarization of the rural population which is occurring in many countries with market economies may be described as very weak and practically insignificant in Poland.

The first factor which contributed to the formation of socioeconomic structure of Polish private agriculture after the end of World War II was Land Reform. Farms larger than 50 ha. in Eastern and Central Poland, larger than 100 ha. in Western Poland, and in so called "regained territories" (German territory given to Poland after the World War II) were expropriated. Most German farmers were also expropriated or left the country, abandoning their land. Part of the expropriated land (one-third of the total, but 40-60% in regained territories) was taken into newly organized State farms. The other part, about 6 million ha., was distributed among about 1 million rural families.

The socioeconomic effects of land reform are often exaggerated. First, the settlement in regained territories had to be excluded from proper land reform. The land was given to Polish farming families who lost their farms because of migration from the territories incorporated into the Soviet Union - West Bielorussia, West Ukrania, and Lithuania. It was not so much land reform, but rather a program of enforced migration and settlement. However, the farms given to the new migrants were usually 10-15 ha. in size, which created more medium sized private agriculture than it was before the war, both in territories incorporated into the Soviet Union and in territories gained by Poland (Tepicht, 1983).

The land reform followed movement of the Soviet Army through Polish territories and depended strongly on land and resources in a given region. In Eastern and Central Poland these resources were not very large and land was mostly given to landless families, i.e. former land laborers in large estates. The average size of newly created farms was 3-5 ha., which means that, in this part of Poland, land reform raised the number of small farms. However, these farms were too small to grant full use of labor resources and secure sufficient income for farm families. Only in Western Poland, where land resources were greater and demand for land much lower, were the newly created farms of a larger size, from 10 to 15 ha.

The socioeconomic effects were less substantial than those
published by the government, but in total it is true that
land reform and settlement in new territory strengthened
the category of medium-sized farms. In 1931 families
owning small farms (up to 5 ha.) constituted about 41% of
all farming families. In 1950 this percentage declined to
28%. Families owning medium (5-15 ha.) accounted for in
26% in 1931 and 37% in 1950. In the same period hired
farm workers in private farming declined from 12% to 2%.
These effects were not important in other Eastern European
countries where private agriculture was later forcibly
collectivized. In Poland collectivization failed and, in
effect, land reform contributed to the formation of the
current structure of Polish agriculture.

The second factor contributing to the formation of
this structure was the agricultural policy in the period
of collectivization (1949-1956). The law of land reform
promised to support the development of private farms of up
to 50 ha. and in the western provinces up to 100 ha.
Contrary to this promise, farms larger than 15-20 ha. were
decimated in the period of enforced collectivization and
in the campaign against kulaks. The elimination of
large-sized family farms, to some extent dependent on
hired labor, strengthened the relative weight of
medium-sized farms.

The third factor was industrialization of the country,
which recruited millions of young people from rural
families. The migration to cities between 1946 and 1965
reached 46% of total population increase in rural areas.
This factor, together with the law prohibiting farm
fragmentation introduced in 1960, diminished the pressure
on inheritance. In the past, the lucky one was the one
who inherited the land, particularly if there were no
siblings to share the land or to pay off. Now the lucky
one was the one who left the farm.

A final important factor was the elimination of market
forces from the economic system. Farmers in Poland are
not in market competition. They may become bankrupt from
heavy taxation, which is the way large private farms were
eliminated in 1951-54, or they may be unable to produce
enough when they grow old and their children have left the
farm. Farmers may have a low standard of living due to
poor prices paid them by the State for products or because
of a lack of inputs distributed by the State, but they
can't possibly be ruined by market competition since it
doesn't exist.

Farmers may queue to deliver products to State

agencies, and if they have resources to bribe administrators, some may get better deals than others. The prices are decided by the State, but even the best price does not leave much for accumulation. Lack of a competitive market drastically restricts the desire to enlarge farms, which would be risky anyway because of progressive taxation. In effect, the demand for agricultural land is very low and land prices depend mostly on local conditions. In 1939 73% of money invested by peasants was spent on purchasing land; in 1950 this percentage declined to 3.4%. After 1956 the land market revived, but most land (small parcels usually labeled as nonagricultural land) was sold to urban dwellers for secondary residences, and demand for land to extend agricultural operation remained very low.

The differentiation of private farms according to size, number of livestock, and tractor possession can be seen in Table 10.2. A deeper insight can be gained by looking at the data provided by farmers keeping records. The accounting is done by farmers under guidelines of the Institute of Agricultural Economics (so called "budget" studies). For many reasons, bookkeeping is an exception on private farms. If done at all, it is carried out only by better equipped, productive farmers who surely constitute the occupational elite. From this point of view, the data on equipment and production are not representative of average private farms, especially smaller-sized farms, but do represent farmers who are well off. The classification of farms according to size is slightly different than that used by the Central Statistical Office, and the group with land up to 1 ha. is omitted (Table 10.3).

Comparing Tables 10.2 and 10.3, we may say that the group of smaller-sized farms -- up to 2 or even 3 ha. -- are mostly of a subsistence character. Even in the most productive farms belonging to to this category, nearly 50% of the income comes from off-farm sources. Usually small farmers keep one hog for family consumption; the most productive farmers also raise one or two to sell. Only half of them maintain a cow for milk, but again the more productive usually have a cow and a calf or sometimes two cows to sell milk to the dairy. Very few keep horses or have a tractor which may also be used for work on other farms. As most of the income is consumed, there is not much left for investment or accumulation.

The next size category, 2-5 ha., is more commercially oriented and better endowed with the means of production,

Table 10.2 THE STRUCTURE OF PRIVATE FARMING IN POLAND

(Agriculture Census 1980)

	Total	Farms of Size in ha:					
		0.5-2	2-5	5-7	7-10	10-15	15 and more
Number of farms 2897 = 100%		30.0	29.5	12.8	13.0	9.7	5.0
Cattle per farm	3.2	0.6	2.1	3.6	5.0	7.2	11.1
Hogs	5.2	1.0	2.9	5.6	8.5	12.9	19.2
Sheep	0.9	0.3	0.5	0.7	1.1	1.8	4.9
Horses	0.6	0.1	0.1	0.9	1.1	1.4	1.3
% Farms with Tractor	12.5	4.3	11.9		29.9		53.9

Source: Statistical Yearbook 1981, Warszawa

Table 10.3 THE STRUCTURE OF PRIVATE FARMING IN POLAND

(Farmers Keeping Books/Records)

Total	Farms of Size in ha:				
	1.1-3	3-7	7-10	10-15	15 and more
Number of farms 1617 = 100%	12.7	25.7	23.1	23.8	14.6
Average size in ha 5.7	2.0	4.7	7.7	11.1	17.5
Cattle per farm total 5.0	1.9	4.4	7.1	9.3	13.2
cows 2.6	1.3	2.3	3.5	4.6	6.1
Hogs total per farm 7.9	2.8	6.6	11.1	16.5	19.9
sows 0.8	0.2	0.7	1.2	1.6	2.1
Sheep per farm 1.5	0.4	1.3	1.4	3.0	7.5
Horses per farm 0.7	0.2	0.9	1.1	1.2	1.2
Tractors per farm 0.3	0.1	0.2	0.4	0.6	0.4
Size of family 3.87	3.11	3.83	4.40	4.76	5.13
Total Labor (days/year) per farm 425	285	428	518	578	634
hired labor 6	1	4	8	15	30
Production total in th zl/farm 191.5	86.7	167.7	250.6	348.8	464.6
Fertilizers Kg NPK per ha 206	210	200	210	206	209
Ag income per family in th zl 116.5	53.7	106.0	154.2	205.1	260.2
Total income per farm 146.6	100.0	135.2	177.2	226.0	278.8
Off-farm % of total 21.6	46.3	21.6	12.9	9.2	6.7
total per person 38.4	32.1	35.3	40.3	47.5	54.3
Consumption % of income 75.7	86.6	77.4	71.7	68.0	65.3

Source: Statistical Yearbook 1981, Warszawa

but only above 5 ha. may we speak about marketable production exceeding subsistence level. In this category most farmers have horses or tractors, raise animals for market, and agricultural production is usually the basic source of income.

The most typical family farms in Poland are the 7-10 ha. and 10-15 ha. sizes, possessing enough land and input to be a full-time family operation. Together these two categories represent about 20% of private farms in Poland.

Farms above 15 ha. have some capitalist features (e.g. hiring labor). The average size of the most productive farms belonging to this category is small, however, and hired labor represents only about 5% of the total labor used in the operation, with 95% of the labor coming from family resources.

The total picture of private farming in Poland tells us that it is nearly exclusively family farming. The largest group of families on farms of up to 5 ha. (about 50%) needs off-farm employment to ensure sufficient income, even if the farm is kept on a relatively high production level. The level of agricultural income for other size groups may be regarded as sufficient. However, it is lower than the average income per person in the country (46,100 zl) and only in 1983 increased to the same level or slightly above.

The differentiation between poor and rich farmers does exist, but it has nothing to do with class polarization into semiproletarian and capitalist farmers -- in Russian terminology bjednjaks and kulaks. There were no capitalist farmers in rural Poland in the proper sense, or at least they were not shown in the available census data. From this point of view, studies done in the Institute of Agricultural Economics in 1947-1962 give better insight into the social structure and processes of differentiation of the population in rural areas (see Table 10.4).

The data about rural social structure resulting from investigations done in the same 120 villages selected as a representative sample were last published in 1966. Later studies done by the Institute of Agricultural Economics or by agricultural universities do not indicate any basic change. As indicated in Table 10.4 rural farm families consist of two basic categories, part-time and full-time farmers. Farms belonging to both are essentially family farms -- most of the work is done by the family and production secures family subsistence or is exchanged for

Table 10.4 Rural Social Structure

(Survey of Institute of Agricultural Economics)
Total number of families living in 120
surveyed villages is 15,675.

%

1. Employees in State agriculture: landless   3.3
   families (owning no more than 0.49 ha.),
   main source of income--employment in State
   farms, agricultural machinery stations,
   other productive services, forestry, etc.

2. Rural proletariat: landless familes employed   0.4
   in nonagricultural institutions, mostly in
   construction and industrial plants.

3. Nonagricultural employees: landless families   12.3
   employed in nonagricultural institutions,
   mostly in construction and industrial plants.

4. Rural semiproletariat: families owning more   0.8
   than 0.5 ha. and employed in private farms
   at least 100 days a year.

5. Part-time farmers with main source of income   17.9
   outside private farming: families owning
   more than 0.5 ha. employed off-farm with
   income from this source(s) amounting to
   60% or more of the total production of
   their farm.

6. Part-time farmers with main income from their   16.7
   farms: families owning more than 0.5 ha. the
   external source of income amounts to 10-60%
   of the value of the total production of their
   farms.

7. Full-time farmers: families owning more than   41.8
   0.5 ha. not employed off-farm (income from
   external sources less than 10% of total
   production of the farm) and not hiring workers
   for more than 150 days a year.

(continued)

8. Capitalist farmers: full-time farmers hiring   0.5
    workers for more than 150 days a year.

9. Families: members of collective farms.   0.5

10. Other rural families (pensioners, holders   4.9
    of unattended farms, etc.)

11. Lack of information about sources of income.   0.9

---

money. The family also owns the land and capital. The
difference between these two categories lies in the role
the farm plays as the source of income and consequently in
allocation of family labor resources. Part-time farmers
are found mainly on farms of up to 0.5 ha. (89%) or
0.5-2 ha. (76.9%), but a significant number are also found
on 2-5 ha. farms (57.8%). The number of part-time farmers
increased in the 1970s, and agricultural census data from
1979 shows that 36.9% of the total farm population lives
in households where most income comes from sources other
than their own farm. Another 31.3% live in households
where the income comes mainly from the farm, but other
sources also play a significant role. Only 31.4% of the
farm population live in households where the income is
exclusively from their own farms. A marginal number of
the farm population (0.4%) live in households with income
exclusively from sources other than their own farm.
Estimates show that today about 60% of farms above 0.5 ha.
are part-time farms. Besides the category of farms of up
to 0.5 ha. which became almost totally nonagricultural,
nearly all farms of 0.5-2 ha. are part-time farmers, and
about 75% of the 2-5 ha. size are also part-time farmers.
        Despite the opinion of some economists and State
administrators, part-time farms are generally no less
productive than the average full-time farms of the same
size. The soil quality is usually poor and the family
large. The permanent food shortage in State owned
groceries and a very poor supply of food in small town and
village groceries requires that part of the food produced
on farms be kept for family consumption, especially on
part-time farms, the family size is often large.
Consequently, market production per ha. is lower on
part-time farms than on full-time farms in the same size
category. Otherwise there are no important economic

differences between part-time and full-time farmers --
both attempt to maximize output. Farming may only be a
secondary income for part-time farmers, but it is worth
allocating spare resources of labor and basic savings from
wages to increase output (Dziewicka, 1976).

The second basic group of farmers in Poland, the
full-time family farmers, was shrinking during the 1970s
but still remains the largest group (nearly 41%) in farm
structure. Two marginal groups of farm population --
semiproletarian and capitalist -- are of special
character. In the first group, as in rural proletariat,
we find people in particularly difficult situations (for
example, handicapped, single women with small children).
Such people are not able to work outside the community and
there are few jobs within, except for occasional hired
labor by farmers in peak agriculture seasons. The service
sector of the economy is underdeveloped and in rural areas
largely neglected.

The size of this category (0.5% of all rural families,
nearly 1% of those owning more than 0.5 ha.) did not
increase in the 1970s, and as the rural proletariat group
it remains marginal.

The other group, called "capitalist farmers" by the
Institute of Agricultural Economics, should be included in
the category of family farms. The number of genuine
capitalist farms, those in which hired labor exceeds
family labor, was much lower in 1962 (about 0.1%). In the
1970s the number of capitalist farms grew. Some small
farms (about 2 ha.) specialized in greenhouse vegetable
production, poultry, fur animals, and other commodities.
They are located mostly around large cities, and are often
owned by urban entrepreneurs. Hired labor comes from
urban areas, mostly women from working class families. In
the 1970s some farms of 25 ha. or more specialized in
cattle and hog production for export. In 1979 both groups
certainly did not exceed 4% of the total number of rural
families. The agricultural policy of the last decade
(1970-80) could explain the growth of this group. A
description of this policy will also explain the recent
situation of family farms and indicate the particular
problems they face in the 1980s.

PRIVATE FARMING IN POLAND AND THE AGRICULTURAL
POLICY OF THE STATE

The evolution of the Polish agricultural policy and

its social and economic consequences were described by
many agricultural economists and rural sociologists in
periods when criticism of the past was tolerated, usually
in periods of political crisis -- 1956-57, 1971, and
1980-81. We must say, however, that in all post war
periods the agricultural policy was oriented toward the
same end -- the elimination or replacement of private
farms with the State and collective farms, both totally
controlled by the State (Galeski, 1983). As Table 10.1
shows, if the change had succeeded, the productivity of
Polish agriculture would be lower and the economic crisis
would be much worse than it is today. The persistent
attempts of "the socialist transformation of agriculture"
did not achieve its goal but succeeded in preventing
private farms from developing their potential.

During the period of collectivization (1947-1956), the
agricultural policy served mostly to persuade farmers to
join collective farms. Heavy progressive taxation,
planned grain purchase (in fact, requisition in 1951), and
later the system of obligatory deliveries with quotas for
private farms established at a level three or four times
higher (per ha.) than for collective farms brought farms
of medium and larger sizes close to bankruptcy. Many
joined collective farms to avoid the consequences of
expropriation for not fulfilling quotas. Collectivization
failed, however. The political crisis of 1956 brought a
change in the agricultural policy in order to calm the
anger of the urban population caused by food shortages.

The new agricultural policy in 1957 proclaimed State
support for a rise in production in private farms. The
system of total State control over market, processing, and
trade established earlier was preserved, however, and
further strengthened. Quotas of obligatory deliveries
were reduced to a more realistic level, but prices farmers
received for products were too low to provide incentive to
raise production. Both State and collective farms
maintain priority in acquiring input, and had access to
subventions and credits. A lack of necessary input
prevented private farmers from raising agricultural
production even if they tried to respond to appeals from
the State. The elimination of market incentives prevented
the revival of capitalist farms, and in this way, Polish
agriculture remains predominantly composed of family
farms. The price paid was the stagnation of agriculture,
as well as the whole economy, in the 1960s.

An influx of foreign credit in the 1970s provided an
opportunity for the State to calm the urban consumer

235

without raising the productivity of agriculture. The
system of obligatory deliveries was abolished; in fact, it
was anachronic considering the State's total control over
the agricultural market. Prices paid to farmers were
raised following inflation, but nothing substantially
changed. Imported inputs, investments, and subsidies were
directed at inefficient State farming where they were
wasted for the most part. Attempts to create an elite
group of specialized farmers engaged in production for
export or production of vegetables to some extent revived
capitalist agriculture. Those farms acquired a
speculative character by profiteering on food shortages,
but did not change the situation of the basic food
producers. Attempts were made to extend the cultivated
area into the socialized sector of agriculture, absorbing
the land from unattended farms (most farms with no
successor) in exchange for a pension for the owner. These
efforts reduced private farming but farms lost were not
replaced by producers who were equally efficient in using
the land the agricultural resources.

The military government established in 1981 made
concessions to private farmers again -- better prices and
supply of inputs -- temporarily improving the situation
for this sector and raising the average income of farming
families. The introduction of market incentives to State
farms and the processing industry improved their financial
standing but did not raise their production. The global
economic system did not change, so the State remains in
full control of the economy. Private farms are controlled
through the distribution of agricultural inputs,
exclusively within the system of contract production.
Until now, this new policy has resulted in raising the
exports of agricultural products, but the internal
consumer has not been better supplied with food and the
basic foodstuffs are rationed. For awhile there were no
attempts to impose socialist transformation of
agriculture, but this cannot be expected to continue for
long because external pressure and interests of
administrative supervisors will soon bring this subject
back.

CONCLUSION

Paradoxically, family farming in Poland was preserved
by the economic system of State socialism. The party and
the State were not able, under the prevailing political,

demographic, and cultural conditions, to impose a system of socialized agriculture like in the Soviet Union and other Eastern European countries. The State's centralized control over the economy eliminated market incentives and forces which would inevitably differentiate family farms into large-scale commercial farming and subsistence oriented farming. Although family farming was preserved, it did not develop productive potential because the agricultural policy oriented towards socialization of agriculture deprived private farms of access to necessary inputs while development strategy of industrialization gave priority to heavy industry and deprived agriculture of required investments.

The industrialization strategy has changed small family farms into part-time farms, at the same time causing a rise in the number of unattended farms and a change in the demographic structure. Younger, better educated people left agriculture. Only recently has a new phenomenon appeared. Young, college educated people are now coming back to private farming, but their reasons for farming are essentially not economic. The main reason is the need for independence, for being their own boss, and to live close to nature. Often they ideologically reject the system of State socialism in the Soviet version. This phenomenon is not strong enough to change the structure of Polish agriculture significantly, but it shows a new alternative. The fact in question is, is it possible to preserve family farming with its ecological, social, and cultural advantages and traditional way of life nostalgically missed by many, particularly the younger generation?

It would seem necessary to avoid both the imposition of centralized industrial farming (statization or collectivization of agriculture) on one hand and the development of industrial type farming of a capitalistic nature on the other. Young, college educated people coming back to family farming believe that preserving the family farm is possible. They look to cooperative institutions fully controlled by farming families, protecting them from market forces which cause the decline of the family farm. They also look toward the development of small business, private and cooperative, in agricultural services. Such alternatives, however, can come into existence only as an effect of the change in the global political and economic system in Poland.

237

NOTES

1. All yield dates from Production Yearbook, FAO,
1982.

REFERENCES

Dziewicka, M. 1976. Dual Occupation in Polish
    Agriculture, in Rural Social Change in Poland, Warsaw,
    Pp. 75-87, J. Torowski and L. M. Szwengrub, eds.
Galeski, B. 1983. Policy Evolution and Current Crisis in
    Polish Agriculture, in Technology and Social Change in
    Rural Areas, ed. G.F. Summers, Westview Press. Pg.
    125-148.
Tepicht, J. 1973/ Marxism et Agriculture, Le Paysan
    Polonais, Armand Colin, Pp. 94-95 and III.,
    Statistical Yearbook. 1981. Warszawa.

11

The Social Economy of Canadian Agriculture: Family Farming and Alternative Futures

**Michael E. Gertler and
Thomas Murphy**

Most Canadian farms are still family farms. Profound changes, however, are taking place in the economic context and organization of farming. The farm sector retains a shrinking fraction of the "value added" in the agro-food system. In this system, a small number of food manufacturing and retaining corporations have amassed significant portions of the market. A parallel concentration of assets also continues within the farm sector. The locus of dynamic growth today is among farm firms whose size, legal organization, and use of hired labor distinguishes them fundamentally from the traditional family farm.

Quantitative and qualitative structural changes have altered the social economy of farming. Farm family roles are recast so that it is necessary to distinguish between the "family-in-farming" and the family farm. People with full- or part-time farming occupations are less likely to be associated with farm operations corresponding to popular conceptions of a family farm, even though families are still the key institution around which farm production is organized. What new forms of farming organization will predominate is a question with profound implications for rural society.

* In addition to the editors, several colleagues kindly read and commented on earlier drafts. Peggy Barlett, Frederick Buttel, Nelson Coyle, Philip Ehrensaft, JoAnn Jaffe, Pamela Smith, and Peter Vandergeest will recognize improvements and also where we have fallen short of intentions.

We begin this discussion of family farms and alternative futures for the family-in-farming with a brief review of the geography, history, and structure of Canadian farming. We then consider factors contributing to farming's transformation, including relations among farmers and between farmers, agribusiness, and quasi-public and state agencies. Finally, we consider group farming and other social innovations. Given appropriate rural and agricultural policies, these may offer the best potential for agriculture based on the family farm.

THE CONTEXT OF CANADIAN AGRICULTURE: CLIMATE AND GEOGRAPHY

According to the 1981 Census of Agriculture, agricultural production employed nearly half a million Canadians. They worked 318,000 farms and marketed commodities worth 15.8 Canadian dollars, about one-half for export. Even so, primary agricultural activities constituted only 4% of the Gross Domestic Product and the farm population only 4.4% of the total population of 24 million (Agriculture Canada, 1981).

Canada is vast but severe winters confine most farming to a relatively narrow band stretching some 3,000 miles along the Canada-United States border. Even in this band, agriculture is not continuous due to soil, topography, and climate limitations. Only 13% of the Canadian land mass, 294 million out of 2,278 million acres total, has agricultural potential (Statistics Canada, 1982). Of this, 162 million acres are now in farms. Two thirds of the land in farms, or less than 5% of the total land surface, is improved farmland.[1]

Nearly 82% of the farmed land is in the Prairie Provinces--Manitoba, Saskatchewan and Alberta (Statistics Canada, 1982). Here cereals predominate, especially Canada's major export crop, spring wheat. Large areas of semiarid rangeland and a grain surplus make cattle and pig production important as well. Climatically favored southern Ontario, with 10% of the nation's farmland, accounts for nearly 30% of farm cash receipts. Here corn, soybeans, tobacco, vegetable, and fruit production are important, as are cattle, dairy, hog, and poultry operations. In southern Quebec, specialized dairy, hog, and poultry operations prevail. The interior valleys of mountainous British Columbia are noted for their

241

horticultural production. The small east coast Maritime
Provinces--New Brunswick, Nova Scotia, and Prince Edward
Island--have only 1.3% of the country's cropland but
account for nearly half of its potato production
(Troughton, 1982; Agriculture Canada, 1981). Even
marginal farming areas, such as those of Newfoundland,
contribute to local food supplies, and their importance in
this regard is proportionately larger than their share of
national production.

A BRIEF HISTORY OF CANADIAN FAMILY FARMING

Prior to the arrival of Europeans, Canada's native
peoples had been cropping wildlife and gathering wild
foods for several millennia. Since before 1000 B.C., some
had also been practicing a slash and burn system for
producing corn and vegetables (Dick and Taylor, 1985).
Shortly after 1600, Europeans started cultivating small
acreages close to fishing ports, trading posts, forts, and
missions, primarily in what are now the Atlantic
Provinces. Farming was at first a minor enterprise next
to furs, fish, timber, and conquest; and the farmer was
often a part-time worker in one of the other staple
industries.

In Quebec, a French colony from 1608 to 1763, most
farming was done under the seigneurial system. Plots were
long and narrow with frontage on rivers or roads. This
pattern facilitated transportation and mutual assistance
in domestic and field operations. British rule brought
new settlers who established freehold family farms. This
together with the farms of the colonists, who had settled
beyond the seigneuries, became the prevalent form. Wheat
was the major cash crop in Quebec under the French and the
British. After American independence in 1783, settlement
and cereal production expanded up the St. Lawrence River
and along the northern borders of Lakes Ontario and Erie.
Because soil and climate were better here, wheat
production soon outpaced Quebec's. As in Quebec, however,
subsistence activities often provided the larger share of
farm livelihoods.

British capitalists, hoping to create conditions for
profitable estate agriculture, sought restrictions on land
grants to settlers. Rather than work for others, however,
people were willing to take their chances on the least
desirable plot (Sinclair, 1981). Independent producers,
owning land and implements, and relying on family labor,

also proved more resilient than the few large estates when grain prices collapsed—as they did in the 1820s and 1830s (Marr and Patterson, 1980).

Colonizing the West meant further displacement of indigenous inhabitants and the extinction of communal tenure (Spry, 1976). On the prairies, ranching preceded subsistence farming and local market production. Ranching companies leased land from the Crown on concessionary terms: up to 100,000 acres at one cent per acre per year for 21 years (Breen, 1973). Population grew slowly at first. To spur immigration, the government encouraged religious and other group settlements, and granted or sold large tracts to colonization companies. It granted the Canadian Pacific Railroad 25 million acres along with cash and existing roadbed in return for constructing a transcontinental railroad which was completed in 1886 (Innis, 1971; Conway, 1984b). Most of the prairie grassland, however, was not broken until the early 1900s when there was no longer desirable land available on the American frontiers and after both dryland farming techniques and short-season grain varieties were developed (Marr and Patterson, 1980).

Land was surveyed into townships containing 36 sections of 640 acres each. Many settlers purchased land from land companies, railroads, or individual speculators. Under the terms of the Dominion Lands Act, homesteaders could also gain title to a quarter section of Crown Land if they met certain obligations designed to ensure that they would be involved in commercial production (Hedley, 1981b). They could acquire another 160 acres from the Crown once they had cleared land and established farmsteads on the home quarter. Every second quarter was initially left empty for this purpose. This checkerboard pattern was broken up with railway lands, Hudson's Bay Company lands, and blocks for school sites. Pioneer farmsteads were thus very isolated (Archer, 1980).

Some immigrant groups arrived and settled in an area together, providing mutual support. Others were allotted settlement land en bloc and recreated villages reminiscent of those they had left in Europe. Requiring individuals to work the particular acreage they had been allotted was, however, disruptive for groups like the Doukhobors who wanted to farm collectively. It was less of a problem for the Mennonites who initially pooled and redivided their land, but who did not draw the attention of governments and neighbors with a more extreme form of communalism (Tracie, 1976).

Wheat for export was the dominant prairie crop, but subsistence activities were important at least through the 1930s. Vegetables and livestock were raised for home use and local sale. Fruit was gathered, game was hunted, and wood was cut for fuel and construction. Draft animals were raised, trained, and worked. Many of these chores fell to women. They handled small-scale production activities as well as domestic tasks, and did field work, especially when men were away (Hedley, 1981b).

Neighbors relied on each other for help with childbirth and the sick; for breaking sod; for building houses, barns, and schools; and for jobs such as threshing, cutting wood, and hauling coal. Major projects were accomplished through work "bees." More routine chores were handled through "change-work," the exchange of labor and services (Hedley, 1980, 1981b).

Although obscured by mutual aid and a mythology of pioneer equality, inequalities in land, capital, and personal capacities were omnipresent in frontier society (Friesen, 1984). Exchange relationships reflected these inequalities. Small farmers and ranchers worked for their larger counterparts, trading labor and loyalty for favors and patronage (Bennett, 1969). Some never acquired a farm while others made money in land speculation. Some hired out while others hired in (Hedley, 1981a). Inequalities were often solidified through inheritance.

As succeeding generations were established, mutual assistance between kin supplanted neighborly exchange. Young farmers received start-up capital from their parents who, in turn, counted on their grown offspring for continued labor input. With mechanization, farms became more self-sufficient in terms of labor requirements; and, with increased dependence on purchased inputs, farmers became more conscious of the monetary value of all farm activities, including labor. Where there was continued sharing, it was increasingly handled as a cash transaction (Hedley, 1981b).

A sizable minority of farmers were politically active in attempting to create an institutional context supportive of family farming. To press for new land, transportation, and tariff policies, farmers founded associations and political parties. In the 1920s, the Progressive Party was an important bloc in the Federal Parliament, and farm parties formed governments in several provinces (MacPherson, 1962; Conway, 1984b). Important reforms were won, but these parties lacked comprehensive economic policies and did not consolidate labor alliances.

244

Farmers turned to cooperatives to gain control over
supply and marketing activities. Cooperatives were seen
as institutional building blocks towards an economy
supportive of family farming, but they were only partially
successful. Cooperatives soon put aside their more
radical agendas as narrow self-interests prevailed over
more socially conscious perspectives on rural society
development. Despite cooperatives, the populist-
progressive politics of many Canadian farmers and the
predominance of family farms, the context of farming--the
dominant ideology, the markets, and the legal
environment--remained distinctly capitalistic and in many
ways inimical to family farming (Johnson, 1981).
Government agricultural policies have never aimed at any
major redirection of trends reflecting rationalization in
this economy.

RECENT CHANGES IN THE STRUCTURE OF AGRICULTURE

The transformation of rural economies and the family
farm is difficult to portray through a brief discussion of
structural parameters. Reliance on aggregate data slights
individual, local, and regional variation. A dearth of
data inhibits exploring business organization, land
tenure, and commodity specialization, as well as
relationships between farmers, agro-industries, and
quasi-public agencies. It is precisely in these areas
that farming is being qualitatively transformed. To
comprehend this change, one must go beyond conventional
analyses of structure. Nevertheless, we start with a
review of relevant structural data.

Farm Business Organization

In 1981, 86.6% of Canadian farms were individual
proprietorships, down from 91.8% in 1971. Corporate
farms, family-owned and otherwise, constituted 2.2% of
farms in 1971, but controlled 4.7% of farm capital, and
accounted for 8.4% of gross farm sales. By 1981, the
proportion of incorporated farms had increased to 3.8%,
while their share of farm assets had expanded to 11.1%,
and their share of cash receipts, to 19%.
In 1971, partnerships constituted 5.8% of all farms,
but they controlled 9.2% of farm capital, and accounted
for 10.6% of sales. By 1981, 9.3% of farms were

partnerships. Their share of total farm capital was
13.6%, and of sales, 14.2%. Thus, in 1981, partnerships
and corporations together accounted for 13.1% of Canadian
farms, had use of 24.7% of farm capital, and accounted for
33.2% of gross farm receipts (Brinkman and Warley, 1983;
Ehrensaft and Bollman, 1983).

Farm Size and Concentration

Due to consolidation and abandonment, farm numbers in
Canada fell from 632,000 in 1951, to 318,000 in 1981.
Over the same three decades, average farm size rose from
279 to 509 acres. The top 5% of farms accounted for 38%
of all farm sale revenues in 1981, and the top quartile,
74%. The bottom 50% of farms measured by gross sales
accounted for only 7% of total farm receipts. Aggregate
shares generated by each quartile changes very little from
1971 to 1981, though a minimum of $12,060 in sales in 1971
and $56,000 in 1981--a large jump even allowing for double
digit inflation--was required to be included among the top
25%. To join the top 5% in 1981, a farm needed gross
sales of at least $160,000 (Ehrensaft, 1983).
This data reflects the existence of numerous small
farm operations along with substantial numbers of
mid-sized units. A relatively few large farms, however,
control a disproportionate fraction of gross sales.
Concentration is particularly evident in beef, poultry,
potato, and vegetable processing production. Hog
production is also moving toward greater concentration as
large confinement operations become commonplace. This
leaves--at least for the time being-- grain, dairy, and
cow-calf production as activities where the moderate-sized
owner-operated family farm remains the norm (Ehrensaft,
1983).
The data does not suggest the imminent disappearance
of middle-size farms--though what constitutes middle size
is being revised upwards and many of these farms are
making changes in organizational and labor use that
distinguishes them from traditional family farms.
Concentration in the Canadian farm sector, however, lags
behind the U.S. as a whole but is similar to that of the
northern U.S. For the states abutting Canada, Lorenz
curves measuring farm sale concentrations are very similar
during comparable periods (Ehrensaft, et al., 1984).

Land Tenure

In 1951, 21.5% of farm operators rented at least some of the land they worked (Troughton, 1982). In 1981, 36.6% did so (Statistics Canada, 1982). The overall proportion of rental land has also increased, reaching 30.9% in 1981. In that year full-owner-occupied farms averaged 316 acres; tenant farms, 561 acres; and part-owner/part-tenant farms, 907 acres.

Land rental is common "entry" strategy as well as a way to accomplish growth (Clemson and Bollman, 1985). Some of the land rental increase may therefore reflect changing demographics. After several decades in which the average age of farmers increased, this trend began to reverse in the 1970s. Between 1971 and 1981, the proportion of farmers under age 35 climbed from 15 to 21%.

Capitalization, Debt, and Income

The farm sector is capital intensive compared with other sectors, though one should take into account the special nature of land as capital. In 1976, capital investment per person employed in the manufacturing sector was $40,000, while in farming it was nearly $175,000 (Forbes, et al., 1982). In the late 1940s, the ratio of capital to value added in farming was 4:1. By the 1970s, it was 8:1, a ratio several times higher than that found in most other sectors (Brinkman and Warley, 1983).

In 1981, the average value of land, buildings, machinery, and livestock was $409,000 per farm, and the total value of farm capital was 130 billion Canadian dollars (Brinkman and Warley, 1983). Measured in 1971 constant dollars, the aggregate capital value of Canadian farms nearly quadrupled between 1951 and 1981. Rising real estate values were the primary reason. During the 1970s especially, increases in land value contributed more to farm wealth than current income (Brinkman and Warley, 1983). Another major factor was an increase in machinery and equipment inventories reflecting both increased mechanization and higher prices.

Net income as a share of gross farm receipts declined from 36.3% in 1961, to 21.5% in 1981. It was down to 14.5% in 1983. Aggregate net farm income has also been falling since the early 1970s (Brinkman, 1985). Declining income and increasing capital requirements are reflected in rising farm debt. As of 1984, Canadian farmers owed 21 billion dollars (Farm Credit Corporation, 1984). Average debt to income ratios rose from 3.7 in 1971 to 5.4 in 1982 contributing to a cash crunch on many farms (Brinkman, 1985). Although declining in recent years, farm equity ratios remain high compared to other industries. In 1981, the "average" farmer had assets of $519,000 and liabilities of $78,000, resulting in a debt-to-asset ratio of 0.15. This ratio increases with farm size. Younger farmers also carry relatively more debt than their more established counterparts (Brinkman and Warley, 1983).

Since 1981, a serious farm depression marked by low commodity prices, high interest rates, and falling land prices has aggravated the debt problem. Farm bankruptcies, foreclosures, forced sales, and voluntary liquidations have reached levels unseen since the 1930s. Data from a 1984 Farm Credit Corporation survey suggest that of 171,465 farmers with gross sales over $20,000, about 19% or 33,000 were in severe financial distress. Another 9% met criteria of moderate stress. Crop farms were particularly likely to be under severe stress (Ashmead and Murphy, 1985).

Updating this data to mid 1985 suggests that 23% of farmers with sales over $20,000 were experiencing cash flow or equity problems corresponding to criteria of extreme financial stress and another 11% were under moderate stress (Ashmead and Murphy, 1985). Even with a protracted depression in agriculture, however, some farmers continue to prosper thanks to relatively protected markets, fortuitous timing, high equity levels, and efficient management.

Commodity Specialization

To take full advantage of available technologies and economies of size, farmers have expanded their operations and become more specialized (Gertler and Fast, 1986). This has frequently involved the separation of crop and livestock production and the curtailment of secondary farm enterprises. By the census definition of specialization—more than half of imputed farm sales from a single commodity group—88% of Canadian farms were specialized in 1961. This proportion had risen to 95% by 1981

(Statistics Canada, 1982). Regional specialization has increased along with farm specialization.

Farm Work and Multiple Job-Holding

The average Canadian farm required the work of 1.4 individuals in 1951. This was still true in 1981, although the total number of individuals with an agricultural occupation had declined 39% and the composition of this workforce had changed. In 1981 the workforce was at least 21% female as opposed to a reported 4% in 1951 (Smith, 1985). A 1983 labor force survey--probably more reliable than the census--found that women represented 70% of unpaid' family workers on farms, 34% of paid workers, and 11% of self-employed workers (Smith, 1985).

The average amount of hired labor employed per year per commercial farm increased from 12.9 weeks in 1951 to 18.6 weeks in 1981. Much of the increase reflects changes in tax law which make it profitable to pay family members a wage. Some of the increase, however, results from the hiring practices of farms employing multiple person-years of nonfamily labor. Between 1971 and 1981, farms hiring one to two person-years of labor increased by 35%; the number hiring two to five person-years increased 90%; and the number of farms hiring more than five person-years increased 75%. These "labor hiring" farms with the equivalent of one or more full-time employees constituted 5.4% of all farms in 1971 and 8% in 1981. Their share of aggregate gross sales grew from 26.8% to 31.5% over the same period (Ehrensaft and Bollman, 1983; Ehrensaft, 1983).[2]

Multiple job-holding by farmers and farm families is an important feature of the rural economy. About one-third of farm operators have reported off-farm work in each census year since 1941 (Bollman, 1982). In 1981, 38.7% reported some off-farm work (Statistics Canada, 1982). The average number of days multiple job-holding operators worked off the farm increased from 75 in 1941 to nearly 175 days in 1976 (Mage, 1982).

THE FAMILY FARM IN THE AGRO-FOOD SYSTEM

Historically, "family farming" has been used to describe a specific set of relationships. It has implied

private ownership of land and equipment--typically by a
male head of the farm household--and no legal or
operational separation between the household and the
farm. This lack of separation has conditioned how the
farm and the household function, affecting working
relationships within the unit, external business dealings,
decisionmaking, and the inheritance pattern. Family
farming has also implied a reliance on family labor and
the absence of significant amounts of hired labor
(Morissett, 1983). Among large farms, the fastest growing
component of the Canadian farm sector, many of these
characteristics are absent. The transformation of such
farms into "larger-than-family-type" and "industrial-
type"[3] operations results from competition in the farm
sector and economic relations with agribusiness firms
which are themselves contesting domestic and international
markets.

To survive, farmers have had to increase their labor
productivity by expanding or intensifying operations. As
farm capital requirements have increased, methods of
transmitting farm property have changed. Prior to the
1940s, it was possible to establish several offspring on
independent farms. The resulting dispersal of resources,
however, impeded the capture of scale economies and
investment in technology. This approach to intergenera-
tional transfer gave way to simple succession--one child
taking over the operation. But this, too, presented
problems. To raise the loans necessary for growth and for
buying out other family members and to gain control of
investment decisions, the inheriting farmer needs title
early. For economic and social reasons, however, the
senior couple may be reluctant to retire (Hedley, 1980).
Even when they accomplish transfer in a timely manner, the
young farmer's debt service can delay investments
necessary to keep the farm viable (Morissett, 1983).

Relations with Processing and Marketing Firms

Structural change in the farm sector has been, if
anything, less drastic than change in the input,
processing, and marketing portions of the agro-food
system. Chain stores now constitute six of the nine
largest firms in the Canadian agro-food complex, dwarfing
in revenues all but the largest distillers, brewers, grain
handlers, packers, and processors (Cote and Lamy, 1982).
Market power allows them to bargain hard with suppliers.

In this environment, most small processors have closed or have been consolidated into larger units.

Food handlers, processors, and manufacturers have, in turn, helped to reshape the farm sector. Contract integration in commodities such as fruit, vegetables, pork, and poultry, gives processors a strong hand in determining who will produce and where they will do it. Contracts also help processing companies control the quantity, quality, and timing of production but leave growers to deal with a disproportionate share of the risk, with the management of agricultural labor, and with the costs of overcapacity and rapid technological change (Debailleul, 1982). In some cases, agribusiness firms find it profitable to enter directly into production. Some grain companies and meat packers run feedlots (Mitchell, 1975), and many vegetable processors produce some or all of the raw product. This corporate-industrial farming usually involves leased land; they contract labor and machinery from underemployed farmers' sons and from former farmers. In other cases, they use wage labor and company land and machinery (Murphy, 1983).

The power to reorganize the sector becomes most obvious when a company switches to a new technology. In Ontario, for example, processors have controlled the timing of converting to mechanical tomato harvesting. As they shift factories and growers over to the small machine-picked varieties, contracts are reallocated to producers judged most cooperative, competent, and capable of expanding to a scale justifying mechanization. They often select farms with more than one operator, on the assumption that they are best able to guarantee deliveries.

Cooperatives, Marketing Boards, and the Role of the State

Agricultural cooperatives account for about one-third of fertilizers, seeds, and prepared feeds sold in the country and are the first handlers for most grain, oilseeds, and milk marketed by farmers. They are, however, less well represented in more lucrative processing and retailing activities (Cote and Lamy, 1982). Cooperatives keep some input manufacture and processing under Canadian ownership, but they have not fundamentally altered the structure and functioning of the agro-industrial complex (Denis, 1979). In part, this is attributable to conservative management and to the power differential among members. This results in policies that meet the priorities of large rather than small operators--to say nothing of co-op employees. Mostly, however, the limited influence of cooperatives reflects their problematic position in the economy.

Cooperative capital is tolerated in competitive, low margin sectors, but when cooperatives enter businesses where they threaten a lucrative oligopoly, they meet concerted resistance. Packer response to the entry of the Manitoba Wheat Pool into meat packing in the late 1960s, for example, cost the cooperative millions and eventually forced sale of the business (Warnock, 1978). Cooperatives have also suffered from spotty and inconsistent support from farmers. With voluntary membership, they have been unable to mobilize effective bargaining on behalf of commodity producers. They have been economically vulnerable, as well, to members using the cooperative as an outlet of last resort or who readily switch to other suppliers or processors when these temporarily offer a few cents advantage.

In response to the Depression, to rapid concentration in the food industry, and to the limited gains they were able to make through cooperatives, farmers and farm organizations fought for the legal mandate to organize effectively in farm commodity marketing. Federal and provincial governments responded in the 1930s with marketing board legislation. "Orderly marketing" has been a major instrument of farm policy in the decades since (Perkin, 1962; Veeraraghavan, 1985).

More than half of the gross dollar value of Canadian farm production is now under the jurisdiction of one or another of more than 100 boards. Some of these boards play a relatively minor role, such as promoting consumption and research. Others represent producers in collective negotiations with processors or act as single-desk selling agencies. Still others, such as the boards governing milk, poultry meats, eggs, and tobacco, exercise supply management and price setting powers as well (Forbes, et al., 1982).

The role of marketing boards in the structural transformation of the farm sector is complex. Farmer controlled boards have secured greater returns for some commodity producers. This may allow more farmers to make a living in agriculture but also rewards expansion and concentration. Where wages are included as a component of cost formulas used in establishing price, this may also help to create conditions under which hired labor can be used (Morisset, 1983). Furthermore, the capitalization of benefits into the prices of land and market quota enriches established operators but may impede the entry of new producers. By 1981 the aggregate quota value was over two billion dollars and the cost of quota for a one-operator unit could exceed $100,000 for milk, $250,000 for turkeys, and $500,000 for eggs and broiler chickens (Forbes, et al., 1982).

Marketing boards and commodity associations lobby for government action on their membership's needs. Their prevalence reinforces the tendency to promulgate commodity-oriented price and income programs rather than comprehensive agricultural and rural development policies. The imperatives of a Western grain, and an Eastern dairy policy dominate farm policy (Forbes, et al., 1982). General fiscal, monetary, and trade policies have reinforced tendencies towards differentiation and capital intensification and have probably had as much impact on agriculture's structure as specific farm programs.

The Canadian state has the contradictory task of showing support for the family farm while facilitating the reorganization of farming as a modern business sector. They must juggle the demands of farmers, agribusinessmen, entrepreneurs outside agriculture, and consumer groups. Foreign ownership of key agribusiness concerns and the need to keep export-oriented agriculture sectors competitive make the task more complex. Faced with conflicting claims, the government has often sacrificed the weakest players and perpetuated convenient mythology. They turn a blind eye to emerging larger-than-family farms and the disproportionate flow of benefits to high volume producers.

An important instance of this tendency to shift burdens on the politically weak is the exemption of agriculture from standard labor codes. This mainly benefits labor-hiring farmers, though they have general support from farmers and businessmen in protecting their special status. It is thus farmworkers who absorb many of the disbenefits of a cheap food policy. When a farm target for austerity measures is found, it has often been the part-time operator. Canadian governments and farm organizations have been quick to vilify and reluctant to defend the rights of the part-time farmer despite the crucial role such operations play in supporting rural infrastructure and providing decent livelihoods and lifestyles for many rural people (Veeraraghavan, 1985).

In the past it has been necessary to speed up or slow

down rural outmigration commensurate with the industrial
sector's needs or with the economy's capacity to provide
new livelihoods (Lianos, 1984). With the farm population
now a relatively small part of the national total, the
present imperative is more one of agricultural crisis
management. International depression and tough
competition with Europe and the United States have led to
low commodity prices and declining earnings for Canadian
producers. Government is under pressure to keep the farm
economy afloat so that land prices do not collapse and
imperil the country's banks. With treasuries under
pressure and conservative economic policy in vogue,
however, the response from provincial and federal
policymakers has been ambivalent at best. Canadians and
their governments seem unwilling to mount a concerted
action to protect rural economies. Compared to their
counterparts in Europe and the United States, Canadian
farmers find themselves relatively on their own in dealing
with financial reverses. Though it has mostly been
everyone for themselves in this situation, some farmers
have banded together to mount coordinated actions against
foreclosure (Wilford, 1984).

THE FAMILY IN FARMING: ALTERNATIVE FUTURES

What does Canadian society expect of the farm sector
and the family farm? People want inexpensive food, but
they also want farming conducted in a way that does not
add to the toxin load, conserves soil, is humane to
livestock, and preserves family-farm based rural
communities. Governments want efficient production and
they want to minimize agriculture's cost to their
treasuries without precipitating a farm revolt.
Agribusiness wants farmers who are businesslike but
without the power to raise prices.
Farmers may disagree on the appropriate configuration
for the farm sector and on what role state and
quasi-public institutions should play. Their disagreement
stems from differences in circumstance and from variations
in philosophy which may not correspond with individual or
group self-interest. Lack of unanimity also stems from
the conflicting roles they assume: manager, worker,
capitalist, debtor, landlord, and tenant. Farmers also
occupy multiple positions in households with functions
relating to both production and consumption (Bennett,
1982).

In general, farmers want fair returns; autonomy in work and business decisions; security in the face of disaster or depressed markets; and opportunity to pass on the farm. Farm women, furthermore, want legal standing as contributors to the value of the enterprise. They may also be particularly concerned about qualities of the rural community. Agricultural workers want the protection of laws covering other workers. Like all potential operators, they also want an economic environment that allows them to become a farmer, rancher, or grower.

Family farming is attractive to many who have grown up in its embrace, and to many who have not. Ideally, it offers workplace and home combined, an attractive situation in which to raise family; participation in a producer community; and the chance to manage people, technology, and natural resources. Many of these desiderata are unattainable in industrial communities and occupations.

Unfortunately, farm life reality often falls short of these possibilities. Operators exploit their own and family labor. Farm wives and farm youth work without legal standing in the enterprise and without much participation in decisions (Hedley, 1982). Family members must seek off-farm employment to subsidize farm income (Graff, 1982). Farmers can look forward to few vacations; to health problems from exposure to chemicals, heavy machinery, and the elements; and to little relief in the event of illness or accident (Strange, 1984). Many face chronic economic insecurity and the prospect that the farm may not be successfully transferred to the next generation (Conway, 1984a). Under these conditions, the stewardship of natural resources is rarely a first priority (Boudier, 1983). Farm employees face low wages and lack the benefits and legal protections that workers in other sectors have (Mitchell, 1975; Cavanagh, 1982). Unless they inherit property, such workers have small prospects for advancing up the "agricultural ladder" (Kloppenburg and Geisler, 1985).

Group Farming as an Alternative

In its present form and context, family farming is an increasingly unreliable vehicle for achieving the goals of most farmers, would-be farmers, and nonfarmers. Increasing farm differentiation and stratification, increasing reliance on hired labor, high failure rates, significant barriers to entry, unsound resource management, and the depressed state of farm communities, also argue for studying alternative approaches to organizing agriculture. Arrangements which preserve attractive aspects of family-based farming, even if not always the family farm as presently construed, deserve consideration.

Farmers are already experimenting with new approaches to keeping their families in farming, their farms in the family, and to assembling the resources necessary for success. These arrangements are typically between relatives and range from sharing equipment to fuller integration as a partnership, corporation, or cooperative.[4] Where there is commitment to owner-operation and family-based production, such integration can accommodate productivity-enhancing techniques and preserve positive aspects of family farming while avoiding the less attractive characteristics of industrial agriculture. Among the formulas tried in Canada, group farms operating as production cooperatives appear to have particular potential for solving capital, labor, and management problems, and for resolving apparent contradictions between social, economic, and resource management goals.

Cooperatives are sometimes formed for a single purpose, such as managing cattle on community pasture or operating a feedlot. We focus here, however, on production cooperatives involving greater integration of farm assets and operations. Such cooperatives probably number fewer than 100, the majority being in Saskatchewan where they have been promoted on and off since the 1940s. These joint enterprises involve up to a dozen farmers or farm families--but typically only two or three--and operate under several related business formats: the machinery cooperatives, the agri-pool, and the cooperative farm.[5] All are managed on a one-member, one-vote basis unlike conventional farming corporations where formal control depends on number of shares owned.

In machinery cooperatives, individual farmers pool their cropland and work it as a unit with jointly owned machinery. Conflicts over equipment access are avoided because each member receives a share of the harvest proportional to his/her land contribution. Members are also responsible for a proportionate share of labor and operating costs. Under the agri-pool arrangement, members lease land to the cooperative which pays them rent and wages. The cooperants equally divide any surplus machinery and sometimes livestock are owned jointly. The cooperative farm goes a step further, dispensing with individual farmland ownership. The cooperative owns or leases land along with machinery, buildings, and livestock. The member/directors pay themselves wages and share any surplus.

Group farming offers many potential advantages: reduced machinery costs and access to larger, more specialized equipment; sharing of labor, experience and skills; possibility for member specialization in particular tasks or enterprises within a larger operation that is more diversified; more possibility for experimentation with technology and techniques; improved decision-making processes; better accounting and planning functions; greater access to credit; security in case of illness or incapacity; and reduced isolation, stress, and physical risk due to sharing work and responsibilities. These advantages are not realized automatically. The complexity of managing a larger multi-member farm sometimes leads to problems in coordinating activities and personalities. Nevertheless, group operations demonstrate the capacity to achieve many of these benefits.

A comparative study of 15 Saskatchewan group farms and 15 neighboring one- or two-operator family farms provides interesting evidence (Gertler, 1981).[6] The groups, with from three to ten operators each, saved about one-third in machinery investment per acre despite having larger equipment than neighboring family-type operations. The groups also made slightly greater use of new technologies and personal safety equipment. Crop rotations were similar on the two sets of farms studied, but crop diversification was positively associated with number of operators. The group operations also had, on average, 50% more livestock per unit land area than was typical of farms in their rural municipalities.

In a predominantly cash grain region like Saskatchewan, livestock facilitate soil conservation as well as stabilizing and strengthening the economy. The groups under study varied, however, in their resource conservation practices, as did the matched conventional family operations. Overall, production practices on the two sets of farms were quite similar. This reflects shared culture as well as the general economic environment of these farmers.

Multi-operator farming arrangements that go beyond the conventional partnership or incorporated family enterprise are found in other provinces also. Manitoba has grain- and livestock-producing cooperatives and joint venture potato farmers. In Ontario and Quebec, dairymen share milking facilities and work together to raise feed and manage stock (Fobes, 1972). In Quebec, as well, cooperative joint ventures--some started with seed money from community agencies--are involved in producing commodities ranging from beef to greenhouse tomatoes (Jean, 1982).[7]

In addition to addressing cost and management problems, group farming arrangements may be useful in responding to other system deficiencies: the unmet needs of part-time farmers, farm women, and hired workers; and the need for new entry and tenure formulas. Some group farming arrangements might also facilitate adopting resource-conserving production practices and provide a socioeconomic base on which to rebuild rural economies.

A significant minority of Canadian farmers are multiple job-holders by necessity or by choice. Even in prime agricultural regions, off-farm work is often a long-term solution to inadequate farm income and underemployment during winter months. Unfortunately, part-time farmers and farm families must often cope with a double work day.

Given the economic benefits of multiple job-holding and the attraction of a life that includes farming, it is reasonable to seek ways to facilitate part-time farming. In a group enterprise, a person with an off-farm occupation can participate in a farm that has the full-time attention of at least one operator. The part-time person is a welcome extra hand but does not take on an inordinate responsibility. With income-pooling, the part-time member gets income from the group operation but may also be an important source of capital and cash for the farm.

In the conventional family farm arrangement, women share the burdens of farm life though they may not participate fully in its rewards: the opportunity to make independent decisions, to interact as equals in a producer community, and to enjoy the security of ownership. In group farming arrangements, women may find themselves even more excluded from management but, where they have obtained full membership, they have sometimes achieved a new relationship to farming, an equal vote and full remunerated participation. For women who choose not to become involved, group operation can also mean a better living, freedom from field work, and time to do other things (Zaleski, 1982).

Large farms in Canada rely increasingly on seasonal

and full-time hired labor. Even full-time farm work is generally poorly remunerated. Due to the circumstances of farm employment, it is unlikely that farm employees can successfully organize to improve income and working conditions (Buttel, 1982). In the present context, farm labor is also not likely to be a step towards farm ownership. It is important that farm labor receive the full protection of all labor laws but also that new avenues for entry into farming be found.[8]

Under some group farming arrangements, it is conceivable that people with little initial equity could join and participate as members, contributing their labor and borrowing enough capital to buy a share in the operation. This would be particularly feasible under arrangements proposed by the Saskatchewan Federation of Production Cooperatives for starting "zero-equity" cooperatives. Program essentials would involve long-term, renewable leases on land owned by a public land bank or nonprofit trust (SFPC, 1973). This approach to land tenure would also provide a way out of the dilemma whereby land prices proscribe the accession of a new generation of farm and nonfarm youth to farmer status--a problem that remains acute even on many incorporated and cooperative farms.

Canada has yet to deal with farming's environmental contradictions. Given agri-food system's present structure, there is little likelihood of a major shift in research agendas or that many farmers will voluntarily risk economic penalities to emphasize stewardship ideals. Other approaches will be necessary to create more ecologically rational farming.

Here, too, group farming arrangements have potential. Groups can operate a number of enterprises, each at a scale which captures available economies, and in so doing can reap the ecological benefits of a more diversified farming system. With more people available to share work and planning, they can adopt some of the more management-intensive aspects of resource-efficient farming, including more complex rotations, crop monitoring, soil testing, and systematic experimentation. Finally, groups can provide the interpersonal support and encouragement necessary to sustain attempts at technical innovation along lines that agribusiness does not promote (LeVeen, 1978). In this case "large" rather than "small" may be--with qualifications--beautiful.[9]

There is no substitute for public participation and coordinated planning of agricultural and rural development. Unfortunately, Canadian experience with integrated development (at home) is limited. Farm sector trends mirror consolidation of manufacturing and marketing activities and, in turn, contribute to dismantling local economies. Farmers have not managed to redirect investment and policy decisions that are at the root of such change, nor have they successfully promoted alternative economic development options.

These realities notwithstanding, multi-family farms may have some potential as vehicles for rural redevelopment. Group farming can increase the number of people gaining a livelihood from agriculture. With sufficient scale and joint enterprise among groups, it could also provide the context for renewed manufacturing, processing, service, and other economic activities.[10]

Perhaps most important is the potential impact of group farming on the culture of agriculture. As organizations that require face-to-face contact and purposeful joint action by farmers, they can become the nuclei of other activities. Experience suggests that production cooperatives and similar group farming arrangements can produce commodities efficiently. They can also produce people with the skills, time, and enthusiasm to rebuild community institutions, including the more traditional cooperatives (Gertler and Buttel, 1981).

CONCLUSIONS

Canada's small population, though increasingly urban, is dispersed over great distances and can often be provisioned most cheaply with imports. Multinational and a few large Canadian firms dominate the agricultural inputs and food processing industries. The farm sector has been shaped, despite sporadic producer resistance, to be a cheap raw materials source and a profitable market for manufactured supplies. Though never as egalitarian as the mythology suggests, the nature of farming and of rural society has been gradually altered as differences between large and small operations become more pronounced. Despite ritual, and often genuine, assertions of official support, family farms are disappearing or being transformed into entities lacking the characteristics historically associated with the term.

Threats to family farm survival are more permanent than the present crisis. Buyers' volume requirements combined with land, machinery, chemicals, borrowed money, and quota costs make a future in agriculture an increasing problem for small- and medium-scale farmers. Many farms may be difficult to refinance even if they survive until the present operators retire. Specialized full-time farmers on the "get big or get out" treadmill are also vulnerable to each market swing and economic downturn. Many will not make it to the turn of the century.

A mostly part-time "subcommercial" small farm segment will persist regardless of concentration among commercial-scale farms--though these small farms will account for a shrinking fraction of resources and output. A middle echelon, constantly revised upwards in terms of average size, will be occupied by a dwindling number of grain, dairy, cattle, and mixed enterprises corresponding more closely to the ideal-typical family farm. A farmer minority with strong backs, thick skins, financial savvy, and good connections will successfully manage large farms. Their success will continue to transform the sector. Trends suggest most of these farms will be organized as corporations and that labor, much of it nonfamily, will be salaried (Ehrensaft, 1985).

Despite the pervasive involvement of government agencies in the regulation and subsidization of farming and farm markets, there is probably little that incremental policy adjustments could now do to reverse structural trends. Nor would there be much support from established farmers or agribusiness for major changes in commodity, credit, trade, and tax policies that might suffice to preserve the dominant position of family farming in its traditional guise as a system of independent, atomistic, family-labor-based units (Buttel, 1982). Ironically, as has been argued in the U.S. by Dillman, et al. (1986), policies that might save family farms in serious straits today might ultimately contribute to a more rapid restructuring of the farm sector. Corporate-industrial farm operations (albeit some of them family owned and managed) seeking the profits that broadly targeted farm programs help to ensure, would increasingly displace family farms.

With depressed markets in several commodities, many aspiring farmers find they must abandon or postpone dreams of independent farm operations. Some of them have given up on farming, but others are working out sharing and pooling arrangements with relatives and neighbors. With greater institutional support for such options, more of these "temporary" measures might become satisfactory

long-term arrangements. Because farm programs whose
rationale rests partly on preserving the family farm seem
ineffective in fulfilling this promise, and because public
concern is aroused, there is political elbowroom for new
approaches.

Frequently, when one goes on a university or
government farm tour, the farms selected for visitation
include one or more long-established group operations.
Several households representing two or more generations
are involved and this contributes to making the operation
a showplace worth showing off to visiting farmers,
scholars, or dignitaries. Rarely, however, does the tour
organizer, the participants, or the farm families involved
acknowledge the nontraditional nature of the farm's
organization.

Where they have received some government support, as
in Saskatchewan, arrangements for cooperative use of farm
resources have shown potential as advanced approaches to
reformulating the family farm. Farmers have adopted these
new forms despite legal obstacles, such as unequal
treatment under inheritance tax law and restrictions on
the number of group farm members participating in various
farm programs. Given some encouragement and the removal
of bureaucratic impediments, there could be many more
pioneers in these new territories of social innovation.

It would, of course, be naive to suggest that by
simply pooling their resources to form multi-operator
joint ventures, agriculture's economic woes could be ended
and the family-in-farming could enjoy the full promise of
farm life. Even group operations, for all the economies,
security, and continuity they can provide, are risky
propositions in the present climate. Like the successful
single-family farm, group operations appearing prosperous
today are those which have had energetic and skillful
management. They have usually also enjoyed some luck in
the form of industrious forebears to inherit and with whom
to share the burdens of building a successful farm
operation.

In the final analysis, the options of family farming
and family group farming both depend on a revised set of
policies and precepts for all involved. Rural development
policies which see families in farming as an essential
element of a vibrant social economy will need to subsume
agricultural policies. Farmers, would-be farmers, and
nonfarmers will need to be considered part of a rural
community system which cannot provide well for one
constituent without providing for all. High unemployment

rates, the Canadian average is nudging 10% again in 1986, may be more devastating to maintaining family-based agriculture than unstable commodity prices. To keep the cycle of farming going from season-to-season and generation-to-generation, farm families need remunerative off-farm employment opportunities. Rural people without property also need good employment opportunities to stay in rural areas and provide the critical mass necessary for services and infrastructure. Family farmers need to understand that rural nonfarmers need good job alternatives so that skilled people remain in the countryside and that those who go to work on farms can insist on dignified, safe, and fair employment terms. A cheap, powerless labor source is probably more critical to the large industrial-style farm than to farms relying mostly on the labor of family, partners, and friends (Dillman, et al., 1986).

To meet the legitimate aspirations of present and future farmers, the family farm must be supplemented in the social economy of Canadian agriculture by new farming arrangements built around the family-in-farming. Some interesting prototypes for innovative redevelopment of the interrelationships between farm families and farm resources are already functioning in rural Canada. As attested by other authors in this volume, additional examples of socially advanced approaches to enhancing the prospects for the family-in-farming can be found in countries with which Canadian farmers have strong ties. There must be tangible support for experimentation with new ways of living and making a living in agriculture. At stake is the future of the family-in-farming and, with it, rural Canada.

NOTES

1. As defined in the census, improved land consists of cropland, seeded pasture, summer fallow, and land used for barnyards, farm roads, and home gardens. The reality of agricultural development has often not resulted in improved production potential for this land. Rather, fertility depletion, erosion, compaction, salinization, and other problems have occurred.

2. Reimer (1983) studied farm labor in Quebec and concluded that paid labor is underestimated by the

census. Because of the informal nature of hiring relationships that involve relatives and neighbors, and because government labor programs often do not apply, much wage work is not reported.
3. Following Rodefeld (1978) who used these terms to denote, in the first instance, large farms with high levels of land and capital ownership by their manager, but with hired labor constituting more than half of the workforce; and in the second instance, large farmers on which there is a high degree of separation between ownership, management, and labor.
4. Only legal partnerships and incorporated farms appear in the census and, although many farm corporations involve more than one principal operator, the number of operators is not recorded. Sharing arrangements in general appear to be interpreted in the census (Carlyle, 1983).
5. To accommodate tax and grain marketing regulations, a variant of the machinery cooperative--the "machinery agency cooperative"--has recently been developed by the Saskatchewan Department of Co-operation and Co-operative Development.
6. The same of group farms included 13 production cooperatives organized as machinery cooperatives, agri-pools, or cooperative farms, and two multi-family, farm corporations.
7. Another form of group enterprise, religiously-motivated Hutterite farm colonies, are found in considerable and growing numbers in Manitoba, Saskatchewan, and Alberta. A typical colony provides for 100 people in a settlement that includes family housing and communal eating facilities, gardens, workshops, and barns. Hutterite farms are diversified and they make selective use of modern technologies (Ryan, 1977).
8. Although only a minority of farmers hire much labor, farmers have generally favored exemption of farm work from regular minimum wage, health, and safety regulations, and other benefits applicable to industrial employees. Special provisions that cheapen hired labor may, however, hasten the demise of family farming, since large labor-hiring farms are rendered more competitive (Buttel, 1982).
9. The qualifications stem from two problems. First, it is not certain that group farmers will take the opportunity to diversify and therefore to gain the advantages of complementarity between various production processes. Second, even if they diversify, their range of choice in modifying production programs may be limited.

They will still operate in a larger economic context that has many ways to impose its logic on decisions.

10. As transportation advances and lifestyle preferences result in the repopulation of commuting-distance rural areas, agriculturalists have found themselves at loggerheads with exurbanites. Joint enterprise arrangements to bring these new rural households into economic alliance with farmers would do much to facilitate co-existence. Under various conceivable formal and informal arrangements, the new partners could gain a say in the management of--and shoulder some of the burdens of--an agriculture furnishing the quality food and environment they seek.

REFERENCES

Agriculture Canada. 1981. Canada's Agri-Food System: An Overview. Ottawa: Minister of Supply and Services.

Archer, John H. 1980. Saskatchewan: A History. Saskatoon: Western Producer Prairie Books.

Ashmead, Ralph, and J. Murphy. 1985. "The myth and reality of the farm financial crisis." Paper presented at the Annual Meetings of the Canadian Agricultural Economics and Farm Management Society, Charlottetown.

Bennett, John W. 1969. Northern Plainsmen: Adaptive Strategy and Agrarian Life. Chicago: Aldine.

Bennett, John W. 1982. Of Time and Enterprise. Minneapolis: University of Minnesota Press.

Bollman, Ray D. 1982. "Part-time farming in Canada: issues and non-issues." GeoJournal 6(4):313-322.

Boudier, Helene. 1983. L'Environnement Vu Par Les Producteurs Agricoles: Leur Perception, Leurs Attitudes et Leurs Comportements. Quebec: Ministere du l'Environnement.

Breen, D.H. 1973. "The Canadian Prairie West and the 'harmonious' settlement interpretation." Agricultural History 47 (April):63-75.

Brinkman, George L. 1985. "Canadian agriculture in the 1980's: conditions, farm performance and policy implications." Pp. 11-19 in Proceedings: Canadian Association for Rural Studies, special issue of Comparative Rural and Regional Studies (Winter).

Brinkman, George L., and T.K. Warley. 1983. "Structural change in Canadian agriculture: a perspective." Working paper prepared for the Regional Development Branch, Agriculture Canada.

Buttel, Frederick H. 1982. "Beyond the family farm." Pp. 87-107 in Gene F. Summers (ed.), Technology and Social Change in Rural Areas. Boulder, Colorado: Westview Press.

Carlyle, William J. 1983. "The changing family farm." Prairie Forum 8 (Spring):1-24.

Cavanagh, Judy. 1982. "The plight of women farmworkers." Resources for Feminist Research 11 (March):6-7.

Clemson, Heather A. and Ray D. Bollman. 1985. "A profile of managers of agricultural resources." Paper presented at the Annual Meetings of Canadian Sociology and Anthropology Association, Montreal.

Conway, John F. 1984a. "The decline of the family farm in Saskatchewan." Prairie Forum 9 (Spring):101-117.

266

Conway, John F. 1984b. The West: The History of a
    Region in Confederation. Toronto: James Lorimer & Co.
Cote, Alain and Etienne Lamy. 1982. "Qui nourrira le
    Quebec? Portrait de l'agro-alimentaire au Quebec."
    Interventions Economiques 9 (Autumn):89-104.
Debailleul, Guy. 1982. "L-Agro-business: strategies et
    contradictions." Interventions Economiques 9
    (Autumn):105-114.
Denis, Wilfrid B. 1979. "Exploitation in Canadian Prairie
    agriculture 1900-1970." Paper presented at the Annual
    Meeting of the Canadian Sociology and Anthropology
    Association, Saskatoon.
Dick, Lyle and Jeff Taylor. 1985. "Agriculture
    history." Pp. 28-31 in The Canadian Encyclopedia,
    Vol. I. Edmonton: Hurtig Publishers.
Dillman, Don A., Frederick H. Buttel, Louis Swanson,
    Daryl Hobbs, William Heffernan, and Donald Beck.
    1986. "The U.S. farm crisis and the future of the
    family farm." Paper presented at the Annual Meeting
    of the American Association for the Advancement of
    Science, Philidelphia.
Ehrensaft, Philip. 1983. "The industrial organization
    of modern agriculture." Canadian Journal of
    Agricultural Economics 31:122-133.
Ehrensaft, Philip. 1985. "Large farms: leading edge
    of structural change." Paper presented at the Annual
    Meetings of the Canadian Agricultural Economics and
    Farm Management Society, Charlottetown.
Ehrensaft, Philip, and Ray D. Bollman. 1983. "Structure
    and concentration in agriculture: a micro-analysis of
    the Census of Agriculture." Paper presented at the
    Annual Meetings of the Canadian Sociology and
    Anthropology Association, Vancouver.
Ehrensaft, Philip, Pierre LaRamee, Ray D. Bollman, and
    Frederick H. Buttel. 1984. "The microdynamics of
    farm structural change in North America: The Canadian
    experience and Canada-U.S.A. comparisons." American
    Journal of Agricultural Economics 66(December):823-828.
Farm Credit Corporation Canada. 1984. "Group farming
    goes hand-in-hand with co-operatives." UCO News 7
    (July-August):8-9.
Fobes, Walter. 1972. "Group farming goes hand-in-hand
    with co-operatives." UCO News 7(July-August):8-9.
Forbes, James D., David R. Hughes, and T.K. Warley. 1982.
    Economic Intervention and Regulation in Canadian
    Agriculture. Study Prepared for the Economic Council

of Canada and the Institute for Research on Public
Policy. Ottawa: Supply and Services Canada.

Friesen, Gerald. 1984. The Canadian Prairies: A
History. Toronto: University of Toronto Press.

Gertler, Michael E. 1981. "A comparison of agricultural
resource management on selected group and individual
farms in Saskatchewan." M.Sc. thesis, McGill
University, Montreal.

Gertler, Michael E., and Frederick H. Buttel. 1981.
"Property, community and resource management:
exploring the prospects for group farming in North
America." Paper presented at the Annual Meeting of
the Rural Sociolgoical Society, Guelph.

Gertler, Michael E. and Sarah E. Fast. 1986.
"Specialization in North American agriculture." In
Frederick H. Buttel, Thomas Murphy, Philip Ehrensaft,
and William H. Friedland (eds.), The Political Economy
of Agriculture in Advanced Industrial Societies.
Washington, D.C.: University Press of America
(forthcoming).

Graff, Lida L. 1982. "Industrialization of agriculture:
implications for the position of women." Resources
for Feminist Research 11 (March):10-11.

Hedley, Max J. 1980. "Reproduction and evolving patterns
of cooperation and resource transfer among domestic
producers." Canadian Journal of Anthropology 1
(Winter): 141-147.

Hedley, Max J. 1981a. "Rural social structure and the
ideology of the 'family farm'." Canadian Journal of
Anthropology 2 (Spring):85-89.

Hedley, Max J. 1981b. "Rural transformation: the
Canadian Prairies." Paper presented at the Annual
Meeting of the Rural Sociological Association, Guelph.

Hedley, Max J. 1982. "'Normal expectations': rural women
without property." Resources for Feminist Research 11
(March):15-17.

Innis, Harold A. 1971. A History of the Canadian Pacific
Railway. Toronto: University of Toronto Press,
(First published 1923).

Jean, Bruno. 1982. "La dualite de la production agricole
en region peripherique. Le cas de L'Est du Quebec."
Interventions Economiques 9 (Autumn): 131-141.

Johnson, Leo A. 1981. "Independent commodity
production: mode of production or capitalist class
formation?" Studies in Political Economy 6
(Fall):93-112.

Kloppenburg, Jack R. Jr., and Charles C. Geisler. 1985.
"The agricultural ladder: agrarian ideology and the
changing structure of U.S. agriculture." Journal of
Rural Studies 1(1):59-72.
LeVeen, E. Phillip. 1978. "The prospects for small-scale
farming in an industrial society: A critical
appraisal of Small is Beautiful. Pp. 106-125 in R.C.
Dorf and Y.L. Hunter (eds.), Appropriate Visions. San
Francisco: Boyd and Fraser.
Lianos, Theodore. 1984. "Concentration and
centralization of capital in agriculture." Studies in
Political Economy 14 (Spring):99-116.
MacPherson, C.B. 1962. Democracy in Alberta, 2nd ed.
Toronto: University of Toronto Press.
Mage, J.A. 1982. "The geography of part-time farming--a
new vista for agricultural geographers." GeoJournal 6
(4):301-312.
Marr, William L., and Donald G. Patterson. 1980.
Canada: An Economic History. Toronto: Macmillan of
Canada.
Mitchell, Don. 1975. The Politics of Food. Toronto:
James Lorimer & Co.
Morissett, Michel. 1983. "La ferme familiale au
Quebec." La Terre de Chez Nous (series of 50 weekly
articles appearing January 1983 to January 1984).
Murphy, Thomas R. 1983. "The structural transformation
of New Brunswick agriculture from 1951 to 1981." M.A.
thesis, University of new Brunswick, Fredericton.
Perkin, G.F. 1962. Marketing Milestones in Ontario,
1935-1960. Toronto: Ontario Department of
Agriculture.
Reimer, Bill. 1983. "Sources of farm labor in
contemporary Quebec." The Canadian Review of
Sociology and Anthropology 20 (August):290-301.
Rodefeld, Richard D. 1978. "Trends in U.S. farm
organizational structure and type." Pp. 158-177 in
R.D. Rodefeld et al. (eds.), Change in Rural America.
St. Louis: C.V. Mosby.
Ryan, John. 1977. The Agricultural Economy of Manitoba
Hutterite Colonies. Toronto: McClelland and Stewart.
Saskatchewan Federation of Production Co-operative.
1973. "Production co-operatives in agricultural
adjustment." Brief to the Government of Canada
presented by the Co-operative Union of Canada.
Sinclair, Peter. 1981. "From peasants to corporations:
the development of capitalist agriculture in Canada's

269

Maritime Provinces." Paper presented at the Annual
Meeting of the Midwest Sociological Society,
Minneapolis.

Smith, Pamela. 1985. "'Not enough hours, our accountant
tells me': trends in children's, women's and men's
involvement in Canadian agriculture." Paper presented
at the Annual Meetings of the Canadian Agricultural
Economics and Farm Management Society, Charlottetown.

Spry, Irene. 1976. "The great transformation: the
disappearance of the commons in Western Canada." Pp.
21-45 in Richard Allen (ed.), Man and Nature on the
Prairies. Canadian Plains Studies 6. Regina:
Canadian Plains Research Center.

Statistics Canada. 1982. 1981 Census of Agriculture:
Canada. (Cat. No. 96-901) Ottawa: Minister of Supply
and Services.

Strange, Marty (ed.). 1984. It's Not All Sunshine and
Fresh Air: Chronic Health Effects of Modern Farming
Practices. Walthill, Nebraska: Center for Rural
Affairs.

Tracie, C.J. 1976. "Ethnicity in the Prairie
environment: patterns of Old Colony Mennonite and
Doukhobor settlement." Pp. 46-65 in Richard Allen
(ed.), Man and Nature on the Prairies. Canadian
Plains Studies 6. Regina: Canadian Plains Research
Center.

Troughton, Michael. 1982. Canadian Agriculture.
Geography of World Agriculture Vol. 10. Budapest:
Akademiai Kiado.

Veeraraghavan, S. 1985. "The role of farm
organizations." P. 121-141 in Anthony M. Fuller
(ed.), Farming and the Rural Community in Ontario: An
Introduction. Toronto: Foundation for Rural Living.

Warnock, John W. 1978. Profit Hungry: The Food Industry
in Canada. Vancouver: New Star Books.

Wilford, Allen. 1984. Farm Gate Defense: The Story of
the Canadian Farmers Survival Association. Toronto:
NC Press.

Zaleski, Halina. 1982. "Women in production
co-operatives: unique problems--special benefits."
Resources for Feminist Research 11 (March):24-25.

12
Family Farming in the United States

**Eugene Wilkening and
Jess Gilbert**

We begin our treatment of the family farm in the
United States with a brief historical overview of land
settlement in the country. This includes the origins of
the variations in farming patterns as one moves from the
more humid East to the semi-arid plains and the
mountainous areas of the West. Next will be an account of
the changing structure of agriculture, various public
policies, and the current crisis, including their effects
on the family farm. The latter part of the chapter will
discuss the social and economic consequences of the
structure of agriculture with special attention to the
affect of farm size upon the use of resources, family
life, and local community.

What is a "family farm?" The concept has changed with
the political-economic development of the U.S. Thomas
Jefferson proposed that the farm family own the land as
well as work and manage a self-sufficient operation.
Throughout the 19th century, self-sufficiency declined as
American farms became increasingly commercialized. By
World War II, influential analysts of the family farm had
dropped the requirement of land ownership and the
prohibition against hiring wage labor. Soon, the family
farmer became an "operator is a risk-taking manager, who
with his family does most of the farm work and performs
most of the managerial activities" (Nikolitch, 1972:248).
This particular view, first proposed in the late fifties,
guided American thinking for the next two decades. Gone
was the idea that a family farm be economically viable and
support the household. Empirically, family farms became
those that hired no more than 1.5 "man-years" of labor and
were not run by a hired manager (Brewster, 1979). By the
1970s, this all-inclusive definition of the family farm

was being questioned (e.g., Rodefeld, 1978; Vogeler, 1981). Several sociologists began reconceptualizing the family farm as simple (petty or independent) commodity production. Goss, et al. (1980) and Buttel (1980) criticized the "family farm" notion as too imprecise and ahistorical, not to say atheoretical. The Marxist concept of commodity production, on the other hand, fit into an historical theory of the capitalist mode of production (Friedmann, 1980). It permitted analysts to gauge structural change in agriculture by focusing on social processes of reproduction, decomposition, differentiation, and transformation. Assuming commercialization, Buttel (1980, 1982) defined the independent commodity producer/family as one who owns and controls most or all of the land and capital, provides most or all of the labor, and supports itself from farm-related income. Although this is close to the Jeffersonian concept, Buttel stressed the historical and geographical specificity of this form of agricultural production: It arose during the transition to capitalism in a few European countries and their colonies, including the U.S. Whichever definition is used, U.S. farms have moved away from a family-oriented institution and toward a commercial business.

AN HISTORICAL OVERVIEW OF THE U.S. FARMLAND SETTLEMENT

The distribution and settlement of land in the United States was affected by a range of public and private forces. The historical conditions under which the land was acquired as well as its geographical and climatic characteristics have had major influences upon farming patterns. Most of the early settlers in the thirteen colonies on the Atlantic Seaboard were not farmers. Many came to seek religious freedom; others were fortune seekers. Prisoners, indentured servants, and slaves were brought to assist in the production of lumber, tobacco, rice, and other products. The British King fostered the expansion of settlement by grants of land to noblemen, churches, and corporations that agreed to colonize the land. In some areas a village type of settlement arose similar to those in Europe. In contrast, the southern colonies with servants and slave labor developed into plantations for producing rice and cotton, a type of settlement which continued into the 20th century. In the middle colonies most land became the property of individual settlers who were primarily subsistence farmers. As the demand for food increased in the urban centers, this area became the "bread basket," producing the native corn and other grains as well as livestock. The independent family farm became dominant as settlers moved westward to the Central and Midwestern regions of the country (Cochrane, 1979).

The Great Plains of the Midwest and the mountains and valleys of the Far West presented special problems of settlement and farm structure. Settlement of this part of the country advanced in the latter 19th century following the Civil War and other land pressures in the East. Although transportation was limited, the open grasslands of the Midwest were attractive, and the railroads encouraged settlement through cheap land sales. While early settlers remained near the water systems, they later spread to the drier rolling lands farther west where livestock ranching became the dominant enterprise. Both grain and livestock production in the West required more capital for initial investment in the larger acreages and for irrigation and livestock caretakers. The Far Western states of California, Washington, and Oregon also had special characteristics affecting farm type and structure. Livestock and grain were adapted to the highlands as well as to the drier lowlands. But the semi-tropical lowlands of California became more specialized in fruits and vegetables as irrigation was provided through government subsidy. Large-scale farms developed here with the use of immigrant hired labor. Similar types of farms also arose in the Southern states of Texas and Florida (Cochrane, 1979).

Despite these regional variations, the national ideal was that families should live on the land they farm and have the freedom to vote and to acquire the public services they desired. This principle was fostered by the Homestead Act of 1862, which gave land to those families who lived for five years on 160 acres (later increased to 640 acres). But the unfavorable climate and the lack of transportation and markets led to instability of family farms in the western regions. By 1900, of some 600,000 homesteads, only one acre in six had gone directly from the government to farmer settlers (Geisler, 1984:13). The rest was sold to entrepreneurs or given to railroads and states for disposition. The principle that people should live on the land they operate represented a contrast to the village form of settlement in most European countries. It reduced the close contact of farm families, increased the costs of public and private services, and also made it easier to develop the larger size of farms in much of the country. But, for the families who owned, worked, and managed the land, rural life had no great social inequalities. Family farming became the predominant type in the diversified agriculture of most of the U.S.

From the 19th century on, the combination of the great expanse of farmland, improved technology, increasing status of the domestic economy, and dependence upon the foreign market have affected the structure and prosperity of U.S. farmers. While families remained the primary landowners and operators in most of the country, the economic orientation pushed the majority of farmers into an enterprise heavily dependent upon large capital investment at increased costs and upon a monetary market system extending well beyond community and even country. The economic depression of the 1930s brought about an increased concern for the structure of agriculture. In 1935 U.S. farm numbers peaked at 6.8 million. The federal government assumed major new roles in directing agriculture. The "New Deal" intervened in farm markets with price supports and production controls. It also attempted to assist the smaller, poorer farmers but was much more successful at saving the larger commercial producers. U.S. farm policies today are based largely on those established in the 1930s. Yet the nature of the problems has changed. Perhaps it is time for another major initiative in agricultural policy. After reviewing changes in farm structure since World War II, we shall mention one or two such possibilities.

STRUCTURAL CHANGES AND PUBLIC POLICIES
SINCE THE 1940s

The structure of U.S. agriculture is the result not only of farm changes but of larger societal forces as well, particularly the political economy. Farming has been different from most sectors of the U.S. economy in two significant ways: its relatively large number of family-based units and its dependence on landed property as the chief means of production (Harrington, et al., 1983:21; Manchester, 1985:16). Yet these traditional characteristics of agricultural production have been increasingly challenged by the forces of a capitalist economy. U.S. agriculture has experienced a transformation since the 1940s, although many family units have managed to reproduce themselves. This section will

address these changes, concluding with a brief review of
public policies and their effects.

In addition to the problem of "overproduction" in a
capitalist economy, the major forces that have led to the
"revolution in U.S. farming" (Schertz, et al., 1979) are
capital-intensive technologies, public policies, and the
increasing non-farm control of agriculture. Combined with
national economic conditions, these interrelated factors
have brought about the following changes in farm structure
since World War II: a decrease in the number and an
increase in the size of farms; greater output and
productivity; concentration of production among fewer,
larger farms; relatively more hired laborers; more
part-time farming; increased debt financing; off-farm
ownership of farmland and new types of tenure; commodity
and regional specialization; contract production; and
internationalization. These are among the ways that
capitalism has penetrated U.S. agriculture.

Most of these changes indicate a movement away from
family farming conceived as independent commodity
production. Let us mention some of the specific trends.
In 1950 the U.S. had over 5.6 million farms, with an
average size of 213 acres. By 1984 there were 2.3 million
farms, averaging 437 acres per enterprise (Marion, et al.,
1986:7). Productivity increased five-fold. The mix of
inputs, however, changed drastically. Since 1950 labor
use has been cut by 75%; now there are more hired than
family workers. Chemical usage went up over 500%, while
feed and seed inputs more than doubled. Overall,
purchased inputs in farming as a proportion of cash
receipts rose from 42% in 1945 to 57% in 1980 (Manchester,
1985:18,30; Marion, et al., 1986:16; U.S. General
Accounting Office, 1985:9). Concentration of production
among the largest 5% of farms has increased moderately
from 39% in 1950 to 50% in 1982. By 1982, nearly half of
all U.S. farm operators worked at off-farm jobs (Marion,
et al., 1986:6-11). Considered as a whole, the survival
strategies of individual farmers (e.g., expansion,
indebtedness, off-farm work) have resulted in a dramatic
social-structural transformation of U.S. agriculture.
After illustrating this point with two contradictory
strategies, we discuss the roles of land, technology,
public policies, and off-farm control vis-a-vis family
farming in the U.S.

Buttel (1980:21) identifies two "master processes"
that ultimately push the family farm along different
paths, one toward transformation, the other toward

reproduction. First is the treadmill of technology, a concept developed by Cochrane (1979:393):

> We know now why farmers adopt new and improved technologies and expand their output even though they complain of low product prices and rising input prices. They do so because each farmer sees the adoption of a new and improved technology as a means of either increasing his profits or reducing his losses. But in a competitive situation, with many producers, there is no way that an individual farmer can hold onto himself the short-run income gains from the adoption of the new and improved technology. Such income gains are lost to him in the longer run through the competitive process. They are lost in a free-market situation through falling product prices. They are lost in a price-supported situation through rising prices of the fixed factors--typically land.

Although allowing an individual to remain competitive in the short run, the technological treadmill differentiates and eventually transforms the family farm system. The second survival strategy operates in the opposite direction. It is the capacity of farm families to "adapt to economic insecurity by reducing consumption in 'bad years'" (Buttel, 1980:21). For instance, the labor of individual members can be allocated so as to maximize the welfare of the whole family. Further, family farming involves more than an "economically rational" attachment to property, especially land. Farmers are reluctant to sell their real property even in the worst of times. Thus, they tighten their belts as required and perhaps hang on to emerge in better economic circumstances. This adaptive capacity, then, works to permit family farms to persist and reproduce themselves over time.

Both of these survival strategies give special importance to land as a unique means of production in agriculture. In the U.S., 75% of farm assets are in real estate. Unlike most European countries, the U.S. has practically no restrictions on the land market. This "free enterprise" derives largely from the early American effort to avoid feudal land tenures. U.S. citizens have an almost unlimited right to buy and sell real estate, including farmland. Such freedom has its costs. An open land market leads, in particular, to the split between farm operator and farmland owner. These two distinct roles, while often fused in the farm family, nevertheless can cause serious tensions. For example, inflation benefits landowners but raises costs for farmers. The main post-war changes in tenure have been the rapid decline of full tenants along with the rise of part-owner operators and non-operator landlords. Full-time farmers now are a numerical minority of farmland owners; however, they own slightly over one-half of all farmland (Gilbert and Harris, 1984). This distinction between owner and operator is increasingly important since land rentals are on the rise (Harrington, et al., 1983:22-24). While tenancy and part-ownership may help preserve certain features of the family farm, these forms of tenure diverge significantly from the concept of independent commodity producer.

Since we already mentioned the technological treadmill, let us add only a few more words on the role of technology in U.S. agriculture. Farm technologies represent the substitution of capital for either land or labor, depending on its form: mechanical (e.g., tractors), biological (hybrids), or chemical (commercial fertilizers, pesticides). In its design and use, technology necessarily involves social relations, and its adoption depends on the likelihood of capital accumulation in the society's economy (Buttel, 1980:24). In agriculture, specifically, technology reinforces the overproduction problem as well as most of the structural trends away from family farming (e.g., concentration of production, indebtedness, specialization). At the same time, its capital intensity has been an important means of preserving the appearance of a family farming system. Moreover, its development is largely supported by public funds in the USDA and the state land-grant colleges of agriculture. Technology is a prime case of agricultural control being transferred from the farm to agribusiness corporations. It thus is intimately tied to the other major forces affecting U.S. agriculture--public policies and increasing off-farm control.

Capital-intensive technology and the growth of off-farm ownership of farmland are two important aspects of the loss of on-farm control of agriculture. Other survival strategies, such as contract production, further exemplify this structural trend. The proportion of commodities produced under contractual arrangements, or by vertically integrated firms, increased from 19% in 1960 to 30% in 1980. Such production is concentrated in fruits, vegetables, poultry, eggs, and sugar cane (Harrington, et al., 1983:5). Contracts with farmers offer a method for the food industry to obtain the quantity and quality of products at the time needed for processing and sales. The contracts often provide the seeds or source materials and sometimes equipment for harvesting; they primarily control the timing and method of planting, fertilizing, pest control, harvesting and delivery of the product. This reduces the freedom of the farmer to adapt these activities to his other farm activities and usually provides no guarantee against losses or damages from the use of chemicals or equipment (Pfeffer, 1982). As contracting for the production of food products increases, the share of the returns to the unorganized family farmer tends to decrease in favor of the concentrated food industry that controls the market and many of the conditions for the use of land, labor, and capital by the farmer. Contract production diverges considerably from the model of family farming.

In addition to technology and off-farm control, public policies have also significantly affected the structure of agriculture since World War II. Three policy areas in particular have been important. The first, general tax policy, is rarely aimed specifically at agriculture, but nonetheless has had deep impacts. At a minimum, policies such as capital gains, cash accounting, and preferential estate taxes have encouraged the following structural changes: the retention of farmland and, thus, the separation of ownership from operation (e.g., rentals); the use of debt capital (credit); the expansion of existing farms, thereby concentrating production and denying entry to would-be farmers; the substitution of capital for labor; the growth of farm corporations; and overproduction, hence lower commodity prices (USDA, 1981: 91-98). Current tax shelters, in other words, subsidize overinvestment in agriculture. They not only distort the farm economy but also function disproportionately for the benefit of the wealthy (Breimyer, 1985; Strange, 1985). Each of the consequences of tax policy has led to further differentiation among family farmers.

Secondly, agricultural commodity policy began in the 1930s as a direct response to low farm incomes. Price supports (via crop loans), income supports (target prices), and production controls (acreage restrictions) are the main instruments of government intervention. As with tax policy, the farm programs have contributed to the structural transformation of U.S. agriculture. They have disproportionately benefited larger farms, thereby abetting the continued growth in size of farms;

capitalized program benefits into land values, thus encouraging higher land prices, as well as the ownership of farmland by nonoperators; promoted both excess production and the misallocation of resources (e.g., to commodities that were most profitable in the short run); and reduced the risk of farming (e.g., disaster protection), thereby adding to the aforementioned trends (USDA, 1981: 101-08).

Finally, agricultural credit policy has succeeded in its original goals of risk reduction and increased capital availability for farmers, yet has had other consequences. For example, plentiful credit has inflated land prices, concentrated production in fewer hands, and effectively "driven" the industrialization of agriculture by providing for energy- and capital-intensive technology (USDA, 1981: 113-15). Like general tax policy, the specific agricultural commodity programs and credit policies have reinforced, if not themselves engendered, the major structural trends away from family farming in the U.S.

CURRENT FARM STRUCTURE, CRISIS AND POLICY

In this section we present an overview of U.S. farm structure in the 1980s, including the current crisis, as well as a policy debate on the family farm. In the 1970s it became clear that a bimodal farm structure had emerged. Over a million and a half small farms survived primarily on the basis of off-farm income while fewer than half a million large farms produced almost all of the agricultural commodities in the country. The largest of this latter group had incomes considerably above the U.S. average. It is the in-between group of farms, neither small nor large, that constitutes the "disappearing middle" of the bimodal distribution. Most of their income is farm-based, and they have achieved most technical economies of size, yet they often lack sufficient volume for an adequate net farm income (Harrington, et al., 1983:20). These, mostly family, farms are struggling to survive. Let us examine in more detail the different types of farms that make up this dualistic structure.

Following the delineation by USDA (1981:46), we shall discuss four size categories, based on gross farm sales. First are the "rural farm residences," places with little agricultural production and relatively high off-farm incomes. These include farms with gross sales of less than $5,000. They constitute the largest grouping (36%)

but account for 8% of all land in farms and merely 1% of agriculture sales (see Table 12.1). Rural farm residences house people who value country living and seek to combine off-farm income (whether from work or transfer payments, such as retirees) with food production for home consumption and occasional sales. On the average these residences generate slightly negative net farm incomes but substantial nonfarm incomes. More of them reside in the South than in any other region. Most are in the tenure category of full-owner operator. They most often raise hay and cattle, principally beef (Brooks, 1984). They will continue to be a significant and probably growing portion of the rural population.

The second class of "small farms," those with gross sales between $5,000 and $40,000, make up over one-third of all farms and over one-fifth of land in farms, but contribute less than 10% of agricultural sales. They also rely heavily on nonfarm income, however, this income is less than for the residential farms. Most of the farm poverty is in this group, for which a number of strategies could improve their incomes: the combination of farm and off-farm work, improved markets, access to credit, technical assistance, appropriate technologies, and specialty products (USDA 1981:144; Harrington, et al., 1983:13). Along other dimensions (tenure, commodities, etc.) they are similar to the rural farm residences. Neither of these two smallest sized farms hire much wage labor.

Farms larger than the first two categories produce almost all of the nation's food and fiber. They are the primary objects of agricultural policy, and their actions are significant causes of structural changes. They may be divided into two equally important groups. "Medium-sized farms" are those with gross sales of over $40,000 but under $250,000. They are one-fourth of all farms, operate 47% of land in farms, and market over 40% of agricultural products. Farming tends to be the major source of income for them. For the most part, they have achieved technical economies of size. Still, their net farm income is often inadequate because of low product prices and high operating costs; their declining financial strength helps explain the bimodal distribution of farms (Harrington, et al., 1983:20). They dominate in the Great Lakes' Dairy Belt, the Northern Plains' Wheat Belt, and the Midwestern Corn and Hog Belt. They hire some wage labor, particularly at peak seasons. While full owner-operators and full tenants are represented, the tenure category of part owner-operator is increasingly important. This group includes most of the "family farms," as defined by USDA. The final category, "largest farms," with gross sales of over $250,000, includes less than 4% of the farms but operates over 22% of land in farms and sells nearly half of all agricultural products. Farm income is the main source of their total income, which is considerably above the national average. They hire most of the U.S. farm labor, much of which is composed of racial or ethnic minorities. Fruit and vegetable growers in the Southwest and West have been able to expand their labor-intensive production by drawing on cheap immigrant workers from Mexico and other countries (Pfeffer, 1986). Some of these are very large operations indeed, including industrial enterprises that maximize profits and minimize family contributions. They are disproportionately represented among farm corporations, which include only 2% of all farms but 23% of farm sales. Most of them are still family-based and incorporated for tax and inheritance reasons. Almost all of the larger, nonfamily corporations are in this size category. They tend to specialize in certain commodities (e.g., fruits, nuts, vegetables, broilers, sugar cane) and in certain states (Texas, Florida, Hawaii, Arizona, Washington, and California) (Krause, 1983).

Another way to present the contemporary structure of U.S. agriculture is to examine the size distribution by acreage. Table 12.2 shows that farms of less than 180 acres, although over 60% of all farms, operate under 10% of the farmland. A middle-sized group of between 180 and 2,000 acres constitutes over one-third of the farms and controls 44% of the land. The very large farms of 2,000 acres or more account for only 3% of the farms yet they hold almost half of all farmland. These data, along with Table 12.1, show the high concentration of production in U.S. agriculture and the bimodal structure consisting of a large number of small farms and a small number of large farms, with the middle-sized farmer seeming to decline.

Let us now turn to an analysis of the farm crisis of the mid-1980s and its effect on the family farm. The roots of the current financial crisis lay in the boom period of the 1970s. The inherent instability of agricultural production and incomes was exacerbated for political-economic reasons. A combination of low interest rates, high inflation rates, and a farm export boom, along with related national economic policies (e.g., devaluation of the dollar), led to speculation in land. During the

Table 12.1. Distribution of Farms by Gross Sales, 1982

Gross Sales	Farms		Gross Sales	
	Number (000)	%	Amount($) (billion)	%
Under $5,000	814.5	36.4	1.6	1.2
$5,000-$39,999	789.6	35.2	12.8	9.7
$40,000-$249,999	548.7	24.5	54.6	41.5
$250,000 & over	86.5	3.9	62.6	47.6
	2239.3	100.0%	$131.6	100.0%

Source: 1982 Census of Agriculture, U.S. Summary
(Table 49).

Note: "Abnormal farms" are omitted.

Table 12.2. Distribution of Farms and Land
in Farms by Size, 1982

Acres	Farms		Land	
	Number	%	Million Acres	%
Less than 10	187,665	8.4	.7	.1
10-49	449,252	20.0	12.1	1.2
50-179	711,652	31.8	74.8	7.6
180-499	526,510	23.5	158.8	16.1
500-999	203,925	9.1	140.5	14.2
1,000-1,999	97,395	4.3	132.4	13.4
2,000 or more	64,577	2.9	467.5	47.4
	2,240,976	100.0%	986.8	100.0%

Source: 1982 Census of Agriculture, U.S. Summary
(Table 4).

1970s, the value of farm assets, primarily land, nominally tripled and increased in real terms by over two-thirds. Debt-to-asset ratios improved. Inflation also drove up production costs, credit demands, and interest rates. Interest payments became farmers' biggest cash production expense, rising from 5% in 1960 to 16% by 1982. Between 1970 and 1982, farm real estate debt more than tripled (Harrington, et al., 1983: 14, 20; Manchester, 1985: 16, 43).

The other contributing factor in the inflationary 1970s was the growth of farm exports. With the sudden rise in foreign demand, U.S. agriculture was truly internationalized. The U.S. became the top farm exporter, accounting for nearly half of the world's grain trade (compared to less than a third in the early 1950s). More than 30% of U.S. crop acres now produce for the world market. Culminating the boom in 1980, over half of all U.S. wheat, rice, and cotton, and well over two-thirds of soybeans and corn, were exported. Farm prices had increased substantially, leading to further specialization, particularly in cereals, feed grains, and soybeans. These factors combined to make U.S. farmers much more vulnerable to fluctuations in world markets, increasing the difficulty of achieving adequate returns from expanded production. Expansion also made it harder to maintain a self-sustaining agriculture, as less productive and more erodible soils were brought into production (Harrington, et al., 1983; Manchester, 1985: 16, 33-36). The era of chronic surpluses appeared to be over. The critical problems of capitalist overproduction, declining commodity prices, and low farm incomes had been forgotten, or at least ignored.

In the 1970s, then, inflation and exports effectively enabled farmers and investors to acquire extremely expensive land. But the overexpanding bubble had to burst. In the early 1980s, both inflation and economic growth ended. The dollar was overvalued and export markets declined. As surpluses built up, farm prices and incomes plummeted (Breimyer, 1985). The most immediate cause of the current farm crisis was federal monetary policy. In late 1979, the Federal Reserve Board shifted to a tight money policy, which lowered inflation and raised interest rates. For agriculture, the effect was forced decapitalization, a massive deflation of asset (mainly land) values. That is, borrowers lost money while savers and lenders gained. Real farm wealth has declined dramatically since 1981, by 19% nationally and over 50% in some Midwestern states. Farmers were especially hard hit because of the switch to variable interest rates. Their average debt/asset ratio rose from 9% in 1950 to 26% in 1982 and has doubtlessly continued to increase (Breimyer, 1985; Manchester, 1985:31,44).

Under such conditions, few farmers can pay for land purchased in the inflationary 1970s. Many of the highly-leveraged farmers who expanded to adopt cost-saving technologies are in serious trouble. These include many larger, more "efficient" farms, some of which will not survive the current debt crisis. The mid-sized, family-based farms are probably suffering the most due to their declining financial strength (e.g., high debt loads, modest farm income, little nonfarm income). This helps explain their "disappearance" in the emerging bimodal structure of agriculture (Harrington, et al., 1983:14, 20, 26). National policies, then, have had the consequence of divesting owner-operators of land and subsidizing tax-sheltered investors who buy farm property. Many more family farmers will likely be dispossessed (Breimyer, 1985).

Few analysts are optimistic that the trends toward differentiation and transformation of the family farm can be reversed, especially not through public policies. Arguing, rather, that the democratization of agriculture (instead of family farming per se) should be the policy goal, Buttel (1983, 1984) suggests three policy directions: 1) a change in federal tax laws, which now favor the concentration of farm ownership and production; 2) direct government intervention in the land market, similar to the policies of most European countries; and 3) improvement in the wages and working conditions of farm laborers. These policy changes would undermine the publicly subsidized "efficiency" of the largest (nonfamily) farms and simultaneously add a considerable measure of economic democracy to U.S. agriculture.

However, there is a more pro-family farm position among some activists and researchers. They contend that public policies have made -- and can make -- a substantial difference in the structure of agriculture. They refuse to assume that the trend toward larger farms is inevitable, but rather see it as the outcome of policy decisions. By drawing on the American traditions of populism and progressivism, they argue that the trend can be slowed, if not reversed; a family farm system might even be re-established. But it will not be easy or painless. Strange (1985), for instance, says that farmers

themselves must recognize and renounce the excessive
speculation and overexpansion of the 1970s. They should
not try to go back to that misguided system. Further, if
farms are to be largely owner-operated, then farmland
cannot be hereditary, especially where the children are
nonfarmers. Rather, an effective inheritance tax could
prevent a "landed gentry" from arising and would keep the
land market open, thus helping insure access for beginning
farmers. As a corollary, land prices must reflect farm
earnings, so that farms can be internally financed.
Farmland cannot remain an object of speculation. In
addition, the government must enforce mandatory production
controls. Currently, farm prices are too low and costs
are too high, due to monopoly control and overproduction.
Higher farm prices should be tied to a food policy for the
poor. In summary, we need to rise above "petty economics"
and recall the Jeffersonian heritage of social justice and
economic democracy. We must work to make the food system
fairer for producers as well as consumers. In the face of
industrial capitalism, there is no guarantee that family
farming can be saved, but it is worth a good fight
(Strange, 1985). One place to begin, Strange argues, is
by changing current public policies that favor the
larger-than-family farm.

EFFECTS OF THE CHANGING STRUCTURE OF AGRICULTURE
UPON FARM, FAMILY AND SOCIETY

Land is the basis of subsistence, residence, and
production in its many forms. It is for this reason that
the nature of our relationship to the land, especially
that used for food production, is of significance to the
larger society as well as to the farmers and their
families. In the early period of settlement and
government formation, the values of freedom and well-being
for all were seen to be supported by land ownership and
farm operation by the family. This was essential for
clearing and settling the land as well as for providing
the conditions for a true democracy. The leaders of this
country felt that family owned and operated farms would
provide the basis for the efficient production of food and
fiber as well as support for the institutions and services
for all. But in recent decades most farmers have
responded to market forces, going much beyond the
resources of the family for land, labor, and capital.
High interest rates, inflated land values of the 1970s,
and low prices of farm products have led to a rate of farm

foreclosures indicative of that of the 1930s. This is particularly true of those farms which have expanded operations to increase returns and to pay for the increased costs of land, labor, and capital. Those who have borrowed less and depended more upon family resources are more likely to survive, although their farm income is low and usually needs supplementing with off-farm work.

The effect of farm size upon efficiency in the use of resources for agricultural production has been a topic of interest in the last two decades. Most studies have shown that economies of size do not go beyond the modernized one- to two-person farm, though larger farms may increase total profits (Miller, et al., 1981). There are also economies in the use of professional management services, the bulk purchase of farm chemicals, machinery, or other inputs as well as in marketing the products. But the diseconomies of scale are usually not considered, such as the ability to vary inputs with changing prices and costs. Large farms with more labor and greater capital investments tend to be less flexible than smaller farms which use unpaid family labor and family-owned land. But this flexibility of the family farm is limited by the interests and abilities of family members as opportunities for education and nonfarm work have increased and as families desire higher incomes to maintain a level of living similar to that of nonfarm families.

The effect of farm size upon soil conservation is less clear. The nature of the land and climate of the U.S. is such that soil loss with wind and water erosion has been a serious problem. While this has affected all regions, it has been more serious in the regions of continuous cropping where heavy winds and rains are common. Following the Great Plains "dust bowl" of the 1930s, farmers have received subsidies for terracing, contour planting and other practices which would reduce soil erosion. This effort has continued, with variations in the extent and nature of the conservation measures supported by state and federal policies, although the problems of soil loss and reduced water levels and contamination are on the increase.

In general, we find that the larger farms are more energy efficient and follow more soil and water conservation practices (Tweeten, 1983; Coughenour and Christenson, 1980; and Heffernan and Green, 1986). They have more resources for conservation practices, receive more benefits and assistance from public programs, and are more likely to have land that needs conservation practices

(Korsching and Nowak, 1983). Yet, there is a feeling that small farmers should receive special attention by government programs since they have not received their fair share of public services (Molnar and Korsching, 1983). Smaller farmers also are less flexible in land use and frequently farm the poorest land, which is subject to greater erosion and where effective conservation practices are more costly. There is a renewed interest in and support for soil conservation, as indicated by the federal subsidy for removing highly erodible land from production beginning in 1986.

The commitment of the family to the farm between generations appears to have a positive effect upon the land. Bennett (1977) finds that the Hutterites communal system favors the viability of the farms and the land in the face of natural and economic adversity. Carlson and Dillman (1983) also find that conservation practices are followed consistently only on those grain farms which are expected to be passed on from one generation to the next, although a study in Illinois finds that age of operator rather than kinship is more positively related with erosion control practices (Van Es and Tsoukalas, 1985). In general a commitment to the land over time is a condition for the long-run sustainability of production.

As indicated earlier, small farms combined with off-farm employment have been increasing as a characteristic of the bi-modal structure of agriculture. While subsistence farmers have engaged in off-farm work since the period of early settlement, off-farm work declined as farming became more market oriented. But, as the terms of trade for agriculture have declined since the 1950s, farm families who wished to continue farming either had to enlarge their operations or were required to supplement their farm income with work off the farm. Hence, off-farm work has become a means for the reproduction of the household and continues as value is placed upon farming as a way of life (Moore, 1984). It also means that living on the land provides for a feeling of self-reliance, freedom, and interest in growing things (Heffernan and Green, 1986).

Part-time farming is no longer primarily a process of moving out of agriculture. In fact, for the younger generation it is frequently a means for accumulating capital for moving into full-time farming. For the most part it has become a permanent form of production in which labor of the household is allocated in a manner to satisfy the needs and values of those involved. This means that farm women are becoming increasingly involved in off-farm work to supplement income from the husbands' work on the farm. Farm men increase their off-farm work as farm labor requirements decrease and capital requirements increase.

It follows that the well-being of farm families is increasingly influenced by the off-farm work of farm family members. In 1978, off-farm income was substantial for all farm sizes and when combined with farm income was above that of the national median family income in 1978. While this may no longer be true, as farm income has declined, it does mean that the welfare of those families living on the land is closely tied to the nonfarm sources of income available to rural residents. At the same time, the income of nonfarm families in rural areas is dependent upon the viability of the farm sector for supporting the institutions and providing the services and a market for farm products. This is indicated in the decline of many rural communities with the current farm crisis.

The off-farm opportunities in rural areas need to be made available for farm families who must supplement their farm income from small enterprises. This could include the processing of food products which is being encouraged in some regions. Rural industries and services can provide opportunities for farm families as well as support for the institutions of rural communities. The positive effects of such developments for farm as well as nonfarm residents require the integration of enterprises into the communities so that the benefits to local residents outweigh the costs which frequently occur (Summers, 1986). In order for farm families to benefit from local as well as other nonfarm opportunities, information and training for such opportunities must be provided. Public funds and local planning are needed to attract nonfarm activities and services into rural areas which will serve both farm and nonfarm families without adding costs and disrupting rural communities and their services.

There is continued concern about the social as well as economic consequences of the loss of family farms. This is occurring near large urban centers as well as in the rural areas. There has been a reduction in the growth rate of rural counties throughout the country to one-fourth that of the metropolitan counties. Farmland near urban areas has increased in value for nonfarm residences and industry. A few states have taken measures to prohibit or discourage nonfamily corporations from entering agriculture. Land trusts which provide an opportunity for farm owners as well as nonfarm persons to

join together and control the land ownership and use will
provide an opportunity for maintaining family sized farms
in some areas. Use of these trusts for controlling land
use for recreation as well as food production are
increasing in the Northeastern states, California and
other areas near large urban centers.

Concerns for the social consequences of large-scale
commercial farming in the U.S. were documented by
anthropologist Walter Goldschmidt in 1944 in California.
His comparison of a small farm community with a community
of a few large-scale farms was quite striking, although
the conditions in the fruit farming community with
immigrant laborers, irrigation, and off-farm residence of
the large operators, were atypical for other regions. He
found that in almost all aspects of family welfare, those
in the small farm community were better off, including
institutions and services of the community. A restudy in
1968 found that these differences still prevailed
(Goldschmidt, 1978). This does not mean that all
increases in farm scale have negative effects upon the
farm families involved in farming (Harris and Gilbert,
1982), but rural income in general declines, and the
number of rural workers with lower income increases. A
more extensive recent study of farms in the Great Plains
and West also finds that counties with more medium-sized
rather than large-scale or small part-time farms have a
higher standard of living (Flora and Flora, 1985).

There is also evidence that the increase in size of
farms has a negative effect upon the social participation
of farm families (Heffernan and Lasley, 1978; Poole,
1981). The time involved in caring for the larger
operations decreases the time available for interaction
within as well as outside the family. Up to a point the
increase in technology may increase income and reduce
labor time which favors increased social contact. Thus,
there are both costs and benefits of increased scale and
mechanization of agricultural production (Flinn and
Buttel, 1980). The benefits are gained by those able to
take advantage of this process, depending upon the type of
agriculture, the region, and the opportunities for
off-farm employment. The greatest effect is the overall
decline in the numbers of full-time, family-sized farms
and an increase in the inequalities among farmers and
between operators and farm laborers. The short-term
economic considerations of food production tend to replace
the personal and social values of family farmers and other
rural residents.

How have changes in farm size and structure affected family relationships within and between generations? In the past, most farms were passed on from father to son or daughter. The parents usually provided livestock and equipment in return for labor and a favorable sale price or low interest rate loans. But this is changing as the value of land, livestock, and equipment has increased greatly and the family becomes more dependent upon nonfamily resources. These external sources must be paid at the market rates, resulting in less favorable arrangements between generations. For this reason, fewer sons take over the family farm and fewer daughters marry farmers' sons. This varies by region, state, and ethnic background. While some states, such as Minnesota, have made it easier for young farmers to take over the family farm or another farm through state subsidized loans, most young farmers now take off-farm work before entering farming.

Women have always performed an important role in farming throughout the U.S. They have always had a major responsibility in producing for subsistence. The amount of time women spend in farm work has increased as less time is required in the household with modern conveniences and less time needed for subsistence activities. According to a national survey (Rosenfeld, 1985), over half of the farm women surveyed considered themselves to be a main operator of the farm and felt they could operate the farm without their husband if necessary. While only 5.2% of all farms were managed by women in 1978, the number is increasing, especially in the Southern and Midwestern states. Women have more difficulty getting credit, obtaining other resources and in marketing their products than do the men (Kalbacher, 1985).

While farm wives may be less involved in farm field work on larger farms, they tend to be more involved in the record keeping and financial matters (Fassinger and Schwarzweller, 1984). This is especially true in the diversified farming regions where the family farm is more dominant. Farm women provide an important role in obtaining information about farm matters through the mass media, and they have also become effective in lobbying for family farm interests, such as changes in inheritance laws. Most of all, they have extended their contribution to the economic as well as social well-being of the farm family through their work on and off the farm.

During a period of economic recession, scale of farming can have increased negative effects upon farm women as well as men, especially when debts are high and production may have to be increased to meet expenses. In 1982 larger farmers in Wisconsin were most dissatisfied with "farming as a way of life," "as a source of income," and especially with "leisure time activities" and "family life" (Wilkening and Moore, 1983). It was the size of the farm debt that had the greatest negative effect upon the satisfaction of the farm wives. Thus, the scale and structure of labor, capital, and income can have negative effects upon the quality of life of farm families, especially during periods of economic recession.

PROBLEMS AND PROSPECTS OF THE FAMILY FARM

It is quite apparent that the structure of American agriculture has changed greatly as it has become a part of a highly commercialized economy. It has shifted from many small-scale family farmed enterprises to less than 3% of the population, and only one-third of these producing most of the products. This shift is likely to continue under the present private and public forces affecting agriculture. This is demonstrated by the continued decline of the middle-sized family farms in favor of large-scale, full-time and small, part-time farms.

The problem of the family farm has become more focused upon how to maintain income levels and stability under prevailing market conditions (Marion, et al., 1986). How can farmer's incomes be maintained comparable to that of other sectors of the economy? Are small farmers especially disadvantaged and require additional support? Are larger-than-family farms and corporate farms able to force out family-sized farms, force up food prices, and be less concerned with the natural resources upon which farming is based? To what extent should farm structure and prices be stabilized? The problem becomes that of how a favorable interaction between the family and the farm can be maintained over time so that both are enhanced.

For the family, it involves the acquisition of the farm at an appropriate stage, with the farm providing sufficient income and other benefits for the family members during the family life cycle and then transferring the farm to the next generation to accommodate both generations. As already indicated, the acquisition of a farm has become more difficult for the younger farmers as land values have increased. Only a few states have assisted in this process through favorable loans or land acquisition programs. Only the fortunate few are able to acquire the family farm at a time and through financial arrangements that do not require a heavy indebtedness in the early years. Many must work off the farm to acquire funds for the initial payment on the farm.

The provision of an adequate income during the life cycle of the family is probably the major problem of the family farm. Off-farm work again provides an opportunity for income for the family which wishes to continue to live on the land for noneconomic as well as for economic reasons. Successful full-time farmers must be good business managers as well as skilled workers. They must acquire special knowledge and skills in production, marketing, financial management, and relationships with others to be successful farm operators. This requires special effort and opportunities which the traditional family farmer often does not have. It requires learning new ways of reducing costs, maintaining resources, and marketing products. These have not received sufficient attention by institutions and organizations serving farmers.

The prospects for the family farm in this country will depend upon the extent to which private interests and public policy provide information and assistance for both beginning and established farmers in solving these problems. At present, information, farm technology, farm credit and price support policies tend to favor the larger farmer. While limits can be placed upon direct payments to farms for low prices and for moving land from production, this is not likely to occur. Even the smaller family farmers have failed to oppose income tax benefits and other policies from which they can benefit little as compared to the larger farmer. Hence, the prospects for the genuine family farm do not appear to be encouraging in the U.S. However, there are activities and organizations which recognize the problems of the family farmer as well as the benefits family farms provide to the families, the farms, and the communities in which they are located. The Natural Organic Farmers Association in the Northeast and centers in Nebraska, Wisconsin and California are giving special attention to the problems of maintaining the family farm.

There is increasing concern by farm as well as nonfarm interests about the problems of soil erosion and heavy use of chemicals in commercial agriculture. Soil erosion has already resulted in the abandonment of much land from crop production. The heavy use of chemicals for fertilizer and pesticides to sustain production as the soil erodes and the pests become more resistant to the chemicals has produced serious problems of groundwater pollution and some food contamination. These problems continue to increase. Environmental and recreational interests are also concerned with maintaining the natural setting and resources which are affected by cash crop expansion and the heavy use of chemicals to control pests. This has been referred to as the long-term crisis in agriculture.

Some agricultural universities and state and federal agencies are giving increasing attention to the problem of developing a sustainable agriculture without the negative consequences for the farm and its products. Garth Youngberg (1984), formerly of the USDA, gave attention to a more "organic" approach to farming. Studies were made comparing farms using few chemicals with those using heavy chemicals (Lockeretz and Wernick, 1980) and found that while production levels differed, net income did not. Other studies have shown that organic farming can be cost effective and can add value to the product through local processing and marketing (Vail and Rozyne, 1984). A more biological approach to farming receives special attention by the Rodale Press, which publishes The New Farm magazine. This publication reports on the research and experience of farmers in moving toward a more sustainable form of food production without the heavy use of chemicals. While family farms involve a concern for the land, there is no assurance that small family farms are any more effective in following a more sound biological approach than larger farms (Buttel, et al., 1986).

Farming systems research (Gilbert, et al., 1980) is another approach with potential benefit to small farmers. This approach brings several disciplines together to determine how to sustain and improve food production under a range of private and societal goals and ecological conditions. For example, intra-disciplinary research is being conducted in three Northwestern states: Washington, Oregon and Idaho, with a grant from the USDA to do research in development for the control of soil erosion. The research grants are made for 15 years to include tillage, plant management, erosion and runoff, pest management, and the socioeconomics of erosion control.

Only small-scale enterprises are adapted to the use of the small and uneven tracts of land in much of the U.S., where topography and soils result in productive areas too small for large-scale machines and operations. States in the Northeast are identifying such areas in public lands and making them available for small-scale producers. This is being done through farmland trusts in which the owners of the land agree to use their land in a way which will protect the resources and the scenic, as well as recreational value, of farmland in return for lower taxes and other benefits. The zoning of agricultural land for protection from urban expansion in many states is providing some protection for small farms, though not always protecting them from larger operators renting them for cash crops.

A somewhat different biological approach to farming is biotechnology, which is more likely to lead to greater control and concentration by the food industry. Research in biotechnology has been done to a great extent by private companies that combine research from various specialties to produce and market the products. This is likely to lead to increases both in production and in dependence of the farmer on commercial seeds, chemicals, and hormones. However, biotechnology research can also address the problems of nitrogen-fixation and plant adaptation to the natural environments. This could aid in the creation of plants which would contribute to a more suitable agriculture in dry land, erodible lands, and other special conditions. But for this to occur, there needs to be an increase in public support for research of this type, which may not only produce high returns in the short run but may also benefit both small and large food producers and consumers in the long run (Jackson, Berry and Coleman, 1985).

There has been a renewed interest in local sales of farm products, especially in the areas near urban centers, such as the Northeastern states which "import" three-fourths of their food. The rising costs of transportation and consumers' greater interest in locally grown food products has stimulated more local marketing. The average molecule of food travels 1300 miles in this country before being eaten. While the percentage of food sold in local markets is small, the amount is increasing as local farmers and food handlers respond to the demand. With the quotas for tobacco acreage declining in certain Southern states, the efforts are being made to provide "mobile markets" for the direct sale of vegetables by small farmers. The needs of small farm families, many of which are in poverty, have been recognized by the university extension programs in almost half the states in the U.S. This is especially important for small black farmers in the Southeast who have a larger proportion in this small farm group (Munoz, 1983). Many of these farmers, of course, supplement their income with off-farm sources. But the focus for the women as well as the men on these farms is to produce, preserve, and market their products for a stable income from units which do not have access to the organizations and markets of the larger scale operators.

What is the significance of the decline of the family farm in the U.S. and why is it of concern to farm families, rural communities, and the nation? Is the shift towards larger and more specialized farms in keeping with a national and international trend that is essential and inevitable? Many inside and outside of agriculture think so. This has happened in businesses other than farming, so why should it be any different?

Farming is different in that it involves the use of natural resources, which are in a process of constant change in time and place. This means that the most effective use of these resources and the maintenance of the living forces requires direct contact with them and concern for their sustainability. This can be done by professionals as well as by general farmers, but it requires attention to the total enterprise over time and its interaction with natural, social, and political conditions as well as short-term economic returns. This suggests that persons who have these concerns be involved in the management of the land. These interests are not necessarily assured by family owned and managed farms. We suggest only that it is more likely if concern goes beyond nostalgia for the family farm to a consideration for the sustainability of the land and well-being of the people affected by farming, both directly and indirectly, in the years ahead. In addition, people's sense of well-being is closely tied to their sense of control and self-fulfillment in their work situation and to their relationship to other people and services in their community (Marans, Dillman and Keller, 1982). This sense is more likely to occur in stable rural communities where the institutions and services are adequate. But it is these social conditions that are declining as the farms become larger and the population base decreases. The immediate effect of this is a decline in the well-being not only of the farmers displaced, but of those who relate with and are served by them as well. In this chapter we have mentioned several ways that such trends may be slowed, if not reversed.

296

REFERENCES

Bennett, John W. 1977. "The Hutterian Colony: A
Traditional Voluntary Commune with Large Economic
Scale." In Peter Dorner (ed.), Cooperative and
Commune. Madison: University of Wisconsin Press.
Breimyer, Harold F. 1985. "The Future of Family Farm
Agriculture." Plenary Address. An Ecumenical Event
on the Future of Family Farm Agriculture, Madison,
Wisconsin.
Brewster, David E. 1979. "The family farm." Pp. 74-79
in Structure Issues of American Agriculture.
Agricultural Economic Report 438. Washington, D.C.:
Economics, Statistics, and Cooperatives Service, U.S.
Department of Agriculture.
Brooks, Nora L. 1984. Minifarms: Farm Business or Rural
Residence? Wash., D.C.:Economic Research Service,
U.S., Agricultural Information Bulletin No. 480.
Buttel, Frederick, H. 1980. "W(h)ither the family
farm?" Cornell Journal of Social Relations.
15(Summer):10-37.
Buttel, Frederick, H. 1982. "The political economy of
agriculture in advanced industrial societies." In S.
G. McNall (ed.), Current Perspectives in Social
Theory. Greenwich, CN: JAI Press.
Buttel, Frederick H. 1983. "Beyond the Family Farm." In
Gene F. Summers (ed.), Technology and Social Change in
Rural Areas. Boulder, CO: Westview Press.
Buttel, Frederick H. 1984. "Agricultural Land Reform in
America." In C. C. Geisler and F. J. Popper (eds.),
Land Reform, American Style. Totowa, NJ: Rowman &
Allanheld.
Buttel, Frederick H., Gilbert W. Gillespie, Jr., Rhonda
Janke, Brian Caldwell and Marianna Sarrantonio.
1986. "Reduced-Impact Agricultural Systems: A
Critique," The Rural Sociologist 6(Sept.):350-70.
Carlson, John E. and Don A. Dillman. 1983. "Influence of
Kinship Arrangements in Farmer Innovativeness." Rural
Sociology 48(Summer):183-200.
Cochrane, Willard W. 1979. The Development of American
Agriculture: A Historical Analysis. Minneapolis:
University of Minnesota Press.
Coughenour, M. and J. Christenson. 1980. "Is Life on the
Small Farm Beautiful?" Paper presented at the 5th
World Congress for Rural Sociology, Mexico
City, August.

297

Fassinger, Polly A. and Harry K. Schwarzweller. 1984.
"The Work of Farm Women: A Midwestern Study." In H.
K. Schwarzweller (ed.), Research in Rural Sociology
and Development I. Greenwich, CN: JAI Press.
Flinn, William J. and Frederick H. Buttel. 1980.
"Sociological Aspects of Farm Size: Ideological
Consequences of Scale in Agriculture." American
Journal of Agricultural Economics 62(December):946-953.
Flora, Cornelia and Jan Flora. 1985. "Emerging Agri-
cultural Technologies Farm Size, Public Policy and
Rural Communities: The Great Plains and the West."
Paper presented for the Office of Technology
Assessment, U.S. Congress.
Friedmann, Harriet. 1980. "Household production and the
national economy." Journal of Peasant Studies
7:158-84.
Geisler, Charles C. 1984. "A History of Land Reform in
the United States." In C. C. Geisler and F. J. Popper
(eds.), Land Reform, American Style. Totowa, NJ:
Rowman & Allanheld.
Gilbert, E. H., D. W. Norman and F. E. Winch. 1980.
"Farming Systems Research: A Critical Appraisal."
East Lansing, Michigan; Michigan State University,
Department of Agricultural Economics, Rural
Development Paper Number 6.
Gilbert, Jess and Craig K. Harris. 1984. "Changes in
Type, Tenure, and Concentration of U.S. Farmland
Owners." In H. K. Schwarzweller (ed.), Research in
Rural Sociology and Development I. Greenwich, CN:
JAI Press.
Goldschmidt, Walter. 1978. As You Sow: Three Studies in
the Social Consequences of Agri-business. New York:
Harcourt, Brace and Co.
Goss, Kevin, Richard D. Rodefeld, and Frederick H.
Buttel. 1980. "The political economy of class
structure in U.S. agriculture." In F. H. Buttel and
H. Newby (eds.), The Rural Sociology of The Advanced
Societies. Montclair, N.J.: Allanheld, Osmun.
Harrington, David H., Donn A. Reimund, Kenneth H. Baum,
and R. Neal Peterson. 1983. U.S. Farming in the
Early 80s: Production and Financial Structure.
Washington, D.C.: Economic Research Service, U.S.
Department of Agriculture. Agricultural Economic
Report 504.
Harris, Craig H. and Jess Gilbert. 1982. "Large-scale
Farming, Rural Income and Goldschmidt's Agrarian
Thesis." Rural Sociology 47(Fall):449-458.

298

Heffernan, William D. and Gary P. Green. 1986.
    "Farm Size and Soil Loss for a Sustainable
    Agriculture." Rural Sociology 5(Spring):31-42.
Heffernan, William D. and Paul Lasley. 1978.
    "Agricultural Structure and Interaction in the Local
    Community." Rural Sociology 43(Fall):548-61.
Jackson, Wes, Wendell Berry, and Bruce Colman. 1985.
    Eds., Meeting the Expectations of the Land. San
    Francisco: North Point Press.
Kalbacher, Judith Z. 1985. A Profile of Female Farmers
    in America. Washington, D.C.: Economic Research
    Service, U.S. Department of Agriculture. Rural
    Development Research Report 45.
Korsching, Peter F. and Peter J. Nowak. 1983.
    "Flexibility in Conservation Policy." In David
    Brewster, et al. (eds.), Farms in Transition. Ames:
    Iowa State University Press.
Krause, Kenneth R. 1983. Corporate Farming: Importance,
    Incentives and State Restrictions. Washington, D.C.:
    Economic Research Service, U.S. Department of
    Agriculture. Agricultural Economic Report No. 506.
Lee, John E. Jr. 1983. "Some Consequences of the New
    Reality in U.S. Agriculture." In D. E. Brewster et
    al. (eds.), Farms in Transition. Ames: Iowa State
    University Press.
Lockeretz, William and Sarah Wernick. 1980. "Commercial
    Organic Farming in the Corn Belt in Comparison to
    Conventional Practices." Rural Sociology 45:708-722.
Lyson, Thomas A. 1984. "Pathways into Production
    Agriculture: The Structuring of Farm Recruitment in
    the United States." In H. K. Schwarzweller (eds.),
    Research in Rural Sociology and Development I.
    Greenwich, CN: JAI Press.
Manchester, Alden C. 1985. Agriculture's Links with U.S.
    and World Economics. Washington, D.C.: Economic
    Research Service, U.S. Department of Agriculture.
    Agricultural Information Bulletin No. 496.
Marans, Robert and Don Dillman with Janet Keller. 1982.
    Perceptions of Life Quality in Rural America. Ann
    Arbor: Institute for Survey Research, University of
    Michigan,.
Marion, Bruce and N.C. 117 Committee. 1986. The
    Organization and Performance of the U.S. Food System,
    Lexington, MD: D.C. Heath.
Miller, Thomas A., Gordon E. Rodewald, and Robert G.
    McElroy. 1981. Economies of Size in U.S. Field Crop
    Farming. Washington, D.C.: Economic Research

Service, U.S. Department of Agriculture. Agricultural Economics Report 472.

Molnar, Joseph J. and Peter F. Korsching. 1983. "Societal Consequences of Concentrated Ownership and Control in the Agricultural Sector." The Rural Sociologist 3(Jan.):34-41.

Moore, Keith. 1984. "Part-time Farming: A Form of Household Reproduction." Ph.D. dissertation in sociology, University of Wisconsin, Madison, Wis.

Moore, Keith M. and Eugene A. Wilkening. 1984. "The Processes of Farm Entry and the Effects on the Structure of Agriculture." Paper presented at the annual meeting of the Rural Sociological Society, College Station, Texas, August.

Mueller, Willard F. 1982. "The Food Conglomerates." In Don F. Hadwiger and Ross B. Talbot (eds.), Food Policy and Farm Programs, New York: The Academy of Political Science.

Munoz, Robert D. 1983. "Small Family Farms in Mississippi and Tennessee: A Comparison of Small Farm Definitions" Washington, D.C.: Economic Research Service, U.S. Department of Agriculture. Agricultural Economics Report 141.

Nikolitch, R. 1972. "Family-sized Farms in U.S. Agriculture." Washington, D.C.: Economic Research Service, U.S. Department of Agriculture. Agricultural Economics Report 499.

Osburn, Howard A. 1984. "Research, Technology and the Small Farm." In Dietrich Knorr and Tom R. Watkins (eds.), Alterations in Food Production. New York: Van Nostrand Reinhold Co.

Penn, J. B. 1979. "The structure of agriculture." In Structure Issues of American Agriculture. Agriculture Economic Report 438. Washington, D.C.: Economics, Statistics, and Cooperatives Service, U.S. Department of Agriculture.

Pfeffer, Max. 1982. "The Social Relations of Subcontracting: The Case of Contract Vegetable Production in Wisconsin." Center for Comparative Studies in the Sociology of Agriculture, Department of Rural Sociology, University of Wisconsin-Madison.

Pfeffer, Max. 1986. "Immigration Policy and Class Relations in California Agriculture." In A. Eugene Havens (ed.) Studies in the Transformation of Agriculture. Boulder, CO: Westview Press.

300

Poole, Dennis L. 1981. "Farm Scale, Family Life and
  Community Participation." Rural Sociology
  46(Spring):112-127.
Raup, Philip M. 1980. "Some Issues in Land Tenure,
  Ownership and Control in Dispersed vs. Concentrated
  Agriculture." In Increasing Understanding of Public
  Problems and Policies, Oak Brook, IL: Farm
  Foundation.
Rodefeld, Richard D. 1978. "Trends in U.S. Farm
  Organizational Structure and Type." In D. Rodefeld,
  et al. (eds.), Change in Rural America:
  Causes,Consequences and Alternatives, St. Louis: C.V.
  Mosby Co..
Rosenfeld, Rachel A. 1985. U.S. Farm Women:
  Interrelationships of Work and Family. Chapel Hill:
  University of North Carolina Press.
Salamon, Sonya. 1985. "Ethnic Communities and the
  Structure of Agriculture," Rural Sociology
  50(Fall):323-40.
Schertz, Lyle P. and others. 1979. Another Revolution in
  U.S. Farming, Washington, D.C.: Economics,
  Statistics, and Cooperatives Service, U.S. Department
  of Agriculture. Agriculture Economic Report 441.
Strange, Marty. 1985. "The Economic Structure of a
  Sustainable Agriculture." In Wes Jackson, Wendell
  Berry and Bruce Colman (eds.) Meeting the Expectations
  of the Land. San Fransisco: North Point Press.
Summers, Gene F. 1986. "Rural Industrialization." The
  Rural Sociologist 6(May):181-186.
Tweeten, Luther 1983. "The Economics of Small Farms."
  Science 219(March): 1037-41.
U.S. Department of Agriculture. 1981. A Time To Choose.
  Washington, D.C.: Government Printing Office.
U.S. General Accounting Office. 1985. Agriculture
  Overview: U.S. Food/Agriculture in a Volatile World
  Economy. Washington, D.C.: GAO-RCED-86-3BR.
Vail, David and Michael Rozyne. 1984. "The Image and
  Reality of Small Organic Farms: Evidence from
  Maine." In Dietrich Knorr and Tom R. Watkins (eds.),
  Alterations in Food Production. New York: Van
  Nostrand Reinhold Co.
van Es, J. C. and Theodore Tsoukalas. 1985. "Kinship
  Arrangements and Innovativeness: A Comparison of
  Palouse and Prairie Findings." Staff Paper,
  Department of Agricultural Economics, University of
  Illinois, Urbana.

Vogeler, Ingolf. 1981. The Myth of the Family Farm:
Agribusiness Dominance of U.S. Agriculture. Boulder,
CO: Westview Press.

Wilkening, Eugene A. and Keith Moore. 1983. "Control
Over Farm Resources and Satisfaction with Farm and
Family." Paper presented at the 1983 meeting of the
Midwest Sociological Society, Kansas City, Missouri.

Youngberg, Garth. 1984. "Alternatives, Agriculture in
the United States: Ideology, Politics and
Prospects." In Dietrich Knorr and Tom R. Watkins
(eds.), Alterations in Food Production, New York: Van
Nostrand Reinhold Co.

13
Conclusions

While the topic of this book is "family farming," it may have been more accurately titled "The Structure of Agriculture in Europe and America." The term family farm has a wide range of meanings and cannot be understood without considering it within the social and economic context of a given country. Most countries have defined the family farm as the family's provision of the labor, land, and management for the farm enterprise. The provision of the capital for machinery and other investments is usually not included, since these are increasingly provided by nonfamily sources in industrial economies; but as technology has increased and the operations specialized, land debit and operating capital becomes the major variable in the cost and returns to the farm enterprise. Also, rather than borrow capital at high interest rates to purchase land to expand operations, additional land is often rented.

So the use of the term family farm varies by the user and has come to be defined in economic terms for the purpose of classifying and studying the changes taking place in the size and structure of agriculture in the industrialized nations. While the specific definitions vary, the assumption is that the family farm is operated by one family, or by an extended family. The fact that the family provides most of the labor and is the risk-taking manager of the farm provides an interrelationship between family and farm that has consequences for both.

What can we learn from the conditions and experiences relating to the structure of agriculture in the industrialized nations of Europe and North America? The nature of the access to land and its products has ranged from the serfs or peasant holdings as part of village or kinship communities to large estates owned by crown and landed aristocracy. New forms of land ownership came with land reforms in France in 1789 and in the 19th century in the rest of Europe. As new lands opened up, both in Europe and America, there were opportunities for new forms of ownership and production of agricultural products. Great expanses of land provided opportunities for land to be acquired by those who worked it. But to rise above subsistence required transportation and storage for the market. Capital was needed for buildings, machinery, and the power to operate them. This has continued over two centuries to result in food production, marketing, and processing as a major economic enterprise which has become increasingly influenced and controlled by economic forces beyond the food producer.

Market forces increasingly have influenced these processes to affect the prices received by the farmer and the prices paid by the consumer. But land ownership, the services needed to maintain the land, and the people who work it are not adequately treated in the market. The reproduction and well-being of the people involved depend upon the family, the community, and government policies at all levels. Some services and policies benefit some more than others; and, frequently, their long-term consequences are contrary to those intended, especially for families and communities. For this reason, it is important to consider the experiences and policies of various countries and how these have affected the structure and functioning of food production and those involved in it.

The major purpose of this book has been to observe the process of change in the structure of agriculture in recent decades and particularly the change in the position of family farming within this structure. The contributions presented indicate that in all countries the family farm is still a major form of production and provides a substantial part of food production for national markets and for export.

It is quite clear that changes are occurring which affect the family based structure of farming. In all countries agriculture has been moving in the direction of larger and more commercial enterprises to increase production. This means a growing role of nonfamily forms of agricultural production and, with improved technology, a change in the ownership, land, and the provision of capital by nonfamily sources. While some families increase their farm size and investment, others shift to off-farm work to maintain an adequate income. Thus, part-time farming as a primary or subsidiary source of income for the family tends to maintain the more traditional patterns, providing the family an opportunity to remain on the land and to share in the social as well as economic values of living on their own land. Hence, the increasing concentration of production on relatively few large farms and the simultaneous increase of small, part-time farms characterizes the current structure of agriculture.

This increasing bi-modal pattern of capital intensive, commercialized, full-time, larger-than-family farms and smaller, more subsistence oriented, part-time family farms, has taken place both in Europe and in North America. While the direction of change is the same, the advancement of these processes differs greatly depending on national and local conditions. The expansion of capital intensive, fully commercialized, full-time family farms may be slowed by the pre-existing structures, such as land fragmentation, the lack of land for sale, difficulty in obtaining the necessary capital for expansion, environmental and/or economic obstacles for full specialization, and restrictive agricultural policy.

The extent and nature of this bi-modal pattern varies with the suitability of natural resources of the region for farming and the presence of other industries. In some parts of the world, such as Scandinavia and regions of North America, forestry, fishing, and recreation have become the major sources of income for family members on small farms. In other countries certain regions provide work in mining and metallurgy, which may be subsidized directly with public funds. In the U.S. and Canada, especially, agri-business is concentrating in large-scale commercial crop production and recruiting seasonal workers from both the local and seasonal migrant workforce. On the large-scale farms this tends to shift the problem from one of maintaining the family farm to the welfare of the hired workers.

The forces of change are similar in market economies of North America and Europe. Farming is affected by technological change and by market forces, although North America is somewhat more dependent upon the export of farm products. But, in general, farms must expand in size and capital investment to maintain an income for producers that is comparable to that of other workers. So some farms expand while others sell out or decline in size. Attachment to place and land, along with some economic and social advantage, keeps many farmers on small plots as the family members seek work off the farm. This is the most common pattern in the advanced industrial countries. The pattern may be encouraged by agricultural and social policy designed to keep the families in the country for cultural as well as economic reasons (e.g. Norway and Germany). In regions of other countries farms have increased in size but jobs or direct subsidy for small farmers have been provided.

Change to large-scale farm units has also occurred in most socialist countries of Eastern Europe. The forces of change here were different, however. They were not market but political forces. The decision to replace family farms with large-scale State or collective farms was made by political authorities and implemented by administrative means. Market incentives to enlarge the operation were nonexistent, and large-scale administered farming units failed to show any economic advantages. Compared to family farms in West Germany, large-scale State and collective farms in East Germany are less productive and less efficient on the basis of the input/output ratio. Family farms survived in Eastern Europe in the form of small plots provided member families of collective farms or to those who worked off the farm. This must be tolerated by authorities because they show very high vitality and contribute significantly to satisfying the needs of consumers troubled by shortages in the food supply. Only in Poland and in Yugoslavia has family farming survived in its full form. In Poland the system of an administered economy did not offer incentives for structural change, and private agriculture is kept in a state of stagnation, although it produced more per unit of land and more in return from inputs than large-scale socialized farms. In Yugoslavia the process of structural change is influenced by market forces but the effects are restricted by administrative regulations (limit of size of farm for instance). In both countries the expansion of full-time family farms is very slow, but part-time farming has grown very quickly and so called "peasant workers" constitute at least one-third of the farming families.

The contributions to this book have indicated the direction and mechanisms of change in the structure of agriculture, the diminishing position of family farming within this structure, and the transformation of traditional family farms into a bi-modal pattern. There is consensus among all contributors that typical family farming is declining. What can we learn from the experiences of agricultural policy's effect on the structure of agriculture in the 11 countries presented in the book?

The agricultural policies vary from open hostility to family farming in Poland to mildly supportive policies in the Scandinavian countries. The hostile policy in regard to family farming in Poland is based on political assumptions that private farming shall be transformed into large-scale collective or State farming. Because of high social and economic costs of such transformation, agricultural policy in Poland was not able to eliminate private family farms but was able to restrain their economic development, slowing at the same time the processes of structural differentiation.

In the market economies of Europe and North America the family farm is threatened by forces which reward farms that increase production and lower costs. It is also threatened by the economic forces of the food industry, public policies which provide returns according to farm scale, and tax policies which provide greater benefits to nonfarm resources. This has enhanced the income of some while decreasing income for others. It has also caused a decline in the social and economic functions of rural communities.

Increased production has gone beyond the demand for both foreign and domestic markets. The result has been the subsidizing of exports by the EEC countries as well as by Canada and now by the U.S. In Great Britain, as in other countries, the subsidy of farm products for export has lead to larger farms and increased production at a cost to the nonfarm taxpayer. In Britain these policies have also lead to the destruction of less productive but scenic and wooded land that is a loss for its recreation and nonfarm use. Price supports in the U.S. and other nations enhance the larger farms, thereby encouraging greater expansion of size of the enterprise.

Production controls are considered to reduce the oversupply for the the market, but have been slow to receive support by the consumers and food industry, as well as by the producers who have large investments in land and capital. Without production controls, the rhetoric of supporting the family farm results in benefits to the larger farms and the decline of the typical family farm. This is happening in the U.S. and Canada and to a lesser degree in Great Britain, France, and Germany. It is also occurring in other countries where the agricultural policy is far more supportive of the family farm.

An increasing influence on the food industry which is affecting both the producer and the consumer is the agri-business enterprise. These national and international structures are increasing their control of food production, processing, and consumer marketing and receive an increasing share of the market price of food products. This is happening in all industrial nations but especially in the U.S., Canada, and Great Britain. These food processing industries seek out and support the farmers in those regions where food production can be extended and controlled. Some are very specialized, such as those for certain fruits and vegetables, poultry, and now for hogs and beef in the U.S. They control the total production process, as well as the place and price in the market. Their costs are also greatly reduced by tax policies which reduce the costs of feeding, breeding, and capital investments. The family farmer has little discretion in the process and receives a relatively low compensation for his efforts. This restructuring of the food industry will continue to affect the structure of agriculture in all nations throughout the world. It will also continue to affect the policies and actions of farmers' organizations and nations with regard to the structure of agriculture and who receives the benefits. Biotechnology presents an even greater challenge with its increasing control of plant and animal production, processing, and the disposition of its products by large-scale private industry which will provide the seeds for farm crops as well as the chemicals for fertilizers and insect and weed control.

Even though most European countries have a long cultural tradition affecting family and farm and have been more effective in maintaining them with the support of public policy, the prospects for the family farm are not very encouraging. All contributors to this book express their concern about the future. The increasing use of energy and other nonrenewable resources in agriculture cause not only concern about environmental consequences but also about the long-term economic consequences--rising costs of food production and relative overproduction--when a very large part of world population is not able to purchase needed food. There are also social concerns related to the crisis of the family farm and its uncertain future. Most nations in

Europe and North America have recognized that the
family-based farm is important for social, political, as
well as economic reasons. Family farms provide for a
larger and more stable rural population with more social
equity and support for local institutions and services.
They are even more important as urban centers present
more problems of employment, housing, crime control,
water supply, and waste disposal. These matters have
been of increasing concern to many as the family farm
disappears or becomes an industrial enterprise governed
by the market or other economic and political forces.

Contributions to this book do not provide consensus
as to what should be done to maintain the family farm as
the basic form of agricultural production. At best they
indicate that some importance is attached to the
ecological, social and cultural, as well as economic,
considerations. Policies and programs for controlling
the economic forces affecting land, labor, and capital
must be formed to balance the short- and long-term
effects upon the welfare of individuals, families, and
the social structures in which they live. The
contributions give some indication of efforts of how this
is being done and what social forces are expected to
support such action at the local, national, and
international levels. But we need a much better
understanding of how agriculture is integrated into the
long-term processes of the ecologic, economic, and social
systems of which it is a part before we can sustain these
systems as they vary across regions, cultures, and
countries. Maintenance of these systems requires public
policies affecting food production and distribution both
within and between countries. These are needed to
provide for a stable agriculture in the future rather
than rely on those policies which lead to only short term
monetary benefits.

Some predict that there will be a major crisis in
food production in the industrial as well as Third World
countries due to increased erosion and pollution of the
natural resources caused by heavy use of chemicals and
continuous cropping of erodible land. Preventing this
will require more attention to the efforts focused upon
the development of farm enterprises which will reduce the
costs and negative effects of the heavy use of chemicals
and limit the continuous cropping of erodible lands.
This is essential to reduce costs as well as to prevent
the negative effects upon the land which is reducing
production in some regions. This means that the

structure of agriculture will need to be adapted to the long-term interests of communities, regions and nations as well as the needs and interests of individuals and families at the farm level. The family farm may do this but not without constant adoption to the larger systems of which it is a part.

About the Contributors

REIDAR ALMAS. Professor of Sociology and Social Studies, University of Trondheim, Dragvoll, Norway.

TORBEN BAGER. Head of Cooperative Research Unit, University Centre of South Jutland, Esberg, Denmark.

RICHARD BREEN. Professor, The Economic and Social Research Institute, Dublin, Ireland.

BOGUSLAW GALESKI. Professor of Sociology, Department of Sociology and Anthropology, University of Wisconsin-Stevens Point, Stevens Point, Wisconsin, U.S.A.

RUTH GASSON. School of Rural Economics and Related Studies, WYE College, Kent, England.

MICHAEL GERTLER. Development Sociology, Cornell University, Ithaca, New York, U.S.A.

JESS GILBERT. Professor of Rural Sociology, University of Wisconsin, Madison, Wisconsin, U.S.A.

D.F. HANNAN. Professor, The Economic and Social Research Institute, Dublin, Ireland.

HUGUES LAMARCHE. Director of Research, Groupe de Recherces Sociologiques, C.N.R.S., Universite de Paris X, Nanterre, France.

THOMAS MURPHY. Development Sociology, Cornell University, Ithaca, New York, U.S.A.

312

ULRICH N[...]Extension
Education, [...]icultural
Sciences,

ULRICH PLA[...]Research,
University

NILS WEST[...]conomics,
University

EUGENE WI[...]ociology,
University